The Miracles of Jesus According to John

The Miracles of Jesus According to John

Their Christological and Eschatological Significance

STEPHEN S. KIM

With a Foreword by J. Dwight Pentecost

WIPF & STOCK · Eugene, Oregon

THE MIRACLES OF JESUS ACCORDING TO JOHN
Their Christological and Eschatological Significance

Unless otherwise stated, Scripture quotations are from the New International Version. Please use standard language for this Bible translation.

Wipf & Stock
An Imprint of Wipf and Stock Publishers
199 W. 8th Ave., Suite 3
Eugene, OR 97401

www. wipfandstock.com

ISBN 13: 978-1-60608-259-1

Manufactured in the U.S.A.

Dedication

THIS BOOK IS DEDICATED to my family: my parents, S. B. and Jackie Kim, my sister, Sylvia, and my brother, James. Thank you all for your support and encouragement throughout my theological journey.

This book is also dedicated to "my own" family: my wife, Sophia, who has unwaveringly cheered me on through the long process of my doctoral studies at Dallas Theological Seminary, and now as my partner in the teaching ministry at Multnomah Biblical Seminary. And, to our two precious daughters, Rachel and Ashley, whose unconditional love and affection for their daddy remind me daily of what is truly important in life. I love you all.

Most importantly, this book is dedicated to my Lord, Jesus Christ, who first revealed Himself to me through the Scriptures many years ago, and who continues to beckon me to discover Him afresh in the Scriptures.

Contents

Foreword

IT HAS LONG BEEN recognized that the miracles of Jesus that John includes in his Gospel from among the many He performed were to authenticate both the Person of Jesus as the Son of God and also to validate the offer of the fulfillment of the promised and covenanted Davidic kingdom to Israel that He made. What is rarely observed is that the miracles had an even wider purpose and that was to give a preview of the nature of the kingdom that would eventually be established under the authority of the coming Davidic King. Thus each miracle has prophetic significance. Dr. Kim, in this study, has developed this significant phase of the study of the miracles in John's Gospel. Based on solid interpretation and by comparing Scripture with Scripture the author gives insight into this significant purpose for the miracles. The parables of Jesus often begin with the words, "The kingdom of heaven is like" in which Jesus reveals the characteristics of the coming millennial kingdom. This study of the miracles adds to the revelation given through the parables with significant disclosures of the conditions in that kingdom when the prayer, "Thy kingdom come" is answered. This work merits careful study.

J. Dwight Pentecost
Distinguished Professor of Bible Exposition, Emeritus
Dallas Theological Seminary

Preface

THIS PRESENT WORK REPRESENTS a revision of my doctoral dissertation completed at Dallas Theological Seminary in May 2001. Three
factors captured my fascination about the Fourth Gospel and the even-
tual study of it. In our age of theological relativism, Jesus' own question to
His own disciples rings ever true: "Who do the people say that the Son of
Man is?" First, its apparent emphasis on the divine Sonship of Jesus was
mesmerizing from the start. It is perhaps the most christological book
in the entire Bible. Through Jesus' seven miracles and His seven "I Am"
sayings, the apostle John provides a clear answer to that all-important
question. And consequentially, does our knowledge of who Jesus is affect
the way we Christians live our everyday life? It most certainly should!
As my esteemed seminary professor Howard Hendricks was fond of
reminding us students, it is our *belief* about the Son that directly affects
our *behavior*.

The second factor that challenged me to probe the Fourth Gospel
was its emphasis on Jesus' miracles. What do they represent? Are they designed to point to something or someone? In our "supernatural-crazed"
culture that affects even evangelical Christianity, it is refreshing to be
reminded that biblical miracles were never arbitrary but were always
purposeful and authenticating God's message and His messenger(s). In
the Gospel of John, the miracles of Jesus are both christological, that is,
they highlight Jesus' Person, and eschatological, that is, they foreshadow
the future work the Messiah will do in His future advent. The miracles
remind us that God's desire for every believer is first and foremost a
spiritual relationship with Him through His Son. Furthermore, Jesus'
miracles also remind us that God's work in and for every believer will be
fully and ultimately realized in the everlasting life.

The third factor that piqued my interest to explore the Fourth Gospel
was its profound relationship to the Old Testament. Whereas the Gospel
of John had been understood by many scholars as being Hellenistic in

its origin for much of church history, the majority of Johannine scholarship has recently "turned the corner" in recognizing the Fourth Gospel's primary antecedent to be Hebraic or Jewish. In my study of this Gospel, it became clear to me how profoundly Jesus' miracles are tied to the Old Testament Scriptures and subsequently their universal implications. In other words, here is a Jewish Messiah who came in fulfillment to messianic prophecies of the Old Testament Scriptures, whose blessings in turn affects people of every race and culture. That God fulfills every promise about His Son made in the Scriptures should remind every believer that He will fulfill His promises to us who belong to His Son.

Stephen S. Kim

Acknowledgements

THIS BOOK REPRESENTS A revision of my doctoral dissertation completed at Dallas Theological Seminary in May 2001. The writing of the dissertation brought to completion my twelve years of biblical and theological training at DTS (ThM, 1993; PhD, 2001). If the writing of a doctoral dissertation is the culmination of one's formal education, then it is also a fitting occasion for acknowledging those who have shaped one's biblical/theological thinking along the way. As I finalize my first book after some eight years following the completion of education at DTS, the impact of my teachers is appreciated all the more. This is an opportune time to express my gratitude to the men who have shaped not only my knowledge of the Scriptures but, more importantly, my life as well.

Above all, I would like to express my gratitude and affection to my beloved and distinguished professor Dr. J. Dwight Pentecost for teaching me God's Word. Your exposition of the Scriptures will always be a model for me in my own teaching ministry. Thank you for loving me as your "Korean son" and praying faithfully for my family and me. Sophia, Rachel, Ashley, and I love you, Dr. P.

I would also like to thank the faculty of Dallas Seminary for training me for the ministry: Dr. Ronald B. Allen, Dr. Mark L. Bailey, Dr. Thomas L. Constable, Dr. Charles H. Dyer (former professor), Dr. Howard G. Hendricks, Dr. Elliott E. Johnson, in the Bible Exposition Department; Prof. Donald R. Glenn, Dr. Eugene H. Merrill, Dr. Allen P. Ross (former professor), Dr. Richard A. Taylor, in the Old Testament Department; Dr. Darrell L. Bock, Dr. Buist M. Fanning, Dr. W. Hall Harris, Dr. Harold W. Hoehner (deceased), Dr. Daniel B. Wallace, in the New Testament Department; Dr. J. Lanier Burns, Dr. Robert A. Pyne (former professor), Dr. Stephen R. Spencer (former professor), in the Systematic Theology Department; Dr. John D. Hannah, in the Historical Theology Department; Dr. William D. Lawrence (former professor), Dr. Timothy S. Warren, in the Pastoral Ministries Department; Dr. David L. Edwards (deceased),

Dr. Michael S. Lawson, Prof. Donald P. Regier, Dr. James R. Slaughter (former professor), in the Christian Education Department; Dr. Walter L. Baker, Dr. Michael Pocock, in the World Missions Department. Thank you, men, for your dedicated service to the Lord.

Reference Abbreviations

BAGD	Bauer, Walter, William F. Arndt, F. Wilbur Gingrich, and Friedrich. W. Danker. *Greek-English Lexicon of the New Testament and Other Early Christian Literature.* 2nd ed. Chicago, 1979.
ISBE	*International Standard Bible Encyclopedia.* Edited by Geoffrey W. Bromiley. 4 vols. Grand Rapids, 1979–1988.
NIDNTT	*New International Dictionary of New Testament Theology.* Edited by Colin Brown. 4 vols. Grand Rapids, 1975–1986.
NIDOTTE	*New International Dictionary of the Old Testament Theology and Exegesis.* Edited by Willem A. VanGemeren. 5 vols. Grand Rapids, 1997.
TDNT	*Theological Dictionary of the New Testament.* Edited by Gerhard Kittel and Gerhard Friedrich. Translated by Geoffrey W. Bromiley. 10 vols. Grand Rapids, 1964–1976.
TDOT	*Theological Dictionary of the Old Testament.* Edited by G. Johannes Botterweck and Helmer Ringgren. Translated by John T. Willis, Geoffrey W. Bromiley, and David E. Green. 8 vols. Grand Rapids, MI: Eerdmans, 1974–.
TWOT	*Theological Wordbook of the Old Testament.* Edited by R. Laird Harris and Gleason L. Archer Jr. 2 vols. Chicago: Moody Press, 1980.

PART ONE

Introduction of Jesus' Miracles in the Fourth Gospel

1

INTRODUCTION

THE PRESENCE AND SIGNIFICANCE OF THE OLD TESTAMENT IN THE FOURTH GOSPEL

THE GOSPEL OF JOHN stands unique in many ways in comparison to the Synoptic Gospels. One of the ways in which the Fourth Gospel distinguishes itself from the Synoptics is in its relative infrequency of quotations or direct references to specific Old Testament passages. For instance, C. K. Barrett observes 124 direct references to the Old Testament in the Gospel of Matthew, 70 in the Gospel of Mark, 109 in the Gospel of Luke, but only 27 direct references to the Old Testament in the Gospel of John.[1] However, it would be erroneous to conclude based on these facts alone that the writer of the Fourth Gospel had a more limited knowledge of the Old Testament than the other three evangelists.[2] Even a casual reading of this Gospel reveals that it is replete with allusions and imagery of the Hebrew Bible.[3] Although the author of the Fourth Gospel does not directly quote Old Testament passages nearly as frequently as the other gospel writers, still his writing as a whole is immersed in Old Testament theology. As Barrett insightfully observes concerning the Fourth Evangelist, "For him the Old Testament was itself a comprehensive unity, not a mere quarry from which isolated fragments

---

1. Barrett, "Old Testament in the Fourth Gospel," 155. These figures vary among scholars, of course, depending on which passages are considered quotations or merely references.

2. Barrett, *Gospel According to St. John*, 29.

3. Because the author uses both the Septuagint (LXX) and the Hebrew Scriptures in quoting or alluding to the Old Testament, the terms "Hebrew Bible" or "Hebrew Scriptures" will be used interchangeably in reference to the Old Testament in general.

of useful material might be hewn."[4] In other words, this Gospel breathes the Old Testament from start to finish.

The Fourth Gospel, which is characterized by its many uses of symbolic language, is immersed in allusions and imagery of the Hebrew Bible. In fact, the frequency of John's allusions to the Old Testament is surpassed only by the Gospel of Matthew. Graham Scroggie attributes 63 Old Testament references to the Gospel of Mark, 129 to Matthew, 90 to Luke, and 124 to John.[5]

Thus, the Gospel of John is second only to Matthew in the frequency of his allusions to the Old Testament.[6] Alfred Plummer is right in saying that "the Fourth Gospel is saturated with the thoughts, imagery, and language of the Old Testament."[7] And, B. F. Westcott is not exaggerating when he confesses, "Without the basis of the Old Testament, the Gospel of St. John is an insoluble riddle."[8] In other words, the richness of John's theology could not be fully comprehended without an adequate knowledge of the Old Testament, whose theology is drawn first and foremost from its deep reservoir. Gerald Borchert concurs that the Hebrew Scriptures play a significant part in the Fourth Gospel: "It is my firm conviction that the place to begin a reflection on the milieu of the Fourth Gospel is with the Old Testament. But the test of John's pervading milieu is not to be measured in terms of direct quotation from the Old Testament because John has fewer quotations than the other Gospels. Yet this Gospel literally breathes the influence of Israel's textbook."[9]

For evidence that the Gospel of John is saturated in Old Testament theology, one needs to look no farther than the opening section of the Gospel, commonly known as the "Prologue" (1:1–18). Emphasizing the eternality of Jesus Christ, the apostle John begins with the words, "In the beginning was the Word, and the Word was with God, and the Word was God. He was with God in the beginning" (John 1:1). These words beckon for a comparison to the opening words of the Hebrew Bible, "In the beginning God created the heavens and the earth" (Gen 1:1). Furthermore, the beginning words of the Fourth Gospel shed further

---

4. Barrett, "Old Testament in the Fourth Gospel," 168.

5. Scroggie, *Guide to the Gospels*, 190, 270, 363, 426.

6. Tenney, "Old Testament and the Fourth Gospel," 303.

7. Plummer, *Gospel According to St. John*, 42.

8. Westcott, *Gospel According to St. John*, lxix.

9. Borchert, *John 1–11*, 61.

light on the creation account of Genesis 1, namely, that God the Father created the world through the Son (cf. Col 1:16–17; Heb 1:2). Thus, God the Son, the eternal Word who was coexistent with the Father in the beginning, is also revealed to be the Creator. This connection is summarized well by Bruce Waltke: "The creation account of the Old Testament finds its full explication in Jesus of Nazareth, the God-man. He is the Creator, the One full of light, life, wisdom, and goodness. As man, He is the One who is bringing the earth under His dominion. . . . John wrote about Him as the Creator."[10]

The use of the word λόγος in John 1:1 also ties itself to Genesis 1:3, where it describes God's creative acts by the simple yet powerful command of His Word.[11] Although scholars have proposed various hypotheses concerning the origin of the λόγος, its nearest and most logical antecedent is again the Old Testament and the Hebrew term דבר ("dabar" meaning Word).[12]

It is especially true in the Old Testament Prophets, where their writings often begin with the words, "the Word of the LORD came to . . ."[13] These words also confirm the opening words of the Epistle to the Hebrews: "In the past God spoke to our forefathers through the prophets at many times and in various ways, but in these last days he has spoken to us by his Son, whom he appointed heir of all things, and through whom he made the universe" (Heb 1:1–2).

The key words and concepts in the remaining parts of the Prologue also reveal their rich heritage from the Old Testament, and they are all developed further in the Gospel narrative itself. Words such as "dwelt" (ἐσκήνωσεν), "glory" (δόξαν), "grace and truth" (χάριτος καὶ ἀληθείας), and "only begotten" (μονογενής), are all familiar words and phrases in the Greek translation of the Old Testament (LXX). They are introduced in the Prologue and developed further in the Gospel narrative. Furthermore, key concepts in the Prologue such as the "wit-

10. Waltke, "Creation Account in Genesis 1:1–3—Part V," 28–41.

11. W. H. Harris, "Theology of John's Writings," 190–91. Harris also points out this connection in Ps 33:6, where it states, "By the word of the Lord were the heavens made, and all the host of them by the breath of His mouth."

12. Allen, "Affirming Right-Of-Way," 8–9.

13. Other examples in the Hebrew Prophets where this phrase occurs include: Jer 1:4, 11, 13; Ezek 1:3; 3:16; Hos 1:1; Joel 1:1; Amos 3:1; Jonah 1:1; Mic 1:1; Zeph 1:1; Hag 1:1; Zech 1:1; Mal 1:1. See also Moloney, *Belief in the Word*, 30. Moloney also sees the comparison especially to the prophets' speaking the word of Yahweh.

ness" (μαρτυρία) motif, "light and life" (φῶς καὶ ζωή) relationship, and "law and grace" (νόμος καὶ χάρις) comparison, all find their antecedents primarily in the Old Testament.[14] These are also introduced in the Prologue and developed further in the Gospel. In sum, then, the Prologue is a sample of the richness of Old Testament theology that the Fourth Evangelist develops in his Gospel. The rest of the Gospel is also flooded with unmistakable references to the Old Testament. The section immediately following the Prologue, commonly referred to as the "Testimonium" (1:19–51), includes testimonies by John the Baptist and Jesus' followers that highlight Jesus' messianic descriptions from the Hebrew Bible. Significant terms such as "the Lamb of God" (ὁ ἀμνὸς τοῦ θεοῦ) (v. 29), "the Messiah" (τὸν Μεσσίαν) (v. 41), "the one Moses wrote about in the Law, and about whom the prophets also wrote" (Ὃν ἔγραψεν Μωϋσῆς ἐν τῷ νόμῳ καὶ οἱ προφῆται εὑρήκαμεν) (v. 45), "the Son of God" (ὁ υἱὸς τοῦ θεοῦ), and "the King of Israel" (ὁ βασιλεὺς τοῦ Ἰσραήλ) (v. 49), all find their source in the Hebrew Bible's description of the coming Messiah.[15] Furthermore, this section concludes with Jesus' clear reference to Jacob's dream and his encounter with heaven (Gen 28) and how, as the Son of Man (Dan 7:13), He is the essence and embodiment of the coming messianic revelations (v. 51).

The sign-miracles (σημεῖα) in the "Book of Signs" (John 2–12)[16] and their attendant contexts in the form of narratives and discourses which demonstrate Jesus to be the promised Messiah of the Hebrew Scriptures and the divine Son of God (cf. 20:30–31), find their primary source of evidence from the Old Testament in supporting that claim.[17]

14. The discovery of the Dead Sea Scrolls in the middle of the twentieth century brought an important turning point in Johannine scholarship. Previous to the discovery, many New Testament scholars interpreted the Fourth Gospel in light of the gnostic background because of the similarities between key Johannine terms to gnostic thought. This view was supported by such prominent scholars as F. C. Baur, R. Bultmann, and others. However, the discoveries at Qumran changed all that and showed how many of John's concepts have their roots in Jewish rather than gnostic material. I discuss this at length later in this chapter.

15. The significance of these titles will be discussed more fully in chapter 4 of the book.

16. Dodd entitles the first part of the Fourth Gospel, the "Book of Signs" (chaps. 2–12) and the second part of the Gospel, the "Book of Passion" (chaps. 13–20). *Interpretation of the Fourth Gospel*, x. R. E. Brown also calls the first section the "Book of Signs," but calls the second section, the "Book of Glory." *Gospel According to John (I–XII)*, cxxxviii.

17. The significance of the σημεῖα will be discussed in detail in chapter 2, while

For instance, the first miracle of Jesus' transforming water into wine in chapter 2 clearly anticipates the joy and abundance in the messianic kingdom described in the Prophets (Isa 25:6; 27:2–6). Also, in connection with the first miracle, the temple cleansing by Jesus in John 2:12–22 anticipates the coming of the Messiah in His eschatological kingdom, when He is expected to begin His ministry in the temple to purify the nation Israel (Mal 3:1–3).[18] And, Jesus' teaching to Nicodemus concerning being "born again/from above" in chapter 3 also hearken back to Old Testament truth of spiritual rebirth (Isa 44:3; Ezek 36:25–27). Further, the unmistakable comparison of Jesus Himself with the raised serpent in the wilderness (Num 21:9) as the basis of forgiveness and eternal life highlights the fulfillment of His messianic work of sacrificial redemption on the cross (Isa 53). Also, Jesus' gift of the living water to the Samaritan woman in chapter 4 brings to mind passages in the Old Testament anticipating the joy from the well of God's salvation in the eschatological kingdom (Isa 12:3), "the fountain of living waters" (Jer 2:13; 17:13), and God's invitation to the thirsty to come to the waters He freely offers (Isa 55:1).[19] Furthermore, the miracle of healing the official's son in chapter 4:46–54, which brings the "Cana Cycle"[20] (chaps. 2–4) to a close, demonstrates yet another important aspect of the Messiah's role as predicted by the Old Testament prophets, namely, His authority to bring healing and deliverance from the brink of death (Isa 53:4; 61:1).[21]

The sign-miracles and their attendant narratives and discourses in John 5–12 are all set in the context of Jewish feasts, namely, the Sabbath, the Passover, and the Tabernacles, as they also signify the anticipatory characteristics and activities of the Messiah.[22] They also refer to the Old

the significance of each of the sign-miracles will be developed in chapters 4–9 of this book.

18. Although many scholars view Jesus' action of cleansing the Jerusalem temple as a fulfillment of the messianic prophecy at His first coming, it is my understanding that Jesus was merely demonstrating His messianic identity to the nation. It is preferable to take the view that Jesus will cleanse the temple and purify the nation at the Second Advent when He establishes the promised kingdom. Jesus' intent was to present His Person, so that the people could believe in Him.

19. Morris, *Jesus is the Christ*, 18–19.

20. See Moloney, "From Cana to Cana," 185–213.

21. Carson, *Gospel According to John*, 238.

22. Borchert refers to these chapters as the "Festival Cycle." *John 1–11*, 224. Moloney also divides chapters 5–12 separately on the basis of their being centered on the Jewish feasts. *Signs and Shadows*. Although Jewish feasts in the Old Testament all have their

Testament as the primary antecedent. Thus, it is imperative to comprehend the basic Old Testament background behind the feasts, as the sign-
miracles and their attendant narratives and discourses are pitted against
it. For example, the miracle of healing of the lame man at the Pool of
Bethesda in chapter 5, although it is set in the context of an "unnamed
feast," the emphasis is on the fact that Jesus healed on the Sabbath.[23] This
miracle provides a glimpse of yet another aspect of the Messiah's work,
namely, the healing of the blind, the dumb, the mute, and the lame (Isa
35:5–6; 61:1).

The following sign-miracles in these chapters are also set in the
context of Old Testament feasts. For instance, the two sign-miracles
recorded in John 6, with the "Bread of Life" discourse in between, take
place during the Passover. The miracle of feeding the five thousand
during the Passover brought natural comparison of Jesus with another
"sign" worker, Moses, who predicted that a prophet like him would arise
(Deut 18:15). People reasoned that, since Moses had fed the people in the
wilderness and also delivered them out of the Egyptian bondage, Jesus
could also lead the nation out of their Roman bondage since He also fed
the people.[24] The Passover background of this miracle is unmistakably
tied to Israel's deliverance from the Egyptian bondage under Moses's
leadership. Moses, as the prophet of God, also worked "sign" miracles
to demonstrate divine authority (Deut 34:11). Apart from the "signs" he
performed in Egypt, he also performed great "signs" in the wilderness
for the benefit of the nation. Throughout the wilderness dwelling, Israel
received "bread from heaven" that fed the nation. Jesus' performing the
miracle of feeding the five thousand is a "sign" to reveal His messianic
identity, for there are indications in the Scriptures that the messianic age

---

historical significance, they also anticipate a future and prophetic significance through
the Person of the Messiah. For a detailed treatment of this, see Hulbert, "Eschatological
Significance of Israel's Annual Feasts." Each of the sign-miracles and their respective
context will be developed in the main body of the book.

23. Although the eschatological meaning of Jesus' Sabbath healings is a matter
of some dispute, some believe that they demonstrate the final rest anticipated in the
eschatological age. The significance of the Sabbath for this particular miracle will be
discussed in detail in chapter 5 of this book. For a good treatment on the eschatological significance of the Sabbath, see R. Griffith, "Eschatological Significance of the
Sabbath."

24. For a good treatment of the people's messianic expectations during Jesus' day,
see Meeks, *Prophet-King*, 1–2.

would be accompanied by signs like those of the Mosaic period.[25] As the Hebrew prophets declared long ago, God's deliverance for Israel at the Messiah's advent will be characterized by signs and wonders that were present when Moses led the nation out of Egypt (Mic 7:15; Isa 48:20–21). The feeding of the multitudes thus anticipates the day when God will abundantly provide for His people in the eschatological banquet.

Continuing the same theme of relating the days of Moses with the coming eschatological age by the similarity of their miracles, the subsequent sign of Jesus' walking on the Sea of Galilee (John 6:16–21) reveals yet another aspect of His identity as the promised Messiah and the unique Son of God. Yahweh's provision for His people in leading them through the Red Sea and exhibiting His control over nature finds similar parallel with Jesus' walking on the Sea of Galilee to protect His disciples. What is even more revealing is the manner in which He identifies Himself to His disciples. Jesus reveals Himself by using the divine name that Yahweh used in revealing Himself to Moses on Mt. Sinai (John 6:20; cf. Exod 3:14).

The healing of the man born blind in John 9 is recorded following the "I Am the Light of the World" discourse of Jesus at the Jewish Feast of Tabernacles, where He claimed to be the Light who defeated darkness of sin and death (cf. 1:5). And, this claim of Jesus was followed with an astonishing promise, "Whoever follows me will never walk in darkness, but will have the light of life" (8:12). The Pharisees, who questioned the validity of Christ's self-testimony, vehemently challenged this "outrageous" claim. The conflict of Jesus and the Pharisees at the Feast of Tabernacles carried over to the particular miracle of healing the blind man who was born blind (9:1–41). This particular miracle also has profound connection with the Old Testament Scriptures where, for example, the prophet Isaiah predicted that the Messiah would be "a light to the Gentiles" (Isa 42:6). Isaiah further predicts Messiah's future work thusly: "To open blind eyes, to bring out prisoners from the prison, those who sit in darkness from the prison house. I am the LORD, that is My name, and My glory I will not give to another, nor my praise to carved images" (Isa 42:7–8; cf. 29:18; 35:5). And, in fulfillment of these messianic prophecies Jesus gave sight to the blind (cf. Matt 9:27–31; 12:22–23; 20:29–34; 21:14).

---

25. Koester, *Symbolism in the Fourth Gospel*, 91–92.

The miracle of healing the blind man was also a sign of judgment for the Pharisees who, being spiritually blind themselves were too proud to admit their blindness, whereas the blind man received his sight from the one who is the true Light who gives light to every man who puts his trust in Him by faith (cf. John 1:9). The judgment of the Pharisees is also highlighted in the following chapter in the "I Am the Good Shepherd" discourse (John 10), where Jesus sets Himself in contrast to the Pharisees. Jesus is the Good Shepherd who lays down His life for the sheep, symbolizing the sacrificial nature of His death. This imagery of Himself as the Good Shepherd is certainly a messianic fulfillment of the Ezekiel passage where it states, "I will establish one shepherd over them, and he shall feed them, My servant David. He shall feed them and be their shepherd. And I, the LORD, will be their God, and My servant David a prince among them; I, the LORD, have spoken" (Ezek 34:23–24; cf. Ps 23; Jer 23; Zech 10).

The remaining two chapters in the Book of Signs (John 2–12) are also saturated with important events and discourses that derive their significance first and foremost from the Old Testament Scriptures. For instance, the climactic miracle of raising Lazarus from the dead in chapter 11 demonstrates that just as Old Testament saints expressed confidence of everlasting hope for the righteous (Ps 16:9–11; cf. Isa 26:19–20; Dan 12:2), Jesus proves that He, as the Messiah, has authority even over death. In the narrative of the miracle account, it is Martha who professes her faith in the eschatological resurrection: "I know he will rise again in the resurrection at the last day" (John 11:24). Jesus then responds to Martha with the familiar words, "I am the resurrection and the life" (11:25). Martha's following statement also reveals her faith in the messianic identity of Jesus: "I believe that you are the Christ, the Son of God, who was to come into the world" (11:27), the same titles that the Evangelist uses in his "purpose statement" in 20:30–31.

The significance of chapter 12 can also be derived from its Old Testament background. The chapter begins with the anointing of Jesus in Bethany, in anticipation of His predetermined and sacrificial death. The anointing symbolizes His messianic identity as the Lamb of God who takes away the sin of the world (1:29; cf. Isa 53). Then, Jesus' triumphal entry into Jerusalem further confirms His messianic identity. By entering into Jerusalem riding on a donkey, Jesus was showing Himself to be the promised Messiah of the Old Testament Scriptures (Ps 118:25–26;

Zech 9:9). Furthermore, the coming of the Greeks provides yet another important aspect of the Messiah and His work. The promised Messiah of the Old Testament Scriptures is more than just a Messiah for the Jews; He is also the Savior of the world, both in the present age and in the one to come (John 4:42; cf. Isa 56:6–8; Zech 14:16–17). In sum, then, it is clear to see the breadth of Old Testament's significance in the content of the Fourth Gospel, particularly the Book of Signs.

Of the many unique characteristics of the Fourth Gospel, one of these is the use of the word σημεῖον in referring to the miraculous signs of Jesus Christ.[26] The word's close association with the Hebrew word אוֹת pits this Gospel all the more in close relationship with the Hebrew Bible.[27] The word σημεῖον is used frequently in the Septuagint (LXX) as the translation of the Hebrew word אוֹת, describing the words "sign," "pledge," or "token."[28] The meaning of both the Greek word σημεῖον and the Hebrew word אוֹת is essentially the same, and they are used in both the Old and New Testaments.[29] For instance, the word σημεῖον is used often in the book of Exodus in describing the miraculous signs of God performed by Moses.[30] Furthermore, these miraculous signs of God were designed to manifest the glory of God, as is also true in the Fourth Gospel.[31] Thus, the sign-miracles in the Fourth Gospel also have their antecedent primarily in the Hebrew Bible.

Apart from the sign-miracles in the Fourth Gospel, the "I Am" statements also find their primary antecedent from the Old Testament. The "I Am" statements are unique to the Fourth Gospel. The Greek phrase ἐγώ εἰμι is used in reference to God's revelation of Himself in the Old Testament (LXX). There are a number of usages of this phrase that are absolute (non predicated) and strongly allude to Exodus 3:14

---

26. The word itself indicates that the miracles signify something. Kysar, *Fourth Evangelist and His Gospel*, 225–32. Although what the signs signify is a subject of much debate in Johannine studies, the Evangelist's own reference indicates a twofold purpose: to demonstrate Christ's messiahship and deity. A more detailed analysis of the Johannine σημεῖα will be discussed in chapter 2 of the book.

27. Rengstorf, "Σημεῖον," 7:243–57.

28. Tenney, "Topics from the Gospel of John—Part II," 145–60. See also BAGD 747–48.

29. Ibid., 146.

30. Rengstorf, "Σημεῖον," 7:256.

31. Ibid., 7:256–57. Rengstorf points out the connection between God's miraculous signs (אוֹת/σημεῖα) and His glory (כבד/δόξα).

and the Isaianic passages (cf. John 46:4) in referring to His deity. There are also seven "I Am" statements that are predicated: the Bread of Life (6:35), the Light of the World (8:12), the Door of the Sheep (10:7), the Good Shepherd (10:11), the Resurrection and the Life (11:25), the Way, the Truth, and the Life (14:6), and the Vine (15:1). Each of these predicated "I Am" sayings, along with the non-predicated ones, has rich Old Testament implications concerning the divine Messiah. To summarize, then, given the presence of the Old Testament and its significance in the Fourth Evangelist's thought, one can only agree wholeheartedly with Westcott's confession, that without the basis of the Old Testament, the understanding of this unique Gospel would certainly be minimized.

THE PERTINENCE AND NEED OF THE STUDY

There is a fourfold need for this study. The first need stems from the rich presence of the Old Testament in the Fourth Gospel and the significant role it plays within the book, as described briefly above. The end of the Second World War in the middle of the twentieth century marks an important turning point in Johannine scholarship, especially in the area of the historical milieu or the background of the Fourth Gospel.[32] There emerged a shift in the scholarly consensus concerning the Gospel's historical milieu, from an essentially Hellenistic background to a Hebraic or Jewish background.[33]

The philosophical background or milieu of the Fourth Gospel has been instrumental in determining the overall message and purpose of the book, especially in the twentieth century. Leon Morris is correct in

---

32. For a survey of recent Johannine scholarship, the following works are helpful: Ashton, "Introduction: The Problem of John," 7–25; R. E. Brown, *Introduction to the New Testament*, 333–82; idem, *Gospel According to John (I–XII)*, xxi–xxii; Carson, *Gospel According to John*, 23–40; Hunter, "Recent Trends in Johannine Studies," 219–22; Kysar, *Fourth Evangelist and His Gospel*, 102–45; Smalley, *John*, 45–74; D. M. Smith, "Johannine Studies," 271–88.

33. Although Bultmann and some other scholars still see a Hellenistic or gnostic milieu of the Fourth Gospel, the majority of Johannine scholars see a predominantly Jewish background. One of the most instrumental elements in this shift in scholarly consensus occurred as a result of the discovery of the Dead Sea Scrolls around the middle of the twentieth century, which contained vital documents from roughly the time period just prior to and around the time of Jesus and the early church. It not only included discoveries of texts and fragments of the books of the Hebrew Bible, it also provided us with vital information about the life and teachings of the Qumran sect. Cf. LaSor, "Dead Sea Scrolls," 2:883–97.

highlighting the importance of this aspect: "A good deal of attention has been given to the background presupposed by this Gospel. This is, of course, important for the interpretation, for we must know the kind of milieu in which the author moved if we are to be sure we understand his meaning."[34] Robert Kysar also echoes the import of recognizing the intellectual milieu of the Fourth Gospel this way:

> One's understanding of a text depends in every case upon the establishment of a context of thought of which the text has been written. To interpret properly any written document it is necessary to have some sort of a concept of the world of thought in which that document was written and hence in the light of which its expressions and concepts are to be understood. This is true no less for a modern text than for an ancient one, but the difficulties in determining what context of thought is to be presupposed for the interpretation of an ancient text are formidable ones when compared to a modern document. The task of determining the degree of affinities an ancient writer has with this or that milieu of thought has been especially burdensome for the biblical student since the dawn of the critical era.[35]

Prior to the twentieth century, however, the subject of milieu for the Fourth Gospel was hardly addressed in the Johannine commentaries.[36] In fact, it was not until C. H. Dodd who in the 1930s wrote an extensive material on the background of the Fourth Gospel and proposed a Hellenistic Judaism as its background that created an interest within Johannine studies concerning the book's background.[37] This interest in the milieu of the Fourth Gospel mushroomed in the 1950s with Rudolf Bultmann's controversial and significant proposal that the Fourth Gospel was written out of the context of Gnosticism. Scholars of the Fourth Gospel soon followed in their footsteps in addressing the possible background, as it surely affects the interpretation of the book in its overall message and purpose.[38] The Old Testament and Hebraic

---

34. Morris, *Gospel According to John*, 60.

35. Kysar, *Fourth Evangelist and His Gospel*, 102.

36. Borchert, *John 1–11*, 60.

37. Dodd, "Background of the Fourth Gospel," 329–43; idem, *Interpretation of the Fourth Gospel*, 10–130.

38. There have been various proposals concerning the possible background influence of the Fourth Gospel, but these can be classified broadly in three categories: gnostic influence, Hellenistic influence, and Jewish influence, with each having sub categories.

Although this topic is not the focus of the book, but because it is somewhat related, each will be surveyed only briefly here.

1. Gnostic Influence. The influence of gnostic ideas on the Fourth Gospel has been proposed by some Johannine scholars because of the much-shared vocabulary and ideas between the two. It was scholars such as F. C. Baur and Bultmann who observed the gnostic background of the Fourth Gospel, as they compared the gnostic redeemer myth to John's idea of a Christ who came forth from God and who returns to God upon dispensing the gnosis that leads to salvation. Morris, *Gospel According to John*, 62. As Beasley-Murray summarizes this teaching, "The fundamental elements of this system are cosmic dualism, redemption from the demonic powers of the earth, and gnosis from the Revealer, by which the way of salvation is known." (*John*, lv). Hence, it is not surprising that some scholars attribute the Fourth Gospel to a gnostic background, as many of these elements find a similar theme in John's gospel. However, each of these elements within the gnostic thought are derived from a vastly different understanding than how the apostle John perceived them. As Renwick puts it, "The Gnostics took over only the idea of redemption through Christ, not the full Christian doctrine, for they made it rather a redemption of the philosophers from matter, than a redemption of mankind from sin." "Gnosticism," 2:484. The Evangelist's thoughts concerning these ideas, on the other hand, are derived first and foremost from the Hebrew Bible. For example, the dualistic understanding of light and darkness between the two worlds find their antecedent not in the gnostic distinction between the spirit world and the physical world, but in the understanding of God as light (Ps 27:1; Isa 42:6) and His way as righteousness (Ps 1). In sum, then, although the Evangelist certainly was cognizant of the vogue philosophical teaching of his day, his primary referent was the Old Testament.

2. Hellenistic Influence. Another commonly proposed milieu for the Fourth Gospel is Hellenistic in background. There are different strands within what is referred to as "Hellenism." Three different strands of Greek thought have been proposed to have had influence on the Fourth Gospel: Greek philosophy, Philo, and the *Hermetica*. The term "Hellenism" may be used in various senses. It may be used, for instance, to describe the whole of distinctively Greek culture, including that of the days before Alexander the Great (336–323 BC); however, it is more commonly used to describe the civilization that spread through much of the ancient world in the wake of Alexander's conquest. Morris, "Hellenism," 2:679. In discussing the "Hellenistic" background of the Fourth Gospel, there is an important distinction to keep in mind. According to R. E. Brown, "There was a strong Hellenistic element already present in the Judaism of NT times, both in Palestine and Alexandria. Therefore, if John was dependent on contemporary Judaism, there was inevitably a Hellenistic influence on Johannine thought. We take for granted, therefore, a Greek strain within Judaism, which had an influence on Johannine vocabulary and thought. But the question we ask here is whether there was another Hellenistic influence on John that did not come through Judaism but came from without. Was the Evangelist particularly familiar with Greek thought so that he reinterpreted the Gospel message in Hellenistic terms?" *Gospel According to John (I–XII)*, LVI. The answer to this significant question raised by Brown has to be in the negative. Although the terms within the Fourth Gospel may find familiarity in Greek philosophical thought, the meaning of the Evangelist is far removed from theirs.

3. Hebraic Influence. Although there are still some scholars who espouse a gnostic or Hellenistic background for the Fourth Gospel, a large number of scholars are coming

background of the Fourth Gospel will be demonstrated throughout this book in interaction with the content of the book, particularly in dealing with the sign-miracles and their attendant narratives and discourses.

The second need for this study includes a detailed look at the Johannine use of the word σημεῖον.[39] There is a need for a careful analysis of the significant word σημεῖον and its Hebrew counterpart

to agree that the principal background influence behind the Johannine thought was Hebraic or Jewish. The place to begin concerning the milieu of the Fourth Gospel is without a doubt the Old Testament. However, the Evangelist did not write his Gospel in a cultural vacuum, and various proposals have been given regarding the historical and cultural milieu of his time. In seeing the Jewish influence of the Gospel, some have proposed a Palestinian milieu and more specifically, rabbinic Judaism as the principal background. Although the dating of the rabbinic sources are difficult and often very late, they do shed much helpful light on the Jewish thought and expectations of first century Judaism. See Dodd, *Interpretation of the Fourth Gospel*, 74–97; and also Daube, *New Testament and Rabbinic Judaism*, 67–71, 97–102, and 325–29. Some NT scholars have pointed out the influence of rabbinic Judaism on the Fourth Gospel, particularly concerning the rabbis' perspectives on the Torah, Sabbath, and the Messiah. See R. E. Brown, *Gospel According to John (I–XII)*, LXI–LXII. Brown highlights the importance of understanding the rabbinic teachings by saying, "Concepts like that of the hidden Messiah and speculations on the creative role of the Torah and on the nature of life in the world to come are all important for understanding Johannine developments." The task of the biblical interpreter is one of distinguishing between the influences derived from the OT and those belonging to rabbinical teachings. The parallels between the two, if anything, at least points to the setting of the Gospel. And, as Guthrie points out, since Jesus was a Jew it is not extraordinary to see such influence in the Gospel. *New Testament Introduction*, 320.

One other source within Jewish thought that is significant in the study of the Fourth Gospel is the influence of the Dead Sea Scrolls and the Qumran community. Until the discovery of the DSS around the middle of the twentieth century, little was known of the Qumran sect in Palestine. These documents also revealed that teachings of ethical dualism in the Fourth Gospel doesn't necessarily derive its milieu from Gnosticism but more likely from the Palestinian background of the Essenes. How much the Fourth Evangelist relied on these writings, if at all, is a matter of debate. For now, however, Borchert's summary seems to be well balanced: "At this stage it seems unwise to posit any literary dependence of the Johannine evangelist upon the Qumran scribes or their manuscripts. Instead, it is clear that both John and Qumran relied heavily on the Old Testament for the starting point of their theological formula." *John 1–11*, 67.

In summary, then, it is significant to see that the principal background in the Johannine thought is not gnostic or Hellenistic but Hebraic, as the Evangelist's primary intent in the Gospel is to demonstrate that Jesus is the promised Messiah of the Old Testament Scriptures and the divine Son of God. Furthermore, it is also evident that the Evangelist's writing demonstrates his cognizance of the cultural milieu of first century Judaism, as shades of rabbinical and Qumran teachings can be detected.

39. Although σημεῖον is used elsewhere in the NT and the OT (LXX), it seems to be used most frequently and significantly in the Fourth Gospel.

אות in their respective contexts. In other words, is there a particularly theological significance in the Evangelist's use of the word σημεῖον in referring to his selected sign-miracles and their attendant narratives and discourses in the Fourth Gospel? The theological significance of the word σημεῖον will be highlighted by surveying the word's uses in other parts of Scripture. In addition to the uses and nature of this significant Johannine word, there is also a need to demonstrate its intended purposes within the book. In other words, what aim did the Evangelist have in presenting these particular sign-miracles? Aside from these important issues concerning the Johannine σημεῖον, there is also a need to clarify which miracles the Evangelist is referring to as the σημεῖον, and how many.[40] Furthermore, is there a particular significance to the order and progression of the σημεῖον that the Evangelist intentionally designed? Many aspects of this word such as mentioned above need to be carefully considered.

The third need for this study is developed in the body of the book, that is, a careful study of the sign-miracles themselves in their respective contexts. If the Evangelist selectively designed these particular sign-miracles to demonstrate that Jesus is the promised Messiah and the divine Son of God as the author's own "purpose statement"[41] in-

40. There are some scholars, for example, who prefer to see the temple cleansing in chapter 2 as one of the σημεῖα. See Köstenberger, *Encountering John*, 70. There are also some who prefer to see eight sign-miracles among the σημεῖα.

41. The purpose of the Fourth Gospel has been the subject of much discussion in Johannine studies. And, although it is not the main focus of the dissertation but because it is somewhat related, it will be treated briefly here. There has been a plethora of proposals by Johannine scholars concerning its purpose throughout church history, and they can be classified broadly by time periods. 1. Earlier Proposals. Based on ancient testimony, the discussions on the purpose of the Fourth Gospel revolved around the understanding that it was dependent on the Synoptic Gospels. In other words, the purpose of John's gospel was dependent on the factors that highlighted the similarities and differences with the other three gospels. This is built upon the assumption, of course, that John knew the other three gospels, and that he wished to present his own version of the gospel story that was distinct. As Beasley-Murray describes, "Earlier discussions on the purpose of the Gospel frequently were dominated by a concern to determine whether the Fourth Gospel was written to supplement the other three, or to interpret them, or even to correct them." *John*, lxxxviii. Or, as Clement of Alexandria summarized long ago, John composed a "spiritual gospel." Windisch, in the 1920s went even further in his description when he concluded that John's Gospel was intended to supercede rather than supplement the Synoptic Gospels. *Johannes und die Synoptiker*, 1–40. Lightfoot wasn't so bold in his characterization as Windisch but argued along similar lines when he describes that John probably sought to

interpret the other Gospels. *St. John's Gospel*, 28. However, this theory that the Evangelist wrote his Gospel to "spiritualize," "supplement," "supercede," or even "interpret" the other three gospels is built upon the presupposition that he was dependent on the Synoptic Gospels. And, while it is possible that the apostle was familiar with the gospel stories of the Synoptics, it is unlikely that he used the other three gospels in their written form and rearranged them for his own purpose. (For a good discussion on the independent theory of John, see D. M. Smith, *John Among the Gospels*.) In sum, it is highly unlikely that John wrote his Gospel in any relation to the Synoptic Gospels.

2. Recent Proposals. Most of the modern commentators' proposals regarding the purpose of the Fourth Gospel spring from a reconstruction of the "Johannine community" that brought forth a specific need for the Gospel. Although there are as many proposals concerning the Gospel's purpose as there are commentators, they can be classified within few categories, with slightly varying details. One of the popular suggestions in the earlier part of this century was a proposal that interpreted the Fourth Gospel as a restatement of the gospel story for the Gentile world in a form that would be intelligible to the Greek mind. Smalley, *John*, 160–61. E. F. Scott saw the Fourth Gospel as a document that resulted from the necessity to translate the gospel story to an audience that lived in the Hellenistic culture. *Fourth Gospel*, 1–28. Thus, he felt that the Evangelist needed to translate the significant Jewish ideas such as the Messiah and the kingdom of God into more popular and intelligible terms like the Logos and eternal life. However, this interpretation reflects the spirit of its time, when the popular view was to see the Fourth Gospel as originating in the Hellenistic milieu. And, as mentioned previously, only a few would see the Hellenistic background as its primary milieu today in light of the discovery of the Dead Sea Scrolls that reflect a Jewish milieu, and with so much of the Gospel alluding back to the Hebrew Bible.

A more popular view concerning the purpose of the Fourth Gospel in recent times has been to view the Gospel as polemical or apologetic in its intent. For example, many scholars see the Fourth Gospel as having arisen from a community of Jewish believers as they were in the midst of a violent dialogue with a synagogue of Jews. A popular proponent of this view is Martyn, whose seminal work was met with wide acceptance within the Johannine scholarship. *History and Theology in the Fourth Gospel*. This proposal was met with wide acceptance among other well-known Johannine scholars as R. E. Brown, Rudolf Schnackenburg, D. Moody Smith, Robert Kysar, Wayne A. Meeks, Robert T. Fortna, with shades of different details, of course. Proponents of this view see as their main support those passages within the Gospel that highlight the expulsion of Jewish-Christians from the synagogue (John 9:22; 12:42; 16:2), and the negative characterizing of the "Jews" throughout the Gospel. However, to see this particular theme as the purpose of the Gospel seems much too narrow, since the book contains and develops many other themes other than this one.

Aside from these proposals, a number of others have also been suggested as the reason for prompting the writing of this Gospel: to evangelize the Jews, to evangelize the Hellenists, to evangelize the Samaritans, to strengthen the church, to catechize new converts, and so on. However, as Carson aptly puts it, the problem of all these suggestions regarding the purpose of the Gospel, is the confusion between purpose and plausible effect. He summarizes his point this way: "Just because John's Gospel can be used to offer comfort to the bereaved in the twentieth century does not mean that is why the Evangelist wrote it. In the same way, just because this Gospel could help Jewish

Christians witnessing to the unconverted Jews and proselytes in the nearby synagogue does not *itself* mean that is why the Evangelist wrote it. To think through all the plausible good effects various parts of this book could have does not provide adequate reason for thinking that any one of them, or all of them together, was the purpose the Evangelist had in mind when he put pen to paper." *Gospel According to John*, 89–90.

3. Alternative Options. The proper place to begin the discussion on the purpose of the Fourth Gospel is with the Evangelist's own "purpose statement" in the Gospel itself: "Jesus did many other miraculous signs in the presence of his disciples, which are not recorded in this book. But these are written that you may believe that Jesus is the Christ, the Son of God, and that by believing you may have life in his name" (20:30–31). Although modern scholars have largely ignored John 20:30–31 in determining the Gospel's purpose, there are good reasons for using these two verses as the primary source in doing so, since it is wise to begin with what is certain rather than what is hypothetical. See Carson, "Purpose of the Fourth Gospel," 639–51.

In using John 20:30–31 as the beginning place in determining the author's purpose, one is left with two options of interpretation because of the textual variant of the verb πιστεύω with the ἵνα clause. The verb can either be read as aorist subjunctive πιστεύσητε, or as present subjunctive πιστεύητε. The aorist subjunctive would indicate an evangelistic message that is directed to unbelievers, in order to convince them to believe. The present subjunctive, on the other hand, would indicate an edificatory or didactic message that addresses believers, in order to strengthen and confirm their faith. Most modern commentators seem to prefer the present subjunctive and thus translate the verse this way: "that you may *continue to believe*." Textually, the evidence seems evenly balanced between the two, and thus cannot be conclusive. Besides, the outcome of the text-critical decision cannot be determinative concerning the Gospel's purpose, since there are examples of both the present subjunctive and aorist subjunctive that occur in both the context of coming to faith and in the context of continuing in faith. Carson, "Purpose of the Fourth Gospel," 640–41. Thus, the determining factor concerning the author's purpose statement in 20:31 is not textual evidence but the context of the book as a whole. Besides, it is also significant that for the apostle Paul, the process of believing is more a process than a point in time. Unlike the apostle Paul, John is not focusing on the point of justification.

Although the purpose statement in 20:30–31 may seem primarily evangelistic in its focus, the content of materials discussed in the Gospel itself seem instructive toward those who are already believers. See Borchert, *John 1–11*, 35–36. The "Farewell" discourse, in chapters 14–17, especially seems to be addressing those who are already believers rather than attempting to evangelize unbelievers. If the Fourth Gospel is addressed primarily for believers, then, what intention did the Evangelist have in mind when he penned his Gospel? The purpose statement of the apostle John seems to suggest that he intends to present Jesus to second and subsequent generations of believers, those who did not "see signs" but have the written account of them. Thompson, "John, Gospel of," 372. Jesus' remarks after Thomas's confession "My Lord and My God" (20:28) may be a clue to John's primary audience. Jesus comments, "Because you have seen me, you have believed. Blessed are those who have not seen and yet have believed" (20:29). Thus, much content of the Gospel seems designed to encourage believers to persevere in the faith they already possess, even in the midst of the hostile world in which they live (15:18–25). In conclusion, then, although the gospel story certainly can be used to

dicates, then there is an important need for a thematic study of these miracles that highlight His Person. Furthermore, if these sign-miracles are designed to demonstrate Jesus as the promised Messiah of the Old Testament Scriptures and the divine Son of God, then there is a need to study the different aspects of His Person and works these miracles highlight. Additionally, if the sign-miracles are designed to highlight the messianic identity of Jesus, then is there also intended future eschatological significance within them, besides the present blessings of the Messiah? While the Fourth Gospel has often been characterized as being more "realized" in its eschatology than the other gospels, it has been done so often at the expense of neglecting the important future aspect of the Messiah's work in the promised kingdom. It is the Messiah's work in the future that provides the significant meaning to His present work. Therefore, although in-depth studies have been proposed concerning the Johannine sign-miracles, many have done so neglecting the future aspect of the Messiah's work in the eschatological kingdom. Thus, this study will attempt to understand the Johannine signs from a premillennial perspective.

The fourth need for this study includes the significance of the Evangelist's emphasis on the inclusive and universal aspect of the Messiah's blessings.[42] Even a casual reading of this Gospel will immedi-

---

bring unbelievers to a saving knowledge in Jesus Christ, the book as a whole seems to be written primarily with the aim of strengthening and instructing those who already possess eternal life.

42. With the shifting of scholarly consensus of seeing the Fourth Gospel from a Hellenistic to a Jewish milieu, many Johannine scholars naturally began to conclude that the identity of recipients was Jewish or Jewish proselytes. J. A. T. Robinson, "Destination and Purpose," 117–31; Carson, "Purpose of the Fourth Gospel," 639–51. Some even narrow the Evangelist's purpose to be a "missionary tract" for the Diaspora Jews. Carson, *Gospel According to John*, 91. It is commonly pointed out by those who propose this view that the purpose statement in John 20:31 to be of little value for Gentiles. In other words, it is argued that since the author's primary aim is to demonstrate that Jesus is the promised Messiah of the Old Testament Scriptures, it must be addressed to Jews since the concept of a messiah would mean little to Gentile readership. However, such a conclusion seems premature and overlooks some significant textual clues.

Several objections can be raised against this conclusion. First of all, it is questionable whether the purpose statement in John 20:30–31 is referring to an unbelieving audience for an evangelistic purpose. Although it certainly does include contents that can lead readers to faith, it is more likely that the Gospel was written primarily to believers with an edificatory and didactic purpose. And, if believers are in view, then the church(es) that was addressed by the Evangelist must have been made up of predominantly Gentile believers. Second, one must be mindful that the first-generation preachers carried over to the Gentiles much Jewish religious terminology. R. E. Brown, *Gospel according to John (I–XII)*, LXXVII. Gentiles who were interested in the gospel message about Jesus had to learn some OT background concerning many spiritual truths. One only needs to glance through the letters of the apostle Paul to see this. He referred to and alluded to the OT constantly to validate his arguments, although he was addressing congregations that were predominantly Gentile believers. Therefore, as Brown concludes, "There is no contradiction in addressing a Gospel to Gentiles in order to persuade them that Jesus is the Messiah." Ibid. Third, it is presumptuous to think that Gentiles were totally ignorant of the Hebrew Bible or were unfamiliar with the concept of the Messiah. One familiar example of a Gentile who had some knowledge concerning the Messiah is the Canaanite woman who came to Jesus on behalf of her demon-possessed daughter. She cried out to Jesus, "Lord, Son of David, have mercy on me! My daughter is suffering terribly from demon-possession" (Matt 15:22). To which confession, Jesus commended her for having a sufficient faith to be healed. Her confession of Jesus as Lord and the Son of David has rich OT implications concerning the Messiah.

Another significant example of Gentiles having some or general knowledge of the OT and the Messiah can be witnessed in the Lucan writings, both in the Third Gospel and the book of Acts. These books, written by a Gentile to a Gentile believer(s), are full of allusions to the Hebrew Bible, especially concerning the promised Messiah and His kingdom, whose salvation encompasses the whole world and not just the Jews. For example, in the angel's announcement to Mary concerning her son, the angel says of him, "He will be great and will be called the Son of the Most High. The Lord God will give him the throne of his father David, and he will reign over the house of Jacob forever; his kingdom will never end" (Luke 1:32–33). Further, after the birth of Jesus, upon seeing the baby Simeon praised the Lord saying: "Sovereign Lord, as you have promised, you now dismiss your servant in peace. For my eyes have seen your salvation, which you have prepared in the sight of all people, a light for revelation to the Gentiles and for glory to your people Israel" (Luke 2:29–32). These verses are filled with allusions to the Hebrew Bible, particularly to the Abrahamic and Davidic covenants, and also to the Isaianic prophecy. Thus, although Gentiles may not have had extensive knowledge of the Hebrew Bible, they did have some knowledge and awareness of the Scriptures and the Messiah, especially if they had been believers for some time and thus received ample instruction in the Old Testament Scriptures (LXX).

Besides the above-mentioned factors that object to the conclusion that the Fourth Gospel had to have been addressed to a Jewish audience, there are also many textual clues within the Gospel that may indicate that the recipients probably were predominantly Gentiles, although first-century churches surely included many Jewish believers also. Although there are many clues within the Gospel that suggest that the intended readers were predominantly Gentiles, only four categories will be mentioned briefly here.

1. Geography. The first important factor that may indicate the Gentile identity of the readers is geography. The Evangelist assumes that his readers have some or general knowledge of the geographical areas of the story, but not specific locations of Palestine. For instance, well-known places like Jerusalem (1:19; 2:13), the region "beyond the Jordan" (1:28; 3:26; 10:40), Galilee (1:44), Judea (3:22), and Samaria (4:4, 5, 7) are assumed to be familiar to the reader, for they are not provided with any clarifying explanations. For a good discussion of this, see Culpepper, *Anatomy of the Fourth Gospel*,

ately detect the obvious universal tone of the message that is peppered

216. On the other hand, specific locations within regions of Galilee and Samaria are explained with clarifying comments. Such cities as Ephraim and Bethany are located with specific explanations. Furthermore, the writer assumes that the readers are unaware of specific topography of Jerusalem. For example, the writer describes, "now there is in Jerusalem . . ." when describing the Pool of Bethesda (5:2). He also adds that it is located "by the Sheep Gate." Therefore, although the recipients of the Gospel were probably cognizant of some geographical locations in the gospel story, they were not aware of specific places.

2. Language. The second significant factor that may hint at the Gentile identity of the readers is the language used by the writer. The Evangelist assumes that his readers only know Greek, for he feels the need to explain even the most basic Hebrew and Aramaic terms. Common terms such as "Rabbi" (1:38), "Messiah" (1:41), and "Rabboni" (20:16) are translated by the author. Further, significant names are translated to convey their meaning such as Cephas (1:42), and Siloam (9:7). And, where Hebrew and Aramaic terms are used such as Bethesda, Gabbatha, and Golgotha, they are referred to as foreign words by adding the phrase "in Aramaic" (5:2; 19:13, 17). Thus, the author seems compelled to explain very common Hebraic or Aramaic terms to the readers, terms of which Jewish readers would be familiar.

3. Jewish Elements. The third factor that hints at the Gentile identity of the readers is the Jewish elements, which include the author's use of the Hebrew Scriptures, the Jewish festivals, and the Jewish practices and customs. Although the author's use of the OT in the Fourth Gospel is extensive, as mentioned previously, it is allusions and not quotations. Whereas the Matthean Gospel is commonly known as the gospel to the Jews, and is characterized with quotations of OT Scriptures and fulfillment formulas, the Johannine Gospel has far fewer quotations and phrases like "that Scripture might be fulfilled" (13:18; 17:12; 19:24, 36; 12:38; 15:25). The fact that the Evangelist alludes to the Hebrew Bible rather than quoting from them may also indicate the Gentile identity of the readers. The apostle John who was a Jew steeped in the Hebrew Bible, but the readers of the Gospel were probably Gentiles who, while not being totally ignorant of the OT were also not deeply learned in them. Thus, the Evangelist probably only alludes to the OT to validate his purpose, namely, to provide evidence that Jesus is the promised Messiah, whose death and resurrection paved the way for the whole world to share in the hope of everlasting life.

Furthermore, the Evangelist's dealings with the Jewish festivals may also indicate that the readers were predominantly Gentiles. For instance, in his mentioning of the Passover as the setting, he explains the festival as "the Passover, a feast of the Jews" (6:4; cf. 2:13; 11:55). This kind of an explanation would have been unnecessary and superfluous if the readers were Jews. In like manner as the Passover, the author explains the Feast of Tabernacles as "the Jews' Feast of Tabernacles" (7:2). In addition, the Evangelist also describes the Feast of Dedication or Hanukkah as taking place in winter (10:22). Surely this would have been unnecessary if his readers were Jewish, since every Jew, Palestinian, or Diaspora, would have known the season of these religious festivals. Therefore, the author's explanations provided with his mentioned Jewish feasts also hints at the Gentile identity of the recipients.

Another significant element that might shed some light on the identity of the readers is the author's comments concerning Jewish customs and practices. For instance, in

throughout the book. Although an important aspect of the sign-miracles in the Fourth Gospel is the Person of Jesus as the promised Messiah of the Old Testament Scriptures, they reveal significant truths concerning the Messiah. A Jewish Messiah has great implications for all the peoples,

---

describing the ritual purification at a Jewish wedding, the Evangelist explained that the stones containing water are said to be "according to the manner of purification of the Jews" (2:6). Furthermore, in describing Jesus' interaction with the Samaritan woman in chapter 4, the Evangelist heightens the drama by explaining that "Jews have no dealings with Samaritans" (4:9). Thus, in providing those explanations attached to the descriptions of Jewish customs and practices, the Gentile identity can be readily seen, since Jewish readership would have known all these customs. Therefore, in the author's dealings with Jewish elements such as his use of the Hebrew Bible, the Jewish feasts, and the Jewish customs and practices, one can conclude that the intended audience of the Fourth Gospel is of a mixed audience at best, or more likely, predominantly Gentile.

4. Universal Salvific Emphasis. The fourth factor that may highlight the Gentile identity of the readers is perhaps the strongest clue. Although the Fourth Gospel is blanketed with OT theology from start to finish, it is also peppered with emphases on the whole world (Jews and Gentiles) as the object of salvation provided by the Messiah. This should not be surprising since, even in the OT, although the Jews were the chosen recipients and primary benefactors of God's promised blessings, the salvations of the Gentile peoples was the ultimate goal of their blessings (Gen 12:3). There is certainly a universal tone that permeates throughout the Fourth Gospel. R. E. Brown, *Gospel According to John (I–XII)*, LXXVII. For instance, Jesus is said to come into the world as a light for every man (John 1:9). Jesus takes away the sin of the world (1:29). Jesus has come to save the world (3:17). When Jesus is lifted up on the cross and in His resurrection, He draws all men to Himself (12:32).

Although the Gospel describes the universal aspect of God's salvation, there are also specific references to Gentiles as well. As Bernard observes correctly, ". . . in the Fourth Gospel the Gentiles are more explicitly than in the Synoptists brought within the range of Jesus' mission. . . ." *Critical and Exegetical Commentary*, 431. For example, in one of those ironic statements that are common in the Fourth Gospel, the Jews in 7:35 predict that Jesus will go to the Diaspora and teach the Greeks. Furthermore, Jesus' public ministry comes to a climactic end when the Greeks or Gentiles ask to see Jesus in 12:20–21. Another significant reference to the Gentiles in the Gospel is Jesus' description of the "other sheep" that are not of the sheep pen but must be brought and made part of the one flock under one shepherd (10:16). That this verse is referring to the conversion of the Gentiles can be concluded from the following chapter (11:52), where Jesus is prophesied to have died not only for the Jewish nation, but also to gather the dispersed children of God and make them one. Therefore, the universal and Gentile emphases concerning the salvation provided by the Messiah also are an indication that the readership may be predominantly Gentile.

In conclusion, then, although the Fourth Gospel is replete with allusions to the Hebrew Bible, this does not by itself warrant a conclusion that the identity of the readers is Jewish. The textual factors within the book indicate rather that the intended readers are probably Gentiles whose hope and eternal destiny are dependent on their faith in the promised Messiah of the Hebrew Bible, who is the Savior of the world.

including the Gentiles. This universal blessing of the Messiah will not only take place in the present age through the church, but also in the promised kingdom of the eschaton. While many Johannine studies have acknowledged the Old Testament emphasis in the Fourth Gospel, there remains a need to see if the sign-miracles themselves and their attendant contexts are also designed to highlight this emphasis. Furthermore, there remains a need for a study of the sign-miracles from a premillennial perspective, where the blessings of the Messiah that are foreshadowed and even experienced in the present age, will be fully realized and fulfilled in the eschatological kingdom.

THE PURPOSE AND OBJECTIVES OF THE STUDY

In close association with the need for this study, the objectives are also fourfold. The first objective of the study is to establish a Hebraic or Jewish milieu of the Fourth Gospel. This will be achieved mainly by focusing on the Evangelist's use of the Old Testament Scriptures throughout the Fourth Gospel. It will not be a comparison with and critique of other philosophical milieus, but recognition of the rich presence of the Old Testament Scriptures in John's Gospel. Beginning with the Prologue and the Testimonium in chapter 1, to the Book of Signs in chapters 2–12, and the Book of Passion in chapters 13–20, the genius of the Evangelist's use of the Old Testament will be highlighted, especially in the sign-miracles and their attendant contexts.

The second objective of the study is to do a detailed analysis of the Johannine use of the word σημεῖον. Is there any special significance in the word that the Evangelist chose to describe Jesus' miracles? The definition and meaning of the word σημεῖον will be traced in its usages in the Old Testament (LXX), and its Hebrew counterpart אוֹת. Furthermore, in relation to the Evangelist's own purpose statement in 20:30–31, the particular sign-miracles designated as σημεῖα will be identified. In addition, the order and progression of these sign-miracles will be defined in its significance.

The third objective of this study is to provide an expositional and thematic study on the sign-miracles themselves in their respective contexts, which according to the Evangelist demonstrate Jesus' messianic identity. Thus, each sign-miracle and its attendant context will be examined with the aim of identifying the Person and works of Jesus as the Messiah. Furthermore, each of the sign-miracles will be examined in their eschatological emphasis concerning the messianic blessings that will be fully realized in the promised kingdom. Although the messianic blessings are being experienced in the present age (i.e., soteriological aspect), there are many others that are highlighted in the sign-miracles in anticipation of the coming eschatological kingdom.

The fourth objective of the study is to highlight the Evangelist's inclusive and universal emphasis in relation to his theme. In other words, how do the sign-miracles demonstrate Jesus to be the promised Messiah of the Old Testament, and what universal and inclusive emphasis can be seen through the sign-miracles? Furthermore, are the sign-miracles of the Messiah fulfilled in the present age, or are they experienced and yet merely foreshadow the fulfillment in the promised kingdom? In other words, the promised Messiah of the Hebrew Bible is the hope for all peoples, and not only in this age through the church, but also in the eschatological kingdom, when the intent of the Abrahamic covenant to bless the nations through the seed of Abraham will be fully realized (Gen 12:1–3; 15:1–21). The purpose of this study, then, is to examine the sign-miracles and their attendant contexts from a premillennial viewpoint.

THE PERSPECTIVE AND LIMITATIONS OF THE STUDY

The limitations of this study will be essentially threefold. First, in establishing the Hebraic or Jewish milieu of the Fourth Gospel, the primary evidence will be the Evangelist's ample use of the Old Testament Scriptures in the book. However, unlike the Synoptic Gospels, particularly Matthew, John does not use many quotations from the Old Testament, although he alludes to them. Besides, it is the breadth of the Evangelist's Old Testament theology that stands out in the Fourth Gospel. Furthermore, the background behind the sign-miracles and the various discourses of Jesus is clearly the Hebrew Bible. Thus, this study will not be a detailed examination of the Evangelist's various uses of the Hebrew Scriptures, but merely the recognition of the apostle's Old Testament theology. Second, the study of the sign-miracles (σημεῖα) will not be an exegetical study on the specific passages that describe the miracles. Rather, it will be an expositional and thematic study of the miracles, as they highlight the Person and works of Jesus as the promised Messiah of the Hebrew Bible. Furthermore, this study will focus mainly on the sign-miracles that are all contained in the Book of Signs (chaps. 2–12), although the content of the Book of Glory (chaps. 13–20) will be broadly surveyed, as the miracles validate the claims made in the Book of Signs concerning the Messiah.

Third, although the blessings of the Messiah that are predicted in the Hebrew Bible are many, this study will mainly focus on the messianic significance and blessings that are highlighted through the sign-miracles in the Fourth Gospel.

THE PROCEDURE OF THE STUDY

The first four chapters will consist of the introductory chapters concerning Jesus' miracles in the Gospel of John, and these chapters will be included in Part 1 of the book. The opening chapter of the book will be an introduction to the whole study. It will begin with the pertinence or need of the study, namely, the rich presence of the Hebrew Bible and its theology in the Fourth Gospel. The Evangelist's purpose statement (20:30–31) seems to indicate that the sign-miracles were intended to demonstrate Jesus to be the promised Messiah of the Old Testament. If so, then how do the sign-miracles demonstrate the messianic identity of Jesus Christ, as they are anticipated in the Old Testament Scriptures? This chapter will conclude with the purpose or objectives of the study, the perspective or limitations of the study, and then the procedure of the study.

Chapter two will be a detailed examination and discussion of the Evangelist's use of the σημεῖον (σημεῖα) in the Fourth Gospel. The study of the apostle John's use of the word will indicate that the sign-miracles in the Fourth Gospel all point to a deeper meaning of Jesus' messianic identity and deeds. The word σημεῖον seems to be used throughout Scripture to convey the idea of demonstrating some significant truths through a miracle, as a sample of what is to take place in the future. In the Fourth Gospel, the main emphasis of the σημεῖα is the Person of Jesus (Christology) who, as the promised Messiah of the Hebrew Scriptures, embodies the fulfillment of God's plan, both in the present age and in the age to come. Furthermore, the miracles that are designated as the σημεῖα in the Fourth Gospel emphasize the Person of the Messiah by the kind of miracles that are expected in the messianic age. The aim of the sign-miracles is primarily to indicate the Person of Jesus as the promised Messiah and the Son of God. In addition, the Fourth Gospel reveals that the messianic identity of Jesus is significant not only for the Jews but also for the Gentiles, whose kingdom will certainly encompass the Gentiles of all the nations. This can be witnessed through the wonderful mixture of all peoples in the present age through the church.

Apart from the significance and purposes of the word shmei=on, this chapter will also discuss the identification and number of the sign-miracles. Which miracles did the Evangelist have in mind in demonstrating the messianic identity of Jesus? Furthermore, the order and progression of the sign-miracles will also be examined. Is there any significance in the order of miracles recorded by the Evangelist? If so, what? These, along with the significance and purposes of the sign-miracles will be included in this chapter.

Chapters 3 and 4 will discuss the significance of John 1 as an introduction to the Book of Signs (chaps. 2–12). They will include both the Prologue (1:1–18) and the Testimonium (1:19–51), as they set the stage for the Evangelist to present the seven sign-miracles. Chapter 3 will consist of the Johannine Prologue (1:1–18) that has often been characterized as the "foyer" to the rest of the Gospel, where many key words, phrases, and concepts that play a significant part in the body of the Gospel are first introduced. Chapter 4 then will focus on the Johannine Testimonium (1:19–51) where John the Baptist and Jesus' disciples attribute seven titles to Jesus. All these titles together prepare the reader for the messianic revelations about Jesus in the Gospel narrative, particularly the sign-miracles in the Book of Signs (chaps. 2–12).

The next seven chapters (chaps. 5–11) will be the major body of the book consisting of the seven sign-miracles of Jesus in the Fourth Gospel. They will all be included in Part 2 of the book. Chapters 5 and 6 will include the first two miracles of Jesus in John's Gospel, both of them performed in Cana of Galilee. They are thus often characterized as the "Cana Cycle" (2:1—4:54). Chapter 5 will focus on Jesus' first miracle of turning water into wine at the wedding (2:1–11) and chapter 6 will develop Jesus' miracle of healing the official's son (4:43–54).

Chapters 7 through 10 will examine the third through sixth sign-miracles in the Fourth Gospel, which are all included in the section often called the "Festival Cycle" (chaps. 5–10). This section is called such because the chapters are all set in the context of Jewish feasts, namely, the Sabbath, the Passover, and the Tabernacles. All these sign-miracles, namely, the healing of the lame man at the Pool of Bethesda (5:1–16), the feeding of the five thousand (6:1–15), the walking on the Sea of Galilee

(6:16–21), and the healing of the man born blind (9:1–41), will be viewed in their significant relationship to their respective feasts.

Chapter 11 will then examine the seventh and climactic sign-miracle of Jesus' raising of Lazarus from the dead (11:1–46). Whereas the first sign of Jesus' turning of water into wine serves as the representative sign among the seven sign-miracles, the seventh sign will be shown to be the climactic and completing sign.

Chapters 12 through 13 will consist of the conclusion of Jesus' miracles that will make up Part 3 of the book. Chapter 12 will also examine the significance of John 12, which serves as a literary "hinge" between the Book of Signs and the Book of Glory. Then, chapter 13 will briefly examine the significance of the Book of Glory (chaps. 13–20) as these chapters fulfill and authenticate the earlier claims and miracles that highlighted Jesus' messianic identity, by both Jesus Himself and His followers. Finally, chapter 13 will consist of the conclusion of the whole study, summarizing each chapter and highlighting its central points as they validate the thesis of the book.

2

Σημεῖα in the Fourth Gospel

INTRODUCTION

ONE OF THE UNIQUE features of the Fourth Gospel is the Evangelist's purposeful and strategic use of the word σημεῖον. In fact, it is the key word in the author's own purpose statement of his book: "Jesus did many other miraculous signs (σημεῖα) in the presence of his disciples, which are not recorded in this book. But these are written that you may believe that Jesus is the Christ, the Son of God, and that by believing you may have life in his name" (John 20:30–31).[1] In other words, it is the sign-miracles (σημεῖα) that demonstrate the Evangelist's main thesis of the Fourth Gospel, namely, that Jesus is the promised Messiah of the Old Testament Scriptures and the divine Son of God. Peter Riga correctly describes the significance of this word when he concludes, "Perhaps no single word can give such a profound insight into the whole theology of the Fourth Gospel as the word σημεῖον."[2]

In fact, some even see the σημεῖον as the key to interpreting the whole Gospel.[3] The study of this significant word will indicate that the sign-miracles in the Fourth Gospel all point to a deeper meaning beyond the miracle itself.[4] A broad survey of the word defines σημεῖον as follows: (1) a sign or distinguishing mark by which something is known; (2) a sign consisting of a wonder or miracle, an event that is contrary to the usual course of nature, either of divine or demonic in nature;

1. Tenney, "Topics from the Gospel of John—Part II," 145.
2. Riga, "Signs of Glory," 402.
3. Rainey, "'Σημεῖον' in the Fourth Gospel."
4. Gordon, "Sign," 4:505–6.

(3) a sign or portent of the last days.[5] Thus, the word σημεῖον seems to be used throughout Scripture to convey the idea of demonstrating significant truths through a miracle, as a sample of what is to take place in the future.[6] In other words, the word σημεῖον is loaded with theological import and plays a strategic role in the interpretation of the Gospel. It is little wonder, then, that many studies have been devoted to this significant word.[7] And, since the proper understanding of this word is paramount in interpreting the sign-miracles (σημεῖα) and the whole Gospel, this present chapter will be devoted entirely to the study of it.

The chapter will be divided into four major sections. The first section will include the uses and nature of σημεῖον. This section will basically consist of a word study on σημεῖον, defining and surveying the word's use in both the extrabiblical and biblical writings, followed by an analysis of the nature of the signs. The second section of the chapter will examine the significance and purposes of the σημεῖα. This section will highlight the theological significance of the σημεῖα by comparing them with other important themes in the Fourth Gospel, followed by an analysis of the purposes of the σημεῖα intentionally designed by the Evangelist, as well as the different aspects of Jesus' Christology that they emphasize. The third section of this chapter will determine the identification and number of the σημεῖα. This section will attempt to determine which parts of the Gospel should be included within the author's intended σημεῖα, following both discussion and speculation on how many should be included. The fourth section of this chapter will include the order and progression of the σημεῖα. This section will attempt to determine whether the Evangelist designed his σημεῖα in a certain significant order, and if so, what significant progression is intended in that order.

---

5. BAGD 747–48.

6. Barrett emphasizes the eschatological aspect of the sign-miracles, "The אוֹת –σημεῖον thus becomes a special part of the prophetic activity; no mere illustration, but a symbolic anticipation or showing forth of a greater reality of which the σημεῖον is nevertheless itself a part." *Gospel According to St. John*, 63.

7. Some of the most extensive studies on the Johannine σημεῖα are the following: Barrett, *Gospel According to St. John*, 75–78; Becker, "Wunder und Christologie," 130–48; R. E. Brown, *Gospel According to John (I–XII)*, 525–32; Fortna, *Gospel of Signs*; Fuller, *Interpreting the Miracles*, 88–109; Guthrie, "Importance of Signs," 72–83; Lohse, "Miracles in the Fourth Gospel," 64–75; Morris, *Gospel According to John*, 684–91; Nicol, *Semeia in the Fourth Gospel*; Richardson, *Miracle-Stories of the Gospels*, 114–22; Riga, "Signs of Glory," 402–24; Schnackenburg, *Gospel According to St. John*, 1:515–28.

These significant issues involving the Johannine σημεῖα will be analyzed in this chapter.

THE USES AND NATURE OF ΣΗΜΕΙΑ

This section will first begin with a brief survey of the word's etymology and its extrabiblical usages, followed by an analysis of the biblical uses of σημεῖον, in both the Old Testament and the New. Then, this section will conclude with a discussion on the nature of σημεῖα, particularly in the Johannine writings.

The Uses of Σημεῖον

This study of the usage of σημεῖον will be divided into two major sections: first, the etymology and its extrabiblical usages in the classical Greek writings, the papyri, the apocryphal books, and the writings of Philo will be briefly surveyed; and second, the biblical usages of σημεῖα will be examined in both the Old Testament and the New.

The Etymology and Extrabiblical Usages of Σημεῖον—Σημεῖον is a derivative of σῆμα and is related to σημήιον (Ionic) and σαμᾶον (Doric).[8] It occurs only in the form of σῆμα in the early Greek epic but σημεῖον became more common in general use later, especially in prose.[9] In either case, it may refer to a sign, mark, or token by which a person or a thing is known. It also may designate an omen or portent of some future event. It also gives reference to certification or to credentials.[10] There seem to be two basic meanings of the word σημεῖον, namely, first, as a distinguishing mark by which something or someone is known, or second, as a reference to a miracle or wonder, that often foreshadows a future event.[11] In other words, the word can refer to a sign in either the natural or supernatural realm.

The meaning of σημεῖον in extrabiblical literature follows a similar sense. For instance, in the classical Greek writings there is a constant search for the hidden meaning in natural phenomena as well as in supernatural phenomena. And, these phenomena are often termed

8. Liddell and Scott, *Greek-English Lexicon*, 1592–93.

9. Rengstorf, "Σημεῖον," 7:201.

10. Liddell and Scott, *A Greek-English Lexicon*, 1592–93.

11. BAGD 747–48.

σημεῖα.[12] Σημεῖον is also used in the papyri in a similar way. It can be used in reference to a hidden meaning or message, to scars or marks on the body such as circumcision, or even in the sense of certification or validation.[13] In the papyri there are also numerous examples of miracles that are called signs with a message attached to them.[14] For instance, in a treatise on divination from the late second or third century BC, there is a description of an event where a lightning struck several statues, and this event is referred to as a σημεῖον because it presumably carried a sign.[15]

Σημεῖον is also used in the apocryphal books such as Tobit (5:2) and Wisdom of Solomon (5:11, 13), with a similar connotation such as certification, validation, evidence, or identifying mark.[16] For instance, on one occasion Tobit is sending his son Tobias on a mission to recover some money from Gabael, and Tobias asks, "What sign (σημεῖον) shall I give him that he may recognize me, trust me, and give me the money?" (Tob 5:2). In this instance, the meaning of a sign connotes a certification or proof. Similar connotation is used in the Wisdom of Solomon 5:11–13 where, like a bird that leaves no evidence (sign) that its wings have moved through the air in flight, so the wicked man leaves no mark or evidence (sign) of virtue as he passes through life. However, there is a different connotation in the same book later when it depicts a miraculous act: "She (wisdom) entered the soul of a servant of the Lord, and withstood dread kings with wonders and signs" (Wis 10:16).

Σημεῖον is also used in the writings of Philo with a symbolic meaning. As Dodd points out, "Philo employs the verb σημαίνειν with especial reference to the symbolic significance which he discovers in various passages of the Old Testament."[17] For example, σημεῖον is substituted as a synonym for σύμβαλον in Philo's comments on such passages as Genesis 2:9, where the trees of paradise are described as "pleasant to the sight, which is a symbol of theoretical excellence; and likewise good

---

12. Rainey, "'Σημεῖον' in the Fourth Gospel," 22–26. Rainey does a thorough study in his dissertation of the uses of σημεῖον in different extrabiblical literature.

13. Ibid., 26–31.

14. Ibid., 30–31.

15. Ibid.

16. Ibid., 31–32.

17. Dodd, *Interpretation of the Fourth Gospel*, 141–43.

for good, which is a token of useful and practical good" (*Allegorical Interpretation*, I.XVII [58]).[18]

In summary, then, the uses of σημεῖον in extrabiblical literature seem to be quite uniform in meaning. The basic meaning of σημεῖον seems to denote a mark or symbol to identify a thing or person which contains a significant message or revelation. Furthermore, σημεῖον also possesses the character of the supernatural, from which the phrase "miraculous sign" is derived.[19]

The Biblical Uses of Σημεῖον—The review of biblical uses of σημεῖον will begin with its use in the Greek Old Testament, the Septuagint (LXX), followed by its usage in the Hebrew Old Testament with its Hebrew counterpart אוֹת. This will be followed by the use of σημεῖον in the New Testament, beginning with the Synoptic Gospels and Acts, followed by the epistles. Then, σημεῖον will be examined in the writings of the apostle John, his Epistles and the Apocalypse, as well as the Fourth Gospel.

THE USES OF ΣΗΜΕΙΟΝ IN THE LXX

The Septuagint provides a rich reservoir for the meaning of σημεῖον. In the LXX σημεῖον is predominantly a translation of the Hebrew word אוֹת and, like it, is used to convey the idea of a sign, mark, token, or a miraculous sign.[20] Rengstorf explains the similarity between the two words this way: "Σημεῖον, which is itself very formal in meaning, which aims at sense impressions with a view to imparting insights or knowledge and which has from the outset no specific religious reference, was obviously regarded by the OT translators as the proper rendering of אוֹת, which is also formal and which also aims at conceptual clarification by means of impressions. If in the LXX אוֹת is normally translated σημεῖον, this is adequate proof how close the two words are by nature."[21] In the Septuagint, σημεῖον occurs some 125 times, but only about 85 times in the Hebrew canonical books.[22] Most of these occurrences ap-

---

18. *The Works of Philo: Complete and Unabridged*, trans. C. D. Yonge (Peabody, MA: Hendrickson, 1993), 31.

19. Hofius, "Miracle," 2:626.

20. Ibid.

21. Rengstorf, "Σημεῖον," 7:219.

22. Ibid., 208.

pear in the Pentateuch and the Prophets, but a comparatively minor role in the historical books and the Wisdom literature.[23]

The meaning and usage of σημεῖον in the LXX is not much different than the extrabiblical uses. It most often refers to a miracle in the Pentateuch and to a symbolic action of a prophet in the Prophets. Physical objects may also be referred to as signs, such as an identifying mark. Or, as Rainey concludes, "The sign may be in the form of a pledge, warning, or portent of something that is going to occur in the future; or it may be a reminder or witness to something that has taken place in the past."[24] And, most importantly, as is common in the Pentateuch, signs may be the credentials to prove that the prophet is a messenger sent from God.[25] This is certainly the case in the life of Moses, God's servant, during the exodus. In fact, many of the instances where σημεῖον is used in the Greek Old Testament are in reference to the miracles displayed in Egypt and the wilderness.

Raymond Brown perceptively connects the main background of the Johannine σημεῖον to the Old Testament, particularly the signs displayed during the exodus.[26] Alan Richardson also insightfully observes the connection between Old Testament signs and the Johannine signs, that they both confirm faith and attest it.[27] He observes that men are tempted to reject the sign which God gives and to demand signs of their own devising, thus provoking or tempting God by their unbelief (cf. Exod 17:7; Num 14:11; Deut 9:22).[28] This is certainly the case in Jesus' rebuke of the Jews in the Fourth Gospel (6:26, 30). Robert Houston Smith also proposes a fascinating connection between the exodus miracles and the Johannine miracles, although he often goes too far in his comparisons.[29] He calls Jesus' signs in the Fourth Gospel antitypes of Moses's signs.[30]

23. Ibid.

24. Rainey, "'Σημεῖον' in the Fourth Gospel," 46.

25. Ibid.

26. R. E. Brown, *New Testament Essays*, 185–86. He makes very interesting observations comparing the similarities between the exodus signs and the Johannine signs: for instance, signs are performed, yet the people refuse to believe (cf. Exod 10:1; Num 14:11, 22; John 12:37); Moses and Jesus are both described as workers of signs (cf. Deut 34:11; John 20:30); the glory of God is connected with signs (cf. Num 14:22; John 2:11).

27. Richardson, *Theology of the New Testament*, 21.

28. Ibid.

29. R. H. Smith, "Exodus Typology in the Fourth Gospel," 329–42.

30. Ibid. Smith makes parallel comparisons of Moses's signs in the Exodus account with the signs of Jesus in the Fourth Gospel. For instance, the changing of water into

While the comparisons of the signs are interesting, they seem too far-fetched when viewed closely and paralleled individually.[31] As Donald Guthrie contends regarding Smith's comparisons, "It is hard enough to believe that the author himself had such parallels in mind and almost inconceivable that any of his original readers would have suspected it."[32] Nevertheless, the study has some value. While the Fourth Evangelist may not have attempted to parallel each of Jesus' signs with Moses's signs, it is not inconceivable that he had these signs in mind generally. After all, some of Jesus' miracles, particularly the feeding of the five thousand and Jesus' walking on water accounts are set in the context of the Passover background. Thus, as Raymond Brown and other Johannine scholars conclude, the primary background behind the sign-miracles in the Fourth Gospel is the Old Testament.

THE USES OF אוֹת IN THE HEBREW OLD TESTAMENT

The Septuagint's use of σημεῖον as a translation of the Hebrew word אוֹת leads to the natural step of examining its Hebrew uses. And, since the significance of both words seems to be very close, the original context of the Hebrew word bears closer scrutiny. The Hebrew word אוֹת appears eighty-three times in the OT, with almost half of these occurrences (42 times) in the Pentateuch and about a quarter of the occurrences (19

---

blood (Exod 7:14–24) and the changing of water into wine (John 2:1–11) are paralleled. The parallel is seen by a way of contrast. Whereas the Moses's sign brings death, Jesus' sign brings life. However, the second, third, and fourth signs of Moses (the frogs, the gnats, and the flies of Exod 7:25—8:32) find no parallels in the Johannine Gospel. Moses's fifth sign concerning the plagues on domestic animals (Exod 9:1–7), however, and the healing of the official's son (John 4:46–54) are paralleled; both afflictions lead to death. Furthermore, the sixth sign of Moses concerning the disease of the body (Exod 9:8–12) is paralleled with the illness of the lame man at the Pool of Bethesda (John 5:2–9). The seventh sign of Moses, the thunderstorm (Exod 9:13–26), is paralleled with the stilling of the storm (John 6:16–21). Moses's eighth sign concerning the locusts (Exod 10:1–20) is paralleled with the feeding of the five thousand in the Fourth Gospel (John 6:1–15). The two miracles are contrasted. Whereas the locusts take food, Jesus gives food. The sixth sign also draws parallels by a contrast. Whereas Moses sends darkness (Exod 10:21–29), Jesus gives light to those blind (John 9:1–7). Finally, the death of the firstborn (Exod 11:1—12:32), the tenth sign of Moses, is the climax of his signs. The seventh sign of the Fourth Gospel of Jesus raising Lazarus from the dead (John 11:1–44) is likewise a climax of the miracles of Jesus.

31. Guthrie, *New Testament Introduction*, 4th ed., 330.

32. Ibid.

times) in the Major Prophets (Isa, Jer, Ezek).[33] In many instances (no less than 18 times), אוֹת appears with מוֹפֵת, especially in the book of Deuteronomy.[34] This is remarkable, in that מוֹפֵת occurs only thirty-six times in the entire Hebrew OT.[35] Furthermore, the word אוֹת occurs most (25 of 83 times) in reference to the plagues of Egypt. In other words, they refer to the miraculous deeds God displayed in Egypt.

Most of the usages of אוֹת in the Hebrew Bible refer to acts performed by God. The use of אוֹת can be classified broadly into seven major functions.[36] First, there are signs of divine knowledge, or signs that are designed to bring about the knowledge of God (Exod 7:3; Deut 4:34). These instances describe God's miraculous signs displayed before men, in order to make Himself known. Second, there are signs of protection or distinction (Gen 4:15; Exod 12:13). These instances describe, for example, a mark of distinction or protection given to Cain.[37] They can also describe a sign of faith on the doorposts of the Israelites by means of blood on the eve of the exodus from Egypt. Third, there are signs of faith that are intended to instill and confirm faith in God (Num 14:11, 22; Deut 11:3; Josh 24:17; Isa 7:11, 14). These signs describe the great works of God performed in Egypt and in the wilderness that serve as a testimony of His power and faithfulness. They also beckon for a response of love and obedience on the part of His people throughout generations.

Fourth, there are signs of remembrance (Exod 13:9; 31:13, 17; Deut 6:8; Josh 4:6). These signs describe observances such as the Passover and the Sabbath that remind the Israelites of God's deliverance of His people. They also describe God's commandments and the stones of remembrance from the Jordan River that are to serve as perpetual reminders of God's goodness and faithfulness. Fifth, there are signs of the covenant. These are signs given by God to remind His people of the covenant He has made with them. For instance, the rainbow is to remind the people of the Noahic covenant (Gen 9:12, 17), circumcision serves as a sign of the Abrahamic covenant (Gen 17:11), and the Sabbath serves as a sign of the

---

33. Kruger, "אוֹת," 1:331–32.

34. Rengstorf, "Σημεῖον," 7:210.

35. Ibid.

36. Helfmeyer, "אוֹת," 1:167–88. Helfmeyer lists seven major functions of אוֹת in the OT (with many of them interrelated and overlapping). These seven will serve as a general guide here.

37. Alden, "אוֹת," 1:18.

Mosaic covenant (Exod 31:13, 17; Ezek 20:12, 20). Sixth, there are signs of confirmation (Exod 3:12; Judg 6:17; 1 Sam 2:34; 10:1, 7, 9). These are signs intended to confirm or authenticate a divine message, and these usages occur frequently in the historical books. Kruger's description is accurate: "The sign as such has nothing to do with the content of the divine word. It merely functions as a legitimation or confirmation of its reliability. In the call narratives a sign is also given as confirmation of the divine commissioning (Moses: Exod 3:12; Gideon: Judg 6:17; Saul: 1 Sam 10:3 ff.)."[38] Seventh, there are symbolic signs. These are signs that function as means of proclaiming God's message (Isa 8:18; 20:3; Ezek 4:3). The seventh category of the word's function differs from the others, in that in this last type the actor is not God but the prophet, who acts in obedience to God's word. As Helfmeyer says, "these signs do not draw attention because they are necessarily miraculous, but because they are peculiar."[39]

These different functions of signs (אוֹת) in the Old Testament have several common traits. First, the basic idea of signs is that they point to and signify something. Second, the medium of communicating signs is either exclusively or primarily visual.[40] In other words, a sign is usually something one sees. Third, the content of signs is mostly theological (i.e., they confirm an act as from God).[41] Fourth, signs are often accompanied by God's word and can only be interpreted and comprehended in the light of it. F. C. Helfmeyer describes accurately: "A sign in itself must not motivate people to believe; crucial instead is the word that accompanies the sign. This word declares in what or whom the sign is intended to motivate a person to believe. Therefore, there is no sign revelation without a corresponding word revelation interpreting the sign."[42] Harold Knight's description is also perceptive: "The essential mark of a miracle for the pious Israelite is furnished not by its supernatural character, but by its richness and depth of significance as a revelatory event. Hence it comes about that faith alone can discern this miraculous quality."[43] And

38. Kruger, "אוֹת," 1:332.

39. Helfmeyer, "אוֹת," 1:186.

40. Gordon, "Sign," 4:505–6.

41. Ibid., 4:506. Although there are secular references of the word in extrabiblical literature, the biblical usages of the word, for the most part, reflect theological referent.

42. Helfmeyer, "אוֹת," 1:177.

43. Knight, "Old Testament Conception of Miracle," 358.

fifth, the nature of signs is mostly miraculous or peculiar. As mentioned above, in many instances in the Old Testament where אֹות is mentioned (25/79x), it is describing the miraculous deeds of God in delivering His people out of Egypt.

THE USES OF ΣΗΜΕΙΟΝ IN THE NEW TESTAMENT

In the New Testament, σημεῖον also has a variety of uses. The word σημεῖον is used for certain at least seventy-seven times.[44] It is used thirteen times by Matthew, seven times by Mark, twenty-four times by Luke (Gospel 11 times and Acts 13 times), twenty-four times by John (Gospel 17 times and Rev 7 times), eight times by Paul and only once in the book of Hebrews.[45] In the New Testament, the linguistic usage of the LXX is generally adopted, and has similar categories: (1) sign (Matt 26:48), mark (2 Thess 3:17), or token (Luke 2:12) of distinction; (2) miraculous sign, miracle (John 2:12, 18, 23; Acts 4:16, 22; 8:6; 1 Cor 1:22); (3) the apocalyptic meaning of sign of the end (Mark 13:4; Matt 24:3; Luke 21:11, 15).[46]

The Uses of σημεῖον *in the Synoptic Gospels and Acts*—The Synoptic Gospels often use σημεῖον in reference to the signs of the expectant Messiah, the true prophet of God, because first-century Jewish people in Palestine expected any true prophet of God to validate His ministry with signs. Thus, the scribes and Pharisees dogged Jesus' ministry by demanding, "Teacher, we wish to see a sign from you" (Matt 12:38; cf. Mark 8:11). The Sadducees also demanded the same kind of signs (Matt 16:1; cf. Luke 11:16, 29; 23:8). It is little wonder, then, that the apostle Paul said, "the Jews ask for signs" (1 Cor 1:22; cf. Luke 11:16; John 2:18; 3:2; 4:48; 6:30; 7:31; 9:16; 12:18; Acts 2:22).[47] Therefore, the use of σημεῖα in the Synoptic Gospels often refers to the signs demanded of Jesus by the Jewish religious leadership. In the Synoptic Gospels, however, Jesus

---

44. Rengstorf, "Σημεῖον," 7:229–30. These figures vary slightly among NT scholars, depending on whether one counts multiple uses in the same verses. For instance, Hofius counts the word (semeion) 77 times in the NT, *NIDNTT* 2:629; and Wigram counts 78 times in his *Englishman's Greek Concordance*, 684–85.

45. Rengstorf, "Σημεῖον," 7:229–30. These facts are according to Rengstorf's general count, and thus vary slightly among other scholars. Therefore, these facts should be considered general and approximate.

46. Hofius, "Miracle," 2:629–32.

47. Gordon, "Sign," 4:506.

refuses to give such signs to the religious leaders because of their demands resulting from unbelief and cynicism (Mark 8:11–12). Besides, the motivation behind their request for a sign was the desire to "test" Jesus (v. 11). Instead, the only sign that will be given the nation and its religious leaders would be the sign of Jonah and Jesus' statement that "the Son of man will be three days and three nights in the heart of the earth" (Matt 12:38–40; Luke 11:29–30). One of the categories of σημεῖα in the Synoptic Gospels, then, is in reference to the demands of unbelief and hardness of heart by the religious leaders of Jesus' day and, therefore, seems to have a negative connotation.

The Synoptic Gospels also use σημεῖα in reference to the future consummation of God's kingdom and the coming of the Son of Man in glory.[48] For instance, when the disciples ask Jesus, "What will be the sign of your coming?" (Matt 24:3; cf. Mark 13:4; Luke 21:7), Jesus says that before the end there will be "great signs from heaven." These signs, which will announce Jesus' Second Advent, will continue throughout the eschaton. In other words, as the religious leaders demanded signs of the expectant Messiah, albeit with wrong motives, certain messianic signs will be characterized in the eschatological kingdom (Matt 11:2–6; Luke 7:18–22). As Hofius explains, the signs in the millennial kingdom will be "signs of God's kingly rule, the dawn of which Jesus announced in his proclamation."[49] He elaborates further concerning the signs: "Jesus' words and works are the beginning of the age of salvation, and the miracles are a foreshadowing and a promise of the coming universal redemption. Ultimately, it is in this eschatological context that the accounts of Jesus' miracles are to be read."[50] This second category of σημεῖα in the Synoptic Gospels, then, seems to include both the eschatological and supernatural aspect of the signs.

The phrase "signs and wonders" (σημεῖα καὶ τέρατα) occurs many times in the book of Acts, but also in several other books of the New Testament (Matt 24:24; Mark 13:22; John 4:48; Acts 2:19, 22, 43; 4:30; 6:8; 7:36; 15:12; Rom 15:19; 2 Cor 12:12; 2 Thess 2:9; Heb 2:4).[51] This phrase appears many times in the LXX in place of the Hebrew words אֹות and מֹופֵת, particularly in Exodus and Deuteronomy in reference to the

48. Ibid.

49. Hofius, "Miracle," 2:631.

50. Ibid.

51. Ibid.

miracles performed in Egypt and the wilderness.[52] Both σημεῖα and τέρατα refer to miracles, but as Tenney explains their distinction, "σημεῖα emphasizes the *significance* or *purpose* of these unusual occurrences, while τέρατα refers to the *marvel* or *wonder* they excite."[53] Nevertheless, they both seem to connote a supernatural event, presumably of great significance.

The Uses of σημεῖον *in the Epistles*—The use of σημεῖον occurs far less frequently in the epistles than the Synoptic Gospels and Acts. Interestingly, the word plays a minor role in the writings of the apostle Paul, for σημεῖον does not even appear in many of his epistles.[54] In all, σημεῖον appears only about eight times in all of Paul's writings. What is more, the word does not appear in any of the remaining epistles (General Epistles), with the exception of its lone appearance in the Epistle to the Hebrews. The use of σημεῖον in the epistles is very similar to the usages in various parts of the Bible, both the Old and New Testaments. Although the number of uses in the epistles are few, the categories are varied and resemble other parts of Scripture: (1) a sign of distinguishing mark or token (2 Thess 3:17); (2) a sign of covenant or rite (Rom 4:11; 1 Cor 14:22); (3) a sign of miracle, either of divine or demonic origin (Rom 15:19; 1 Cor 1:22; 2 Cor 12:12; 2 Thess 2:9; Heb 2:4).

The Uses of σημεῖον *in the Johannine Writings*—Of all the New Testament writers, no one uses σημεῖον as frequently, uniformly, or significantly as the Fourth Evangelist. In the Johannine writings, σημεῖον is used at least twenty-four times (17 times in the Fourth Gospel and 7 times in the Apocalypse).[55] Interestingly, this significant word is not used in any of his epistles. However, the use of the word in John's Apocalypse seems to have much the same meaning as in his Gospel.[56] Because of the well-documented distinction of John's use of σημεῖον from the other gospel writers, this section will be devoted to comparing the similarities as well as distinctions between them.

---

52. Rengstorf, "Σημεῖον," 7:209–10.

53. Tenney, "Topics from the Gospel of John—Part II," 146.

54. Σημεῖα does not appear in any of Paul's following epistles: Gal, Eph, Phil, Col, 1 Thess, Phlm, 1 & 2 Tim, and Titus.

55. Wigram, *Englishman's Greek Concordance*, 684–85.

56. Tenney, "Topics from the Gospel of John—Part II," 146.

Although there are many distinctions between the Synoptists and the Fourth Evangelist in their use of σημεῖα, there are also some similarities. First, John knows and uses σημεῖον in the usual sense to mean "sign," "pointer," or "mark."[57] For instance, σημεῖον means "sign" or "portent" of the eschaton (Rev 12:1, 3; 15:1), "proof" of self-authentication (John 2:18), and "miracles" or "acts" of supernatural kind, whether by Jesus or demons (Rev 13:13–14; 16:4; 19:20). Second, like the other biblical writers, Johannine signs are also usually visible. As Karl Rengstorf explains, "The basic thrust of the term is clear in John, for no matter what specific nuances are given by the context the essential reference here again is to visual perception and the assurance this gives."[58] Terms such as θεωρεῖν (John 2:23), ὁρᾶν (John 6:2), ἰδεῖν (John 6:14, 30; Rev 15:1), and ὤφθη (Rev 12:1, 3) are used to indicate that signs are something that one can see visually. Third, as is common in the Synoptic Gospels, John also uses σημεῖον in reference to a sign being demanded of Jesus.[59] However, this usage occurs only twice in the Fourth Gospel, once after the cleansing of the temple (2:18), and the other after the feeding of the five thousand (6:30). In short, John is cognizant of and does employ σημεῖον in the synoptic tradition.

Although there are some similarities between John and the Synoptists in their use of σημεῖον, there are also significant differences that must be highlighted. First, both in the Gospel and the Apocalypse, σημεῖον has replaced the role that δύναμις plays elsewhere in the New Testament, particularly the Synoptics, in reference to the miracles.[60] If the Synoptists narrate Jesus' miracles primarily to highlight His power (δύναμις), particularly over the forces of evil, the miracles (σημεῖα) in John's Gospel seem to primarily emphasize Jesus' identity as the Messiah of God and the divine Son of God. As Rengstorf observes perceptively, "Johannine σημεῖα and the person of the one who does them cannot be separated. In some way the σημεῖα also bear the nature of him who is

---

57. Rengstorf, "Σημεῖον," 7:243.

58. Ibid.

59. Ibid., 244.

60. Morris, *Gospel According to John*, 684–85. He explains that δύναμις, which is a favorite word used by the Synoptists in reference to Jesus' miracles (Matt uses it 12x, Mark 10x, Luke 15x), is never used in John. He also points out, interestingly, that although the Synoptists use σημεῖον (Matt 13x, Mark 7x, Luke 11x), none of them uses the word in reference to Jesus' miracles.

at work in them."[61] In short, the emphasis of the sign-miracles in John's Gospel is primarily christological.

Second, the Johannine usage of σημεῖα is generally restricted to the selected miracles of Jesus in the Fourth Gospel and to ungodly powers in the Apocalypse.[62] In both the Gospel and the Apocalypse, σημεῖα generally point to the supernatural and the miraculous. As Nicodemus confessed to Jesus during his nocturnal encounter, "For no one can perform these miraculous signs (σημεῖα) you are doing if God were not with him" (John 3:2). Furthermore, the selected few miracles in the Fourth Gospel are messianic in their focus. They are the kind of miracles expected with the dawn of the messianic age (Isa 35:5; cf. Matt 11:5; Luke 7:22).[63] Hofius highlights the eschatological emphasis of the Johannine miracles thusly: "The eschatological reference of Jesus' miracles is also expressed in its particular way by John's Gospel. The miracles are understood as signs pointing beyond themselves to the one who performs them. They prove Jesus' identity as the Christ of God (John 20:30), who brings the fullness of eschatological salvation."[64] Thus, Rengstorf calls the Johannine miracles "messianic epiphany-miracles."[65] In short, the Johannine signs are both miraculous and messianic.

Third, the use of σημεῖα in John's Gospel occurs predominantly on the lips of the Evangelist himself (John 2:11, 23, 4:54, 6:2, 14, 12:18, 37, 20:30).[66] This is significant because the author himself presents Jesus' signs positively. Whereas σημεῖα in the Synoptic Gospels seem to have negative connotations because they are demanded by the skeptical religious leaders, John's presentation of Jesus' signs serves both as a source of knowledge about Him and a motivation to believe (or, continue to

61. Rengstorf, "Σημεῖον," 7:245.

62. Ibid.

63. Ibid., 245–46.

64. Hofius, "Miracle," 2:632.

65. Rengstorf, "Σημεῖον," 7:246.

66. Ibid., 7:247. There are a few instances where the word was used by someone other than the Evangelist. For instance, Jesus' opponents used the word on two occasions when they asked Him what sign He showed (John 2:18; 6:30). Additionally, Jesus' opponents also asked themselves whether the Christ would do more signs than Jesus when He came (7:31). There were also couple of occasions when Jesus Himself used the word, once when He lamented that His hearers would not believe unless they saw "signs and wonders" (4:48), and another when Jesus referred to those who sought Him out because they ate the loaves, and not because of the signs (6:26). But, other than these, every other occasion σημεῖα was used it was by the Evangelist himself.

believe) in Him.[67] Furthermore, the signs selected and presented by the Evangelist are theological. As defined previously, the word σημεῖον suggests the sign-miracles are full of meaning. As Morris explains, "It is not an end in itself, but it points men beyond itself."[68] In short, then, although there are some similarities between the Synoptists and the apostle John in their use of σημεῖον, there are also significant differences that distinguish the Fourth Evangelist from the other biblical writers. For John, the sign-miracles primarily emphasize the Person of Jesus as the promised Messiah and the divine Son of God. Further, they are also miraculous and theological in their nature.

The Nature of Σημεῖον

A survey of the uses of σημεῖον in both the extrabiblical and biblical writings reveals that the word has a wide range of meanings, referring to both the miraculous and non miraculous. Whether the word has the same wide range of meanings in the Johannine writings, however, has been a matter of disagreement. For instance, in his purpose statement of the Gospel, the Evangelist himself wrote: "Jesus did many other miraculous signs (σημεῖα) in the presence of his disciples, which are not written in this book. But these are written that you may believe that Jesus is the Christ, the Son of God, and that by believing you may have life in his name" (20:30–31). By σημεῖα, is the Evangelist referring to his selected miracles in the Gospel, or does he include more than the miracles such as Jesus' other acts and sayings? Or, as some scholars point out, does σημεῖα refer to everything written in the Fourth Gospel?

A significant number of scholars contend that σημεῖα referred to in John 20:30–31 are not limited to the miraculous acts of Jesus, but include more than that.[69] Some scholars recognize certain non miraculous significant acts as σημεῖα. Dodd explains this point: "Those acts to which the term σημεῖα is explicitly applied in the gospel are in point of

---

67. Gordon, "Sign," 4:506.

68. Morris, *Gospel According to John*, 686.

69. An impressive number of scholars hold this view. Carson, *Gospel According to John*, 103; Dodd, *Interpretation of the Fourth Gospel*, 142–43; Fuller, *Interpreting the Miracles*, 108; L. Johnston, "Making of the Fourth Gospel," 1–13; Köstenberger, *Encountering John*, 74–79; Riga, "Signs of Glory," 402; Ruland, "Sign and Sacrament," 450–62; E. F. Scott, *Value of the Fourth Gospel*, 21–22; T. C. Smith, "Book of Signs," 441–57.

fact all such as are also regarded as miraculous; but as we have seen, the miraculous is no part of the original connotation of the word, nor is it in usage always applied to miracles. We can hardly doubt that the Evangelist considered such acts as the cleansing of the Temple and the washing of the disciples' feet as σημεῖα. In both these cases he suggests a symbolic interpretation. I conclude that the events narrated in the Fourth Gospel are intended to be understood as significant events, σημεῖα."[70] Andreas Köstenberger, for instance, includes the temple cleansing in chapter 2 also as one of the σημεῖα, while surprisingly omitting the miracle account of Jesus' walking on water in chapter 6.[71] L. Johnston describes the Johannine σημεῖα as including all the actions of Jesus in the Gospel that have special significance.[72]

There are some scholars who also include the words of Jesus recorded in the Gospel as σημεῖα. Riga, for instance, understands σημεῖα as including both miracles and discourses in the Gospel.[73] T. C. Smith argues in similar vein, emphasizing the close relationship between Jesus' words and works in the Fourth Gospel.[74] There are some who even go further in interpreting the scope of σημεῖα. Vernon Ruland explains, for example, that "σημεῖον includes not only a miracle but any event, person, or discourse pregnant with divine meaning by which the Father presents an option between belief or unbelief in Christ."[75] Or, as D. A. Carson concludes in light of John 20:30–31, "the entire Gospel is a book of signs."[76]

However, this view that interprets the σημεῖα as including more than the selected miraculous signs seems inconsistent. For instance, do σημεῖα also include just other "significant" acts of Jesus, or does it include His discourses also? And, what about the narratives surrounding the miracles? Does it also include the Evangelist's parenthetical statements? Surely the narratives and discourses surrounding the sign-miracles are related and help to interpret them more significantly, but that is not the same as identifying each of them as σημεῖον.

70. Dodd, *Interpretation of the Fourth Gospel*, 142.

71. Köstenberger, *Encountering John*, 74–79.

72. L. Johnston, "Making of the Fourth Gospel," 7–10.

73. Riga, "Signs of Glory," 402.

74. T. C. Smith, "Book of Signs," 441–57.

75. Ruland, "Sign and Sacrament," 458.

76. Carson, *Gospel According to John*, 103.

It seems preferable, therefore, to limit the scope of σημεῖα to the miraculous acts of Jesus in the Fourth Gospel.[77] In surveying the usage of σημεῖα, it is certainly evident that the word has a broader meaning than just the miraculous. However, in the writings of John, the word has a narrower scope, particularly, in reference to miracles. Morris argues, for instance, that John's σημεῖα refers exclusively of miracles.[78] Brown echoes this view when he asks rhetorically, "Are there non-miraculous signs in John? Every use of σημεῖον refers to a miraculous deed."[79] E. Earle Ellis also supports this view in saying that, "In John, a sign is a miracle of Jesus, selected and interpreted by the evangelist, which points to Jesus' messiahship."[80] William Hendriksen also concurs when he defines σημεῖον as "a miracle viewed as a proof of divine authority and majesty."[81]

It seems clear that the Fourth Evangelist uses σημεῖον as referring to the miraculous acts of Jesus. This is consistent with the Evangelist's quotation of Nicodemus's words during his nocturnal encounter with Jesus, "Rabbi, we know you are a teacher who has come from God. For no one could perform the miraculous signs (σημεῖα) you are doing if God were not with him" (3:2). This is also consistent with the people's statement concerning John the Baptist's ministry, namely, that he never performed a miraculous sign (σημεῖον) (10:41). Some scholars such as Dodd, for instance, suggest that the Evangelist considered Jesus' actions such as cleansing of the temple as σημεῖον. However, that is unlikely because immediately following the temple cleansing incident, the Evangelist records the Jews' demand of Jesus: "What miraculous sign (σημεῖον) can you show us to prove your authority to do all this?" (2:18).[82] In other words, if the Evangelist designed the temple cleansing action of Jesus as one of the σημεῖα, it seems incongruent with the Jews' demand for a sign immediately following the incident.

77. There are a number of scholars who prefer to limit the σημεῖα to the miraculous acts of Jesus: R. E. Brown, *Gospel According to John (I–XII)*, 528; Ellis, *World of St. John*, 55–56; Gordon, "Sign," 505–6; Hendriksen, *Gospel According to John*, 1:117; Morris, *Gospel According to John*, 686; Rengstorf, "Σημεῖον," 7:247; Robertson, *Divinity of Christ in the Gospel of John*, 29–31.

78. Morris, *Gospel According to John*, 686.

79. R. E. Brown, *Gospel According to John (I–XII)*, 528.

80. Ellis, *World of St. John*, 55–56.

81. Hendriksen, *Gospel According to John*, 1:117.

82. R. E. Brown, *Gospel According to John (I–XII)*, 528.

The view that includes the sayings and discourses of Jesus in the σημεῖα, is also unlikely. It seems clear that, at least in John, every instance where σημεῖον is mentioned, it is in reference to Jesus' miraculous deeds (John 2:11, 18, 23; 3:2; 4:48, 54; 6:2, 14, 26, 30; 7:31; 9:16; 10:41; 11:47; 12:18, 37; 20:30).[83] Thus, Rengstorf concludes, "John never calls a saying of Jesus a σημεῖον."[84]

In conclusion, although the word σημεῖον can and often does include a wide range of meaning, in the Johannine writings, and especially in his Gospel, the word seems to be restricted specifically to the selected miracles of Jesus (cf. 20:30–31). In summary, although the meaning and usages of σημεῖα throughout the Scriptures are broad and varied, the word seems to have a narrower focus in the Johannine writings in referring to the miraculous events.

THE SIGNIFICANCE AND PURPOSES OF ΣΗΜΕΙΑ

This section will first begin by highlighting the significance of σημεῖα by comparing this word in its relationship with other important words in the Fourth Gospel. This will be followed by a discussion of the theological purposes of σημεῖα as intentioned by the Evangelist.

The Significance of Σημεῖα

The significance of σημεῖα will be highlighted through its comparison with other significant words in the Fourth Gospel, namely, δόξα and πιστεύω. The first word (δόξα) will emphasize the significance of the sign-miracles (σημεῖα) as they manifest the glory of Jesus Christ, while the second word (πιστεύω) will accentuate that the selected miracles in the Fourth Gospel were not designed to merely impress its readers by their wonder but to encourage them to believe.

The Relationship of σημεῖον *to* δόξα

The relationship of σημεῖον to δόξα is significant because according to the words of the Evangelist himself, the σημεῖα of Jesus reveal His δόξα. In John 2:11, for instance, the manifestation of Jesus' glory (δόξα) is linked closely with the first sign-miracle (ἀρχὴν τῶν σημείων) of Jesus at the wedding in Cana. Significantly, Jesus' δόξα also stands in a

---

83. Rengstorf, "Σημεῖον," 7:247.
84. Ibid.

causal relation to the disciples' faith in Him, according to the Evangelist.[85] His δόξα is also said to be manifested in the same way at the σημεῖον of the raising of Lazarus, the seventh and last of the sign-miracles in John's Gospel (11:4, 40).[86] Interestingly, the Evangelist seems to form an inclusio or bookends around his σημεῖα with the theme of Jesus' δόξα. Furthermore, John also closes the Book of Signs (chaps. 2–12) with a connection of the recorded σημεῖα with Jesus' δόξα (12:37–41). The significance of the theme of Jesus' δόξα is anticipated in the Gospel's Prologue (1:1–18) where the Evangelist eloquently declares, "The Word became flesh and made his dwelling among us. We have seen his glory (δόξα), the glory (δόξα) of the One and Only, who came from the Father, full of grace and truth" (1:14). In fact, the theme of Jesus' δόξα in the Fourth Gospel is so significant that some even considered calling John's Gospel, the gospel of the divine glory.[87]

The profound relationship between Jesus' σημεῖα and His δόξα can be seen also in their common background, the Old Testament (LXX), particularly the book of Exodus. As God revealed His glory through the wondrous works He performed on behalf of His people in Egypt (Exod 15:11), so now Jesus performs His σημεῖα in order to reveal His δόξα. Riga perceptively summarizes the connection between Jesus' σημεῖα and His δόξα with the Old Testament: "The miracles of the Book of Exodus made a great impression on the mind of the Jews as God's direct intervention in their favor. St. John explains that this same marvelous power of God which was revealed to the Jews in the Old Testament for their salvation has now become incarnate in Christ in whom the presence and the power of God are in their full and perfect form (John 2:11; 4:54; 11:40–41; 12:41). . . . By believing in Christ, the disciples saw the glory of Christ as the Israelites of old saw the glory of God in contemplating and understanding the great wonders performed for them in the Exodus."[88] In other words, just as God revealed His glory by His wondrous works

---

85. Ibid., 7:253.

86. Tenney, "Topics from the Gospel of John—Part II," 159.

87. Rigg, *Fourth Gospel and Its Message*, 46. Rigg points out that Bultmann in his commentary also divided John's Gospel around the theme of δόξα. Bultmann makes the following divisions: the revelation of glory (δόξα) before the world (chaps. 2–12); the revelation of glory (δόξα) before believers (chaps. 13–17); the revelation of glory (δόξα) (chaps. 18–20).

88. Riga, "Signs of Glory," 402–24.

to His covenant people, Jesus reveals His δόξα to the people through the σημεῖα He performs.

Another significant aspect that springs forth from the comparison of Jesus' σημεῖα with sign-miracles in the Old Testament, is that in the Old Testament σημεῖα were given not only for the benefit of the covenant people, but also that God's δόξα could be manifested to the Gentiles. As Barrett observes concerning the σημεῖα in the Old Testament, "A sign is a part of the proclamation of the glory of God to the Gentiles."[89] The prophet Isaiah records the purpose of such manifestation of divine glory this way: "I will set a sign (σημεῖον) among them, and I will send some of those who survive to the nations. . . . They will proclaim my glory (τήν δόξαν μου) among the nations" (66:19 LXX). Thus, just as God's σημεῖα has a universal scope in manifesting His δόξα in the Old Testament, the σημεῖα of Jesus also have a universal aim of revealing His δόξα to the world, including both Jews and Gentiles, and believers and unbelievers alike. In sum, then, in line with its Old Testament precedent, the σημεῖα of Jesus are given to reveal His Person to the whole world through the manifestation of His δόξα. Rengstorf's summary of the relationship between Jesus' σημεῖα and His δόξα is appropriate: "In His σημεῖα Jesus in some sense makes Himself transparent and causes His true being, His sonship, to be manifest in its δόξα."[90]

The Relationship of σημεῖα *to* πιστεύω

The significance of Jesus' σημεῖα can also be perceived by their relationship with another key term in the Johannine Gospel, πιστεύω (faith). According to the Evangelist's own purpose statement of his Gospel (20:30–31), the aim of the Johannine σημεῖα is the faith of his readers in Jesus as the Christ, the Son of God. As Rengstorf aptly describes, "John refers to the σημεῖα of Jesus in such a way as to leave the impression that they are the decisive thing in establishing faith in Jesus as the Messiah."[91] The selected σημεῖα of Jesus in the Fourth Gospel are recorded, then, not merely to impress the readers of their wonder but to foster and

---

89. Barrett, *Gospel According to St. John*, 63.

90. Rengstorf, "Σημεῖον," 7:253.

91. Ibid., 250.

strengthen their faith in Him. It is little wonder, then, that Merrill Tenney has characterized the Fourth Gospel as the "Gospel of Belief."[92]

The vital relationship between the σημεῖα of Jesus and πιστεύω is obvious in the Evangelist's emphasis of faith in the presence of the sign-miracles. For instance, following the first miracle of Jesus at the wedding in Cana, the Evangelist points out that the disciples believed in Him (ἐπίστευσαν εἰς αὐτόν) (2:11). The second miracle of Jesus healing the official's son in Cana also stresses the importance of faith in Jesus and His word, where it records that the man believed Jesus and His word (ἐπίστευσεν ὁ ἄνθρωπος τῷ λόγῳ ὃν εἶπεν αὐτῷ ὁ Ἰησοῦς) (4:50). The seventh and climactic sign-miracle of Jesus raising Lazarus from the dead also underscores the import of faith, when the Evangelist describes that many who witnessed the miracle believed in Him (ἐπίστευσαν εἰς αὐτόν) (11:45).

Unfortunately, the sign-miracles do not always achieve their desired effect, however. The σημεῖα of Jesus were often met with a temporary and even superficial faith in John's Gospel.[93] At the beginning of the Fourth Gospel the Evangelist indicates that Jesus performed numerous sign-miracles in Jerusalem during the Passover Feast which resulted in belief, but that Jesus did not entrust Himself to them because He apparently knew that their faith was somewhat shallow (2:23–24). Further, at the request of the official for his son's healing Jesus decries the people's eagerness to witness His miracles, because He did not want their faith to be only sign-based: "Unless you people see miraculous signs and wonders, you will never believe" (4:48). In addition, Jesus also rebukes the crowd who witnessed the miracle of feeding the five thousand by saying, "You are looking for me, not because you saw miraculous signs but because you ate the loaves and had your fill" (6:26). In other words, many people desired to see Jesus' miracles primarily because of their physical appetite. In summary, then, it is significant that the σημεῖα of Jesus must be received with a proper πίστις if one desires to see the δόξα of Jesus.

---

92. Tenney, *John*.

93. Tenney, "Topics from the Gospel of John—Part II," 158–59.

The Purposes of Σημεῖα

The purpose statement of the Fourth Gospel recorded by the Evangelist reveals his twofold purpose in selecting Jesus' σημεῖα: "Jesus did many other miraculous signs (σημεῖα) in the presence of his disciples, which are not recorded in this book. But these are written that you may believe that Jesus is the Christ, the Son of God, and that by believing you may have life in his name" (20:30–31). The first purpose of the sign-miracles is revelatory. In other words, the Evangelist presents them to portray Jesus as the promised Messiah of the Old Testament Scriptures and the divine Son of God.[94] The second purpose of the sign-miracles is pragmatic. They are designed to lead the readers into a life of faith in Jesus. These two purposes will be the subject of discussion in this section.

The Revelatory Purpose of σημεῖα

According to the Evangelist's purpose statement in 20:30–31, the aim of Jesus' σημεῖα is first and foremost christological. The object of the recorded sign-miracles in the Fourth Gospel is primarily to reveal the Person of Jesus who, as the promised Christ (ὁ Χριστὸς) and the divine Son of God (ὁ υἱὸς τοῦ θεοῦ), embodies the fulfillment of the divine plan, both in the present age and in the age to come. As Rudolph Schnackenburg explains correctly, all the sign-miracles "focus the attention entirely on the worker of them and manifest the majesty and saving power bestowed upon him."[95] The Johannine σημεῖα are indissolubly linked with the Person of Christ.[96] Thus, the Person of Christ is the overarching theme and aim of the sign-miracles in the Fourth Gospel. There

94. The Johannine sign-miracles emphasize the Person of Jesus as both the promised Messiah and the divine Son of God. The deity of Jesus, as the divine Son of God, is a theme that is obvious in the Fourth Gospel. Beginning with the Prologue (1:1–18) and the Testimonium (1:19–51), all the miracles in the Book of Signs" (2:1—12:50) demonstrate Jesus' deity. In addition, the seven predicated "I Am" statements, as well as the non predicated ones, certainly affirm Jesus' deity. Because the significance of Jesus' deity in the Fourth Gospel has been sufficiently developed in the field of Johannine studies, it will not be developed here in detail. However, the emphases of Jesus' deity in the sign-miracles themselves will certainly be dealt with in the context of the miracles. Jesus' messianic identity and work, on the other hand, has not been developed deeply as they should be, as least in their relationship with the miracles. Thus, Jesus' identity as the Messiah will be the focus of this chapter.

95. Schnackenburg, *Gospel According to St. John*, 1:515–28.

96. Ibid.

are three closely related aspects of Jesus' Christology that the Johannine sign-miracles manifest in the Fourth Gospel, namely, the messianic, eschatological, and universal emphases. If Christology is the overarching umbrella of the Johannine sign-miracles, these three aspects of Jesus' Christology are the main spokes that support it. Thus, these three aspects of Jesus' Christology will be the focus of this particular section. They will only be introduced briefly in this chapter, but will be developed more fully and demonstrated in the subsequent chapters that analyze the sign-miracles in their respective contexts.

THEIR MESSIANIC EMPHASIS—The first and most important aspect of Jesus' Person that the Johannine miracles reveal is His messianic identity. The miracles that are designated as the σημεῖα in the Fourth Gospel, highlight the Person of the Messiah by the kind of miracles that are expected in the messianic age (i.e., Isa 35:5).[97] Jesus quotes this Isaianic passage when John the Baptist inquires concerning His identity whether or not He was actually the promised Messiah of the Scriptures (Matt 11:2–6; Luke 7:18–23). Apparently, the identity of the Messiah was to be recognized by the kind of miracles that accompanied His ministry. Guthrie confirms this connection when he explains, "The connection of Messianic claims with signs is not surprising, for it was generally expected that the Messiah, when he came, would authenticate his claims by means of signs. The absence of signs would have been unthinkable for a claimant to the Messianic office."[98]

The expectation that the messianic age would be characterized by miracles was foreseen in the Hebrew Scriptures. There were expectations that signs like those of the Mosaic period would be characterized in the eschatological period.[99] The Hebrew prophets declared long ago that in the messianic kingdom God would perform wonders like those with which He brought Israel out of Egypt (Mic 7:15; Isa 48:20–21). Furthermore, the prophets of old also hoped for the eschatological day when the Messiah will perform miraculous healings and deliverances for the sick (Isa 35:5–6; 53:4; 61:1). The Old Testament saints also waited in expectation for the day when they would be raised to life everlasting (Ps 16:9–11; cf. Isa 26:19–20; Dan 12:2). The sign-miracles of Jesus in the

97. Saucy, "Miracles and Jesus' Proclamation," 303.

98. Guthrie, "Importance of Signs," 72–83.

99. Koester, *Symbolism in the Fourth Gospel*, 91–92.

Fourth Gospel demonstrate and foreshadow the Old Testament hope for the messianic deeds during the eschatological kingdom.

The expectation that the messianic age would be characterized by miracles was also expressed in the extracanonical witnesses written during the intertestamental period. Although the fact that the Messiah would be a miracle-worker is not explicitly stated in the extracanonical literature, there were nevertheless expectations that wondrous works would be characterized in the messianic age.[100] For example, 2 Baruch 73 describes the miraculous blessings of the Messiah's kingdom as a time when "joy will be revealed and rest will appear. And then health will descend in dew, and illness will vanish, and fear and tribulation and lamentation will pass away from among men, and joy will encompass the earth."[101] Furthermore, Psalms of Solomon 17:37–40 describes the power and might that will characterize the Messiah in the eschatological kingdom: "And he will not weaken in his days, (relying) upon his God, for God made him powerful in the holy spirit and wise in the counsel of understanding, with strength and righteousness. And the blessing of the Lord will be with him in strength, and he will not weaken; His hope (will be) in the Lord. Then who will succeed against him, mighty in his actions and strong in the fear of God?"[102] In short, although the explicit statements concerning the coming Messiah as a miracle-worker are not common in the intertestamental literature, they nevertheless speak aplenty concerning the wondrous nature of the coming kingdom.

The messianic identity of Jesus is confirmed most clearly in the New Testament, by the miracles He performed throughout His ministry. Both the Synoptic Gospels and the Fourth Gospel record Jesus' miracles to portray Him as the one about whom the Old Testament Scriptures spoke. The crowds who witnessed Jesus' miracles certainly made the messianic connections. For instance, Luke records the miracle of Jesus' raising of the widow's son in Nain (7:11–17) and includes the crowd's response who witnessed the miracle: "They were all filled with awe and praised God. 'A great prophet has appeared among us,' they said. God has come to help

---

100. For a good treatment of the Jewish apocalyptic hope, see Russell, *Method and Message of Jewish Apocalyptic*, 309–10. Russell explains that the works in the eschaton emphasize "not so much on the Messiah and his ushering in of the kingdom as it is on the kingdom itself as a mighty act of God."

101. Klijn, "2 Baruch," 645.

102. Wright, "Psalms of Solomon," 668.

his people" (v. 16). Even the Jewish religious leaders such as Nicodemus could not deny the messianic implications of Jesus' works when he asked Jesus, "Rabbi, we know you are a teacher who has come from God. For no one could perform these signs if God were not with him" (John 3:2). On another occasion, the Jews gathered together and asked Jesus a similar question after witnessing many of His miracles: "How long will you keep us in suspense? If you are the Christ (the Messiah) tell us plainly" (10:24). To which Jesus replied, "I did tell you, but you do not believe. The miracles I do in my Father's name speak for me" (v. 25). In other words, it was the miracles that Jesus performed throughout His ministry that most clearly testified to His messianic identity.

The Fourth Evangelist also explicitly states that the selected miracles of Jesus are intentioned to reveal Jesus as the Messiah. From his purpose statement towards the end of the Gospel (20:30–31), to the declarations of the disciples concerning Jesus' messianic titles in the Testimonium (1:19–51), to the sign-miracles and their attendant contexts through narratives and discourses in the Book of Signs (2:1—12:50), and even to the Farewell Discourse and the Passion Narratives in the Book of Glory (13:1—20:31), the whole Johannine Gospel is a testimony regarding Jesus' identity as the Messiah of God. In short, then, the New Testament explicitly characterizes Jesus' miracles as messianic.

THEIR ESCHATOLOGICAL EMPHASIS—Another significant aspect of Jesus' Christology that the miracles of Jesus reveal is the eschatological emphasis, which is closely related to His messianic identity and deeds. As Mark Saucy correctly explains, "the miracles of Jesus are revelatory deeds of the eschatological kingdom He preached and that in the Gospels they provoked people to make decisions regarding Him."[103] This is certainly true of the Johannine sign-miracles. Otfried Hofius argues in similar vein when he explains that Jesus' miracles are signs of God's kingly rule, the dawn of which Jesus announced.[104] He elaborates further thusly: "Jesus' words and works are the beginning of the age of salvation, and the miracles are a foreshadowing and a promise of the coming universal redemption. Ultimately, it is in this eschatological context that the accounts of Jesus' miracles are to be read."[105] Schnackenburg depicts the

103. Saucy, "Miracles and Jesus' Proclamation," 282.
104. Hofius, "Miracle," 2:631.
105. Ibid.

Johannine σημεῖα as a means of assuring the "eschatological presence" in Christ.[106] Sebald Hofbeck correctly concludes that the Johannine σημεῖα are intended to demonstrate that Jesus is the expected Messiah of the eschaton, so that they are both messianic and eschatological in their meaning.[107]

The most important element within the eschatological aspect of Jesus' Christology that the Johannine σημεῖα reveal is the Person of Jesus as the Messiah of the coming eschaton. Some scholars interpret the σημεῖα in the Fourth Gospel as an indication that Jesus' eschatological kingdom was present during His ministry.[108] This view interprets Jesus' miracles as being more than signs or indicators of the kingdom; they were the kingdom itself. R. E. Brown also echoes this thought when he says, "The miracle was not primarily an external guarantee of the coming of the kingdom; it was one of the means by which the kingdom came."[109]

However, this view seems to err on the focus and function of Jesus' miracles, particularly the sign-miracles in John's Gospel. First, the Johannine sign-miracles' primary aim is to emphasize the Person of Jesus as the promised Messiah who will inaugurate His eschatological kingdom. Their aim is not to demonstrate that the kingdom had begun. The emphasis of Jesus' miracles is His Person, namely, that He is the eschatological King (John 1:49; 12:13) who will inaugurate His promised kingdom. The messianic kingdom can only be inaugurated, however, when the nation Israel repents of her sin and returns to Yahweh as her King (Acts 3:19–21). The miracles reveal, then, that the one who will inaugurate the messianic kingdom is here (demonstrated by the nature and power of Jesus' miracles), and whose messianic blessings (i.e., soteriological) are dispensed also in the present age. Thus, as the promised messiah Jesus grants eternal life to those who believe in Him, here and now. In short, the focus of the Johannine σημεῖα are primarily person-oriented rather than kingdom-oriented.

106. Schnackenburg, *Gospel According to St. John*, 1:522–23.

107. Hofbeck, *Semeion*, 161–66.

108. For an example of this, see Dodd's *Parables of the Kingdom*, 21–59. He articulates his so-called "realized eschatology," arguing from the parables and passages like Matt 12:25–28 that Jesus' miracles showed the full presence of the kingdom in His earthly ministry.

109. R. E. Brown, "Gospel Miracles," 187. Other notable scholars who share Brown's view include: Beasley-Murray, *Jesus and the Kingdom*, 80–83, and Schnackenburg, *God's Rule and Kingdom*, 127.

Second, it is important to keep in mind the function of a sign. The miracles in John's Gospel in particular are designated specifically as signs (σημεῖα) (20:30–31). As it has been the case throughout in both the extrabiblical and biblical usages, the word σημεῖον indicates that a sign points to something else. Saucy describes it accurately, "It either authenticates or predicts a coming event (e.g., Exod 4:8–9; Isa 7:14), but it is not to be identified with that event."[110] Besides, the miracles that Jesus performed were primarily to reveal the identity of Jesus as the messiah, and also to demonstrate the nature of His coming kingdom. In other words, the miracles of Jesus were not designed to demonstrate that the kingdom itself was present, but that the one who will one day establish His kingdom was present. Saucy's clarification of Jesus' miracles is insightful: "Jesus' miracles did not bring about the final rest and restoration of the kingdom promised in the Old Testament. Those who were healed would again fall sick and die; the demons would escape complete subjugation until the 'hour,' and the creation would continue to suffer under the cosmic oppression of the evil one—all indications that the kingdom was not yet established."[111] Thus, as Saucy aptly concludes, there is a distinction between what Jesus' miracles were and what they foreshadowed.[112] Or, as Reginald Fuller describes Jesus' miracles, they are "foretastes," "anticipations," or "foreshadows" of the eschatological kingdom.[113] But more importantly, the main focus of Jesus' miracles is to demonstrate that Jesus is the one who will one day inaugurate the promised kingdom.

In sum, then, the focus of the Johannine σημεῖα is to reveal that Jesus is the eschatological King who will inaugurate His promised kingdom, and their function is to demonstrate the nature and power that will characterize that kingdom. Saucy's succinct summary is an appropriate conclusion highlighting the eschatological emphasis of Jesus' Christology: "Jesus' miracles indicate the presence of kingdom power, and yet they are not the presence of the kingdom because they are not the kingdom itself in its fullness; of this reality they are only signs. Also miracles show why the eschatological kingdom was not established in Jesus' First Advent. They provide a unique angle from which to observe

110. Saucy, "Miracles and Jesus' Proclamation," 303.

111. Ibid.

112. Ibid., 304.

113. Fuller, *Interpreting the Miracles*, 40.

Jesus' initial offer of the Old Testament prophetic hope, its rejection by all quadrants of Israel, and finally its subsequent change and delay."[114]

The future eschatological emphasis in the Fourth Gospel can be easily overlooked, however, because unlike the Synoptists, the Evangelist hardly uses the word kingdom. Instead, the apostle John seems to substitute "eternal life" where "kingdom of God" is often used in the Synoptic Gospels. This has led many to suggest that the Evangelist has replaced the Jewish "kingdom of God" with "eternal life" for his Hellenistic readership. However, the term "eternal life" is also used frequently in the Synoptic Gospels (Matt 19:16–17, 29; Mark 10:29–30; Luke 18:29–30; cf. Matt 7:14, 19:25; Mark 10:26; Luke 18:26), and in the places they do appear they are used interchangeably with "kingdom of God" (Mark 9:43, 45, 47, 10:17–30; Matt 19:23–29; Luke 18:24–30).[115] In addition, the concept of eternal life has a Jewish background primarily and it appears in their writings prior to the New Testament (Dan 12:2; cf. Pss Sol 3:12; 13:11; 14:10; 1 Enoch 37:4, 58:3).[116] For instance, Daniel's vision of the end times states, "Multitudes who sleep in the dust of the earth will awake, some to everlasting life, others to shame and everlasting contempt" (12:2). And, Psalms of Solomon also states, "This is the share of sinners forever, but those who fear the Lord shall rise up to eternal life, and their life shall be in the Lord's light, and it shall never end" (3:12).[117] The Evangelist thus seems to use "eternal life" in exchange for "kingdom of God" in order to emphasize the present reality of life in Jesus Christ without minimizing the future aspects of the eschatological kingdom. As Marianne Meye Thompson insightfully explains, "John does not abandon the Jewish conception of 'eternal life' as entailing the gathering of the people of God, nor does he spiritualize the hope for the resurrection of the body. Eternal life is present now insofar as through Jesus knowledge of and fellowship with God is mediated. Thus eternal life is also appropriation by faith of unseen yet present realities that shape one's life in this world and become more fully realized in the next."[118]

114. Saucy, "Miracles and Jesus' Proclamation," 307.

115. Thompson, "John, Gospel of," 380.

116. Ibid.

117. Wright, "Psalms of Solomon," 655.

118. Thompson, "John, Gospel of," 381.

THEIR UNIVERSAL EMPHASIS—Another significant aspect of Jesus' Christology that the Johannine sign-miracles reveal is the universal emphasis of the messiah and His eschatological kingdom. Jesus is the promised Messiah of the Old Testament Scriptures, to be sure, but His kingdom will certainly encompass not only the Jews but the Gentiles as well. And, the messianic blessings will also be universal and thus dispensed to all the nations. This is true, not only in the present age through the Church, but also in the messianic kingdom in the age to come. The prophet Isaiah predicted this glorious sight, when all the nations will stream to Yahweh's mountain to receive His blessings in the messianic kingdom (Isa 2:2-3; cf. Gen 12:1–3; Ps 87). The natural question arises, however, what relation a Jewish messiah has with Gentiles, both in the present age and particularly in the eschatological kingdom.

Although the significance of the Messiah and His promised kingdom has been correlated mostly with the fate of the Jewish people, it has often been done so at the expense of overlooking the vital implications of the Messiah and His future kingdom that will also encompass the Gentiles. Furthermore, although the divine concern for the salvation of the Gentiles has often been portrayed as the concern of only the New Testament, this is far from scriptural truth. The Hebrew Bible is woven with the fabric of missiological concern for the salvation of the whole world from beginning to end.[119] George Peters' excellent summary of the Old Testament stands in contrast to the erroneous but common perception that views the Old Testament as being exclusivistic and unconcerned with the salvation of the Gentiles, or if it is, it is a peripheral concern at best. He correctly demonstrates this point in saying, "The universality of salvation pervades the Old Testament. It is not peripheral but rather constitutes the intent of the Old Testament revelation because it constitutes the dominant purpose of the call, life and ministry of Israel. The Old Testament does not contain missions; it is itself 'missions' in the world."[120]

That the Old Testament is in essence the story of God's mission to the whole world is clearly evident from the opening chapters of the

---

119. Strickland, "Isaiah, Jonah, and Religious Pluralism," 28. Strickland surveys the books of Isaiah and Jonah, in order to demonstrate the "missions" heart of God for the pagan nations surrounding Israel.

120. Peters, *Biblical Theology of Missions*, 129. Particularly helpful is the chapter in the book that is entitled, "Missionary Theology and the Old Testament," 83–130.

Bible's first book. The first eleven chapters of the book of Genesis, which can be called a "prologue" to the book, contain the foundational motivation behind the story that takes place subsequently in the rest of the Scriptures.[121] Following the story of man's creation and his fall to sin, the promise is given concerning the coming Redeemer in Genesis 3:15, often called the "protevangelium," and is universal in its extent.[122] In other words, through the seed of the woman, the coming Messiah, there is salvific hope for all mankind. The rest of the Bible story, then, is the outplaying of that original plan of God to reconcile the rebellious human race to Himself. And, the Abrahamic covenant (Gen 12:1–3; cf. 15:1–21) is the means by which God has chosen to fulfill His glorious plan of blessing all the peoples of the earth. Although the recipients and primary beneficiaries of this promise are Abraham and his descendants, to be sure, the aim of God's blessings upon Abraham and his descendants is that all the peoples of the earth may receive God's blessings that come through the Messiah. In other words, the divine blessings on the nation Israel are for the ultimate purpose of magnifying God's glory to the nations, in order that the peoples of the nations might join Israel in the worship of Yahweh (Ps 117).[123] Besides, this was Israel's specific function granted her as a nation when God called Israel to be a "kingdom of priests and a holy nation" (Exod 19:6).

The "mission" heart of God to bless the nations is clearly evident even in the Old Testament, in that He blesses Israel for the ultimate purpose of revealing His glory to the nations. God blesses His covenant people so that He can make His name known among the peoples of the earth. This "sacred magnetism" of drawing the nations toward God by blessing Israel to be the envy of the nations is referred to as the "centripetal" method of missions.[124] One of the most significant means by which God reveals His glory in the Old Testament times is through the worship of His people. Whether it is through the sacrificial offerings by the patri-

121. Allen, "God Reached Out to Abraham," 38.

122. Peters, *Biblical Theology of Missions*, 83–87.

123. Allen, "Surprise of Wonder," 36–39. In this short but insightful article, Allen exposits Ps 117 as an invitation of the Gentile nations to join in on the worship of Yahweh, which is really the spirit of the whole Bible.

124. Grisanti, "Israel's Mission to the Nations"; See also his dissertation on the subject, "Relationship of Israel," 40–55." In both his journal article and his dissertation, Grisanti carefully discusses the "centripetal" method of missions in the book of Isa. Cf. Peters, *Biblical Theology of Missions*, 21.

archs in the patriarchal age, or through the Levitical sacrifices in the tabernacle during the Mosaic period, or through the worship of God in the Solomonic temple during the monarchical era, Israel was the envy of the nations in their worship of the one true God, Yahweh. And, throughout Israel's history, foreigners from the pagan nations were invited to join Israel in the worship of Yahweh (1 Kgs 8:41–43). Examples of foreign individuals who put their faith in Israel's God as the one true God of the universe are Rahab the Canaanitess, Ruth the Moabitess, Uriah the Hittite, and Naaman the Syrian, to name a few.[125] These foreigners who came into contact with Israel through various circumstances put their trust in Yahweh as the one true God of the universe. Thus we see the marvelous "missions" heart of God for the nations throughout the Old Testament in the history of the covenant nation.

However, it was through Israel's disobedience and rebellion against God that caused her to cease being the channel of God's marvelous blessings to the peoples of the earth. As a result, during the "times of the Gentiles" (Luke 21:24) Israel has been set aside temporarily, and the church of Jesus Christ has assumed the role of manifesting the glory of God to the peoples of the earth. With the death and resurrection of Jesus Christ, and with the coming of the Holy Spirit on the day of Pentecost, the church has assumed Israel's role being the witness to the world (Matt 5:13–16; 1 Pet 2:9–10). As a result of both Jews and Gentiles becoming one in the body of Christ through the common indwelling of the Holy Spirit in individual believers, the church is called to go forth into the world to make disciples of the nations (Eph 2:11–22; 3:1–13; 1 Cor 12:13; Matt 28:19–20). In contrast to the Old Testament times, the church is called to go into the world and actively evangelize and make disciples of the peoples of the world, as can be witnessed in the book of Acts.[126] As a result, the church is to be the witness of God to the world during this period known as the "church age," as we "shine as lights in the world, holding fast the word of life" (Phil 2:15–16).

Following the Rapture of the church and the advent of Jesus Christ when He comes back to set up His promised kingdom on earth, however, Israel will once again enjoy the privilege of being God's primary agent of drawing the Gentile nations unto the Messiah. And, whereas Israel

125. Allen, "Surprise of Wonder," 38.

126. This method of going out to the world and actively witnessing is called the "centrifugal" method of missions. See Peters, *Biblical Theology of Missions*, 21.

failed in the role of being God's kingdom of priests unto the world, in the eschatological kingdom, however, she will experience the joy of being the light for the Gentile nations, and thus the Abrahamic covenant will be completely fulfilled. The Hebrew prophets looked forward to such a glorious time when universal blessings will come from Yahweh and His Messiah, who will fulfill the ancient promise to bless all the families of the earth (Gen 12:1–3; cf. Isa 66:19–23; Jer 3:17; 16:19; Hos 14:6–7; Zech 14:16–19).[127] Furthermore, in that glorious day God will fulfill the desire of His "missions" heart, when foreigners will join Israel in the worship of Yahweh in His temple so that it actually does become "a house of prayer for all the peoples" (Isa 56:6–8; cf. Zech 14:16). After all, this is what Jesus probably had in mind to demonstrate when He cleansed the Jerusalem temple at the beginning of His earthly ministry (John 2:1–22). He wanted to demonstrate that as the Messiah He will usher in His promised kingdom, which will one day be filled with Gentiles who, following the lead of the Jews, will worship Yahweh in the Jerusalem temple. Therefore, the significance of the Messiah and His kingdom cannot be overemphasized for the Gentiles.

The universal blessing of the Messiah is also a significant theme that runs across the Fourth Gospel. From the beginning of the Gospel to the end, although the Evangelist highlights the Person and works of the Messiah in the context of the Hebrew Scriptures and the Jewish festivals, the Gospel is decorated with universal overtones concerning the Messiah's blessings, particularly its soteriological aspect. For instance, the Evangelist's emphases on the Samaritans and the royal official in chapter 4, the Greeks in chapters 7 and 12, and the Gentiles ("other sheep") in chapter 10, clue his readers concerning the universal focus of the Messiah's Person and works. The Fourth Gospel reiterates the scriptural truth that the promised Messiah of the Hebrew Bible is not only the Savior of the Jews but of the whole world (John 4:42). The messianic blessings of the Savior are dispensed and experienced even in the present age, as the Evangelist "translates" many Old Testament and Jewish terms into universal terms for a church, which is predominantly Gentile in its makeup. The claim that Jesus is the Christ (Messiah), would also have meaningful connotations for the Gentile members of the church, who

---

127. Strickland, "Isaiah, Jonah, and Religious Pluralism," 31.

would have been trained and taught in the Septuagint (LXX), regarding the foundation and hope of their faith.[128]

The Pragmatic Purpose of σημεῖα

According to the Evangelist's own purpose statement of the Fourth Gospel (20:30–31), the second purpose of the sign-miracles is pragmatic in aim. The Johannine miracles are designed not only to reveal Jesus as the promised Messiah of the Scriptures, but also that his readers might come to (or continue to) believe in Him. They are intended to produce faith in his readers. There are two significant factors concerning the Johannine σημεῖα that are relevant to the concept of faith, and these factors will be the focus of this particular section.

The first factor of the Johannine sign-miracles that is relevant to faith is that the sign-miracles are primarily decision-oriented. As Schnackenburg perceptively describes regarding Jesus' miracles, "although they stimulate reflection (John 3:2; 7:31; 9:16, 11:47), they are ineffective in themselves to bring about the full Christian faith if they are perceived only externally or sought for as sensations (cf. 4:48)."[129] Although many witnessed Jesus' miracles that testify of His messianic identity, only some believed. Some, such as the Jewish religious leaders who were hostile to Jesus rejected His claims flatly, but most of the crowd remained passive. However, Jesus' miracles by their nature demand an active response of faith. William Dembski is insightful in pointing out the following principles about signs in regards to guiding human decision, which reflect what has been developed in this paper: first, a sign must be clearly specified, otherwise it can be rationalized away; second, a sign must be extraordinary, but not necessarily miraculous; and third, a sign must be clearly tied to some decision.[130] In short, σημεῖα by their nature and aim demand a response of faith.

The second significant factor of the Johannine sign-miracles that is related to faith is that Jesus' miracles are also divisive in their nature. Although the Johannine sign-miracles are designed to lead people to a decision of faith, they also have an opposite effect of resulting in unbelief and rejection. As Riga perceptively describes, "The 'divisive' element is

128. Guthrie, "Importance of Signs," 72–83.

129. Schnackenburg, *Gospel According to St. John*, 1:519.

130. Dembski, *Intelligent Design*, 28.

present in σημεῖα, for they become a stumbling block—a point of separation between those who believe in Christ and those who, remaining in the material understanding of the signs, cannot or do not wish to penetrate their deeper spiritual meaning."[131] A good case in point of this principle is the crowd who witnessed Jesus' feeding of the five thousand, when they failed to perceive the spiritual meaning of Jesus' bread and cared only for their physical appetite (John 6:26–27). Sign-miracles can be said to have a double effect, one to those who approach them with faith and another to those who regard them with skepticism and unbelief. Schnackenburg is correct in saying, "They (σημεῖα) 'show' true believers the glory of Christ as he works on earth, but where faith is weak and inadequate they show only the visage of the marvelous and hence do not lead to full faith (12:37)."[132] Kysar similarly describes the Johannine σημεῖα as having a double character of revealing and veiling at the same time.[133] According to Kysar, "For belief, signs are a revelation; they unveil the divine glory of Christ (2:11, 11:4, 40), while, for unbelief, they only veil the true identity of Christ, and they result in confusion and misunderstanding."[134]

In summary, the Johannine σημεῖα are designed not only to reveal Jesus to be the promised Messiah of the Old Testament Scriptures, but they are also intended to lead people to faith in Him. The nature of σημεῖα demands an active response of faith, after having witnessed the miracle. However, this desired effect of faith does not always take place and the opposite effect of skepticism and unbelief is often the result. Thus, in truth, the Johannine σημεῖα also have a divisive element, having a double character of revealing and veiling at the same time, depending on whether the miracles are received by faith.

THE IDENTIFICATION AND NUMBER OF ΣHMEIA

This section will first begin with identifying the selected miracles of Jesus in the Fourth Gospel, which the Evangelist specifically refers to as

---

131. Riga, "Signs of Glory," 408.

132. Schnackenburg, *Gospel According to St. John*, 1:519–20.

133. Kysar, *Fourth Evangelist and His Gospel*, 227.

134. Ibid. For a detailed-treatment of this see Hofbeck's *Semeion*, particularly 178–82 under the section, "Zeichen und Glauben."

the σημεῖα. This will be followed by speculation on how many of these miracles should be included in the Evangelist's σημεῖα.

The Identification of Σημεῖα

Although there are some who view the scope of σημεῖα in the Fourth Gospel as including more than the miracles of Jesus, the argument has been made that the Evangelist's reference to σημεῖα specifically point to the miraculous acts of Jesus.[135] As mentioned previously, each instance where σημεῖον is used in the Fourth Gospel, it is in reference to Jesus' miraculous deeds (John 2:11, 23; 3:2; 4:48, 54; 6:2, 14, 26, 30; 7:31; 9:16; 10:41; 11:47; 12:18, 37; 20:30).[136] Besides, this fits well with Nicodemus's description of Jesus' deeds: "Rabbi, we know that you are a teacher who has come from God. For no one could perform the miraculous signs (σημεῖα) you are doing if God were not with him" (3:2). Therefore, although the word σημεῖον can and often does include a wide range of meaning, the scope of the word is narrower in the Fourth Gospel and includes just the miracles of Jesus.

The following are Fourth Gospel miracles of Jesus that are commonly designated as σημεῖα:

1. The turning of water into wine at the wedding in Cana (2:1–11)

2. The healing of the official's son in Cana (4:43–54)

3. The healing of the lame man at the Pool of Bethesda (5:1–16)

4. The feeding of the five thousand (6:1–15)

5. The walking on water on the Sea of Galilee (6:16–21)

6. The healing of the man born blind (9:1–41)

7. The raising of Lazarus from the dead (11:1–44)

Other miracles or deeds of Jesus that have been commonly suggested to be among the Johannine σημεῖα include the temple cleansing by Jesus in chapter 2 and Jesus' miraculous catching of fish in chapter

---

135. A more detailed treatment of the miraculous nature of the Johannine σημεῖα was discussed previously in this chapter under the subheading, "The nature of σημεῖα."

136. Rengstorf, "Σημεῖον," 7:247.

21. Each of these will be discussed briefly here but will be treated more extensively in later chapters, where the sign-miracles will be discussed in their contexts.

Before discussing these three incidents, however, it is important to set the above-mentioned seven miracles in the broad context of the whole book. The seven miracles are all narrated in the first half of the book (2:1—12:50), commonly referred to as the Book of Signs.[137] The chapters generally describe the public ministry of Jesus consisting of approximately three years, while the second half of the book (13:1—20:31) mainly narrates the private ministry of Jesus with His disciples. The second section of the Fourth Gospel describes the last week He spent with them before His death, and is thus often referred to as the Book of Passion or the Book of Glory. Thus, it seems probable that the sign-miracles recorded in the Book of Signs are the intended σημεῖα by the Fourth Evangelist, since chapter 12 describes Jesus' impending death based on the rejection of Him as the Messiah by the nation's religious leaders. The Evangelist adds a clear parenthetical statement, that the nation rejected Jesus as their Messiah even after having witnessed His sign-miracles (12:37). Their rejection of Jesus as the Messiah leading up to the passion week had already sealed their fate. Therefore, in the words of the Synoptists, there were no more signs to be given the nation except the sign of Jesus' resurrection (cf. Matt 12:38–42; Luke 11:29–32).

One act of Jesus that has been suggested as one of the Johannine σημεῖα is the cleansing of the temple by Jesus at the beginning of His ministry in Jerusalem, following His first recorded miracle (2:11–22). Köstenberger, for instance, designates the cleansing of the temple as one of the σημεῖα, while omitting the fifth sign of Jesus' walking on water (6:16–21).[138] According to Köstenberger, the temple in Jesus' day

---

137. These distinctions, which were first coined by scholars such as Dodd and R. E. Brown, seem justified by several important literary factors. First, all of the seven miracles of Jesus are narrated in the first part of the Fourth Gospel, while none is recorded in the latter chapters, except the miracles of Jesus' resurrection in chapter 20 and His catching of the fish in chapter 21. However, it is doubtful that the Evangelist regarded these miracles as σημεῖα. Second, each "book" ends with a "summary statement" in 12:37–50 and 20:30–31. And third, the seven sign-miracles are "book-ended" by the theme of glory, as the first and the seventh miracles are stated to reveal Jesus' glory. And, in chapter 12, this theme of Christ's glory is equated with the glory of Yahweh, which the prophet Isaiah saw in his vision. Thus, there are good literary indications that the selected sign-miracles in the Fourth Gospel all fall in the first half of the book.

138. Köstenberger, *Encountering John*, 74–79.

had deteriorated into a place of religious profiteering and perfunctory ritual, and Jesus' predicted destruction of the temple was a clear sign of God's disapproval of Israel's apostasy from the true worship of Yahweh.[139] Köstenberger further explains that Jesus' cleansing of the temple is also a prophetic sign: "Jesus' cleansing of the temple provides a symbolic act that points to the inner meaning of Jesus' crucifixion and bodily resurrection, which render him the replacement of the temple in the life and worship of his people (2:19–21)."[140]

Although Köstenberger makes an argument for Jesus' act of cleansing the temple as being one of the Johannine σημεῖα, there are some convincing arguments against it also. First, as previously discussed, there are good reasons to conclude that the σημεῖα in the Fourth Gospel specifically refer to the miraculous acts of Jesus. Every instance where the word σημεῖα/σημεῖον appears, it is in reference to the miraculous deeds of Jesus (John 2:11, 18, 23; 3:2; 4:48, 54; 6:2, 14, 26, 30; 7:31; 9:16; 10:41; 11:47; 12:18, 37; 20:30). Second, Jesus' cleansing of the temple pericope may serve an important literary function of confirming the claims of the first miracle in John 2:1–11, rather than being a separate σημεῖον. If the first sign provides a messianic message to the nation that Jesus Himself is the promised Messiah of the Old Testament Scriptures, and that He is the one who will usher in the promised kingdom, then this particular act of Jesus' cleansing the temple is His "sequel" public declaration concerning His messianic identity. At the coming of the Messiah in His eschatological kingdom at the Second Advent, He is expected to begin His ministry in the temple to purify the nation Israel (Mal 3:1–3). Upon cleansing the temple at the beginning of His First Advent, Jesus was revealing Himself as that one who will one day inaugurate the kingdom. Furthermore, Jesus' expression, "My Father's house," was also a self-claim to His messiahship (Ps 69:9).[141] Thus, although Köstenberger makes convincing arguments for Jesus' cleansing of the temple pericope to be a separate σημεῖον, it is preferable to see it as a literary addendum to the first sign-miracle.

Another act of Jesus that has been commonly suggested to be one of the Johannine σημεῖα is the miraculous catch of fish by Jesus

139. Ibid., 74.

140. Ibid., 75.

141. The significance of Jesus' cleansing of the temple will be discussed more extensively in chapter 3 of the book, where the passages will be explained in their context.

during His postresurrection ministry to His disciples (chap. 21). The miraculous catch of fish by Jesus is indeed a miracle, but its inclusion among the σημεῖα is questionable. To begin with, it is placed outside the Book of Signs (2:1—12:50), and furthermore, it is also placed after the Evangelist's purpose statement in 20:30–31. Furthermore, it is doubtful that this particular miracle would reveal the messianic identity of Jesus like the other previous sign-miracles. Besides, because of the similarity of this miracle with the one Jesus performed at the beginning of His earthly ministry (cf. Luke 5:1–11), the purpose of this miracle seems to have been to enable His disciples to identify Him and recognize His ability to perform miracles even after His resurrection.[142] Thus, this particular miracle should not be categorized along with the previous sign-miracles. In conclusion, although there are other acts of Jesus such as His cleansing of the temple in chapter 2 and His miraculous catching of fish in chapter 21 that deserve consideration of being included in the selected σημεῖα, there are good reasons for omitting them from the Evangelist's theologically designated sign-miracles.

The Number of Σημεῖα

It has customarily been understood by most Johannine scholars that there are seven miracles in the Fourth Gospel that belong in the Evangelist's designated σημεῖα.[143] Is the number seven an arbitrary number, or does it have some symbolic significance? Schnackenburg, for instance, wonders concerning the Johannine sign-miracles: "It has been long customary to count seven of these. Is the number accidental?"[144] Richardson also tentatively suggests regarding the miracles in the Fourth Gospel, "The number seven is probably symbolic."[145] Colin Brown is more specific when he concludes, "The choice of seven may reflect the idea of perfect number, completeness, the days of creation, or the restoration of creation."[146] The symbolic significance of the number seven in the Old Testament demands a closer look regarding the sign-miracles of the

---

142. Blum, "John," 344–45.

143. Blackburn, "Miracles and Miracle Stories," 555. See above for a list of the seven miracles that are commonly designated as the Johannine σημεῖα.

144. Schnackenburg, *Gospel According to St. John*, 1:516.

145. Richardson, *Miracle Stories of the Gospels*, 115.

146. C. Brown, "Miracle," 376.

Fourth Gospel, since so much of the Evangelist's thoughts originate from and reflect the Hebrew Bible.

The number seven is the most significant symbolic number in the Bible, appearing in almost six hundred passages, especially in the Old Testament.[147] It was used as a sacred number in virtually all the ancient Semitic cultures.[148] This was especially true in the sacred Scriptures of the Hebrew people. In the Old Testament, the number seven is associated with many sacred cultic elements that highlight the idea of completion, fulfillment, and perfection.[149] R. A. H. Gunner lists scores of examples of sevens used throughout the Hebrew Bible that signify the events or items they represent:

> In the creation narrative God rested from his work on the 7th day, and sanctified it. This gave a pattern to the Jewish Sabbath on which man was to refrain from work (Ex. 20:10), to the sabbatic year (Lv. 25:2–6), and also to the year of jubilee, which followed 7 times 7 years (Lv. 25:8). The Feast of Unleavened Bread and the Feast of Tabernacles lasted 7 days (Ex. 12:15, 19; Nu. 29:12). The Day of Atonement was in the 7th month (Lv. 16:29), and 7 occurs frequently in connection with OT ritual, e.g., the sprinkling of the bullock's blood 7 times (Lv. 4:6) and the burnt-offering of 7 lambs (Nu. 28:11); the cleansed leper was sprinkled 7 times (Lv. 14:7), and Naaman had to dip 7 times in Jordan (2 Ki. 5:10). In the tabernacle the candlestick had 7 branches (Ex. 25:32).[150]

Besides these important events and items that are associated with the number seven in the Old Testament, particularly impressive also is the seven biblical feasts that make up Israel's religious calendar: the Passover, the Unleavened Bread, the Firstfruits, the Weeks, the Trumpets, the Day of Atonement, and the Tabernacles (Lev 23). These seven feasts, which were given to His covenant people by Yahweh, were to serve as a perpetual reminder of their holy relationship to their Redeemer. As John J. Davis explains, the number seven is a "sacred number of the covenant between God and man."[151] And, this definition is certainly true of Israel's feasts.

147. For a good discussion of the significance of numbers, see Davis, *Biblical Numerology*.

148. Birch, "Number," 3:559.

149. Gunner, "Number," 834.

150. Ibid.

151. Davis, *Biblical Numerology*, 122.

The number seven is also used significantly in apocalyptic literature such as 1 and 2 Enoch and 2 Esdras, but more importantly, it is used particularly frequently by the apostle John in his Apocalypse.[152] The apostle John describes many events and persons associated with the number seven: seven churches (1:4), seven golden candlesticks (1:12), seven stars (1:16), seven angels (1:20), seven lamps of fire (4:5), seven spirits of God (1:4; 3:1; 4:5), a book with seven seals (5:1), a lamb with seven horns and seven eyes (5:6), seven angels with seven trumpets (8:2), the dragon and the beast with seven heads with seven crowns (12:3; 13:1), seven last plagues (15:1), and seven golden bowls (15:7). Needless to say, the apostle John uses the number symbolically to represent some meaning as well as literally. Thus, it is no surprise to find such common use in the Fourth Gospel as well.

If the apostle John is also using the number seven symbolically concerning Jesus' miracles, could it be that the seven sign-miracles perfectly and completely reveal Jesus to be the promised Messiah of the Old Testament Scriptures and the Son of God, as the Evangelist's own purpose statement (20:30–31) indicates? Is it coincidental that there are also seven "I Am" statements in the Fourth Gospel, which describe Jesus' Person and work?[153] The sign-miracles are therefore perfect and complete in their revelation concerning the messianic identity of Jesus Christ. Furthermore, these seven sign-miracles may also emphasize the perfect and complete nature of the Messiah's future kingdom when all of the patriarchal promises, namely, to provide blessings for all the nations (peoples) under the Messiah's reign will be completely fulfilled (Gen 12:1–3).

In summary, then, although the symbolic significance of the number seven may only be speculation, the frequency and meaning of its use throughout the Hebrew Bible at least demand a consideration concerning its description of the sign-miracles in the Fourth Gospel. This is especially pertinent since the apostle John was Jewish and thought in terms of Hebrew theology, which is certainly the case in this particular

---

152. Birch, "Number," 3:559.

153. The following seven are the "I Am" statements that are predicated: the Bread of Life (6:35), the Light of the World (8:12), the Door of the Sheep (10:7), the Good Shepherd (10:11), the Resurrection and the Life (11:25), the Way, the Truth, and the Life (14:6), and the Vine (15:1).

book. Furthermore, the apostle John's symbolic use of the number seven is clearly evident in his Apocalypse.

THE ORDER AND PROGRESSION OF ΣΗΜΕΙΑ

The study of the Johannine σημεῖα reveals that the Evangelist intentionally selected seven sign-miracles to present Jesus as the promised Messiah of the Old Testament Scriptures and the unique Son of God (cf. John 20:30–31). Based on the symbolic significance of the number seven throughout the Hebrew Bible (considering John's frequent use of the OT), and the apostle John's ample use of the number seven symbolically in his Apocalypse, it is probable that the Evangelist chose seven specific miracles through which to present Jesus as the promised Messiah of the Hebrew Scriptures. It is also possible that the Evangelist intentionally arranged the order and progression of his sign-miracles for a purpose. Certain textual clues indicate that the apostle may indeed have had a certain order and progression in mind, particularly concerning the first and last miracles.[154]

The first textual clue that hints at the Evangelist's intention to purposefully arrange his miracles in a certain order is his numbering of the first two miracles (cf. 2:11 and 4:54). Even more suggestive is the word he chooses to number the first miracle. He uses the word ἀρχή (ἀρχὴν τῶν σημείων) instead of the more commonly used word to simply indicate sequential order, πρῶτον, which would have been certainly more parallel to the δεύτερον of 4:54. Although ἀρχή can denote the idea of being "first,"[155] it is more commonly used to convey the sense of a "beginning" or "primacy."[156] If the Evangelist's intention was simply to number his miracles, he probably could have used the word πρῶτον. However, in using the word ἀρχή the Evangelist suggests a theological meaning to the number. The word ἀρχή could have been chosen by the Evangelist to convey a double meaning of being both first in sequence and also symbolically as a representative sign.[157] If the first sign-miracle of Jesus turning water into wine identifies Him as the promised Messiah of the Scriptures who will one day inaugurate His eschatological king-

---

154. Guthrie also sees a certain sequential order in the Johannine σημεῖα, especially regarding the first two sign-miracles. "Importance of Signs," 72–83.

155. BAGD 111–12.

156. Delling, "ἀρχή," 1: 478–89.

157. Foubister, "Nature and Purpose of Jesus' Miracles," 320.

dom, then the following miracles also are similar in kind in revealing His messianic identity and the kind of power and conditions that will ultimately be present in the promised kingdom.

Therefore, what the first sign-miracle reveals as a representative sign concerning the Messiah's Person and His coming kingdom, is indicative of the subsequent miracles, including the seventh miracle, which can be characterized as a climactic sign.[158] The seventh miracle of Jesus raising Lazarus from the dead (11:1–44) climactically reveals that Jesus possesses the power to do what no one else ever has or will do, that is, raise to life someone who has been dead for four days.[159] This climactic sign is the last sign-miracle performed by Jesus in His public ministry. The Jewish leadership was set on killing Him, especially after having witnessed this particular miracle (11:46–53). In the familiar words of the Synoptists, after this miracle no more signs would be given the people except for the sign of Jonah, or the resurrection of Jesus Christ (cf. Matt 12:39–42).

Another textual clue that hints at the fact that the Evangelist may have intentionally arranged his sign-miracles in a certain order is the close relationship between the first miracle and the seventh miracle of Jesus raising Lazarus from the dead (11:1–46). As mentioned previously, these two miracles are commonly joined by two significant themes. First, the first and seventh miracles are both profoundly related to the theme of Jesus' glory. The theme of Jesus' glory, which is first introduced in the Prologue (1:1–14), brackets all the seven sign-miracles by being explicitly highlighted in the first and seventh miracles (2:11 and 11:40; cf. 12:41). Second, the first and seventh miracles also are commonly joined by the theme of faith, or more accurately, believing.

As the Evangelist's own purpose statement (20:30–31) suggests, the aim of the sign-miracles is that his readers might *believe* that Jesus is the Christ, the Son of God. Thus, as a result of the sign-miracles of Jesus, the Evangelist emphasizes that the disciples believed in Him (2:11 and 11:45). In sum, then, based on certain textual clues in the Fourth Gospel, it is perhaps possible to assume that the Evangelist intentionally arranged his seven sign-miracles in a theological order to most effectively reveal Jesus' identity as the promised Messiah of the Scriptures and highlight

---

158. Ibid., 341.

159. R. E. Brown explains that there was an opinion among the rabbis that the soul hovered near the body for three days but after that there was no hope of resuscitation, *Gospel According to John (I–XII)*, 424.

the kind of miracles that will be present in His kingdom. It is significant to keep in mind, however, that a numerical order was not the intent of the Evangelist. The second miracle of Jesus' raising of the royal official's son is explicitly numbered, in order to indicate that it was the second miracle Jesus did in Cana of Galilee.

CONCLUSION

The purpose statement of the Fourth Gospel (20:30–31) explicitly states that the Evangelist selectively chose certain miracles of Jesus in order to reveal His identity as the promised Messiah of the Hebrew Bible and the divine Son of God. And, these selected miracles of Jesus that are recorded in the Gospel of John are designated as σημεῖα. A broad definition of this intensely theological word conveys the following ideas: (1) a sign or distinguishing mark by which something is known; (2) a sign consisting of a wonder or miracle, an event that is contrary to the usual course of nature, either of divine or demonic in nature; (3) a sign or portent of the last days.[160] Thus, the word σημεῖον seems to be used to convey the idea of demonstrating significant truths through a miracle, as a sample of what is to take place in the future. And, this certainly is the case with the sign-miracles in the Johannine Gospel. In short, the word σημεῖα is loaded with theological import and plays a strategic role in the interpretation of the Fourth Gospel. And, since the proper understanding of this significant word is paramount to the interpretation of this book, an etymological and theological study of σημεῖα is necessary before studying the miracles in their respective contexts.

This chapter is divided into four major sections: first, the usages and nature of σημεῖα; second, the significance and purposes of σημεῖα; third, the identification and number of σημεῖα; and fourth, the order and progression of σημεῖα. The first section defines the etymological meaning of the word and surveys the word's usages in both the extrabiblical and biblical literature. The word's usages in the extrabiblical and biblical literature seem to be similar to its basic definition, in that they convey the meaning of a mark or symbol to identify a thing or person which contains a significant message or revelation. And, it often possesses the character of the supernatural, although sometimes it does not.

---

160. BAGD 747–48.

However, in the writings of John the word σημεῖον is always associated with supernatural miracles, whether it is of divine or demonic origin.

The second section begins by emphasizing the significance of the Johannine σημεῖα, as they are so closely related to other important themes in the Fourth Gospel, namely, δόξα and πιστεύω. Δόξα highlights the significance of the σημεῖα as they manifest the glory of Jesus Christ, while πιστεύω accentuates the fact that the Johannine σημεῖα were not designed to merely impress its readers with their wonder but to encourage them to believe. This section also includes a discussion on the twofold purpose of the Johannine σημεῖα, namely, their revelatory and pragmatic purposes. The sign-miracles are first and foremost christological, that is, they are designed to reveal Jesus to be the Christ, the Son of God. And, in the Johannine sign-miracles the messianic, eschatological, and universal aspects characterize Jesus' Person, or His Christology. The sign-miracles are not only revelatory, however. They are also pragmatic in their aim, that is, they are designed to encourage people to make an active decision of faith regarding the Person about whom the σημεῖα testify. The Johannine σημεῖα are also characterized with a divisive element of having a double character of revealing or veiling at the same time, depending on whether the miracles are received by faith.

The third section begins by identifying the seven miracles of Jesus that are commonly designated as the Johannine σημεῖα. They are the following: the turning of water into wine at the wedding in Cana (2:1–11); the healing of the official's son in Cana (4:43–54); the healing of the lame man at the Pool of Bethesda (5:1–16); the feeding of the five thousand (6:1–15); the walking on water on the Sea of Galilee (6:16–21); the healing of the man born blind (9:1–41); and the raising of Lazarus from the dead (11:1–44). Although other deeds of Jesus have been proposed as belonging within the Johannine σημεῖα, there are reasonable grounds for excluding from the Evangelist's selected sign-miracles. This section then closes with a discussion on the symbolic significance of the number seven. Based on ample evidences concerning the symbolic significance of the number seven in the Old Testament Scriptures, and knowing the Evangelist's close affinity with the Hebrew Bible throughout the Fourth Gospel, this study proposes that the number seven that characterizes the sign-miracles is not just arbitrary nor coincidental but intentional. Besides, the book of Revelation, which is also written by the apostle John, is filled with visions and symbols characterized by the number seven.

The fourth section of this chapter includes a discussion concerning the order and progression of the Johannine σημεῖα. In other words, are the recorded sign-miracles in the Fourth Gospel placed arbitrarily, or are they intentionally placed in a certain order by the Evangelist? This study proposes that the first and the seventh miracles form an inclusio within the Book of Signs (2:1—12:50), by being bracketed with the themes of glory and faith. Furthermore, the first sign-miracle is stated to be first not only in sequential order but also as a representative sign of the subsequent signs that follow. And, the seventh sign is a climactic sign to end the public ministry of Jesus. In the familiar words of the Synoptic Gospels, no more signs were given to the people after the sign-miracles except the sign of Jonah, or the resurrection of Jesus Christ (cf. Matt 12:39–42).

3

The Prologue (1:1–18)

INTRODUCTION

THE PROLOGUE OF THE Fourth Gospel is one of the most profound passages in all of Scripture. It is crafted with an unparalleled literary beauty and at the same time possesses a unique theological depth. Thus, John B. Polhill is not exaggerating in calling the Johannine Prologue a "theological masterpiece."[1] Its masterful presentation of Jesus as the eternal λόγος of God has provided a unique and vital angle from which to view the Son of God. The distinctiveness of the Johannine Prologue can be appreciated also in comparison with the "prologues" of the other Gospels. For instance, the Gospels of Matthew and Luke begin their presentation of Jesus from His birth, while the Gospel of Mark begins its presentation of Jesus from the commencement of His earthly ministry. The Fourth Evangelist, on the other hand, presents Jesus as the divine Son of God who exists from eternity past with the Father. Although some thought-provoking studies have been done to show certain similarities between the Johannine Prologue and the "prologues" in the Synoptic Gospels,[2] the uniqueness of the Johannine Prologue stands out in many

---

1. Polhill, "John 1–4," 445.

2. For instance, see Lightfoot, *Gospel Message*, 18–19. Lightfoot draws parallel between the opening words of Mark's Gospel with the Johannine Prologue because they both emphasize the important role of John the Baptist to the ministry of Jesus at His commencement. See also Hooker's significant article, "Johannine Prologue," 40–58. Hooker points out some interesting parallels between the Fourth Gospel and the Gospel of Mark. For instance, she draws attention to the opening words of Mark's Gospel in identifying Jesus as the Christ, the Son of God (1:1). These two titles of Jesus are the cornerstone of Mark's Gospel as they are both repeated in the pivotal points of the book (Peter's confession of Jesus as the Christ at Caesarea Philippi in 8:29 and the centurion's

respects, just as the Fourth Gospel is distinct in many ways from the Synoptic Gospels.

THE PLACEMENT OF THE PROLOGUE

The uniqueness of the Johannine Prologue, along with its stark contrast in its literary form to the rest of the Gospel, has thus caused many Johannine scholars to question its authenticity and conclude it to be a later addition by a redactor.[3] However, there are solid grounds for accepting the Prologue as being part of the original. Although there are various arguments for the authenticity of the Johannine Prologue, perhaps the most convincing is the close thematic connection between the Prologue and the rest of the Gospel. As D. A. Carson correctly summarizes, "The tightness of the connection between the Prologue and the Gospel render unlikely the view that the Prologue was composed by someone other than the Evangelist."[4] Morris echoes this sentiment based also on the close relationship between the Prologue and the rest of the Gospel: "It

confession of Jesus as the Son of God at the cross in 15:39). Interestingly, these are the same two titles that appear in the Fourth Gospel's purpose statement (20:30–31).

3. For a good survey of the various proposals concerning the formation of the Johannine Prologue, see R. E. Brown's commentary, *Gospel According to John (I–XII)*, 21–23; see also Schnackenburg, *Gospel According to John*, 1:221–81. These two authors, for instance, in addition to providing valuable surveys of the views of others, provide their own reconstructions of the Prologue source. Brown, for example, sees a source of four strophes:

1. vv. 1–2	The Word with God
2. vv. 3–5	The Word and creation
3. vv. 10–12b	The Word in the world
4. vv. 14, 16	The Word and the community

The remaining pieces, supplements made at later stages, are the following:

1. vv. 12c–13	added to explain how men become God's children
2. vv. 17, 18	added to explain "love in place of love"
3. vv. 6–9, 15	materials about John the Baptist

Schnackenburg, on the other hand, finds original Prologue in verses 1, 3, 4, 9, 10, 11, 14, 16, while seeing others as later additions.

Although many Johannine scholars such as Brown and Schnackenburg view the Prologue (1:1–18) and the Epilogue (21:1–25) to be later additions to the original document, I support the authenticity of both to being original. Because it is not the aim of this book to discuss the authenticity of the Gospel, the argument will be based on the presupposition that it is an authentic part of the book.

4. Carson, *Gospel According to John*, 111–12.

is more likely that it is the original, for it accords so well with what follows. These verses bring before us some of the great thoughts that will be developed as the narrative unfolds; the excellency of Christ, who is the Word of God, the eternal strife between light and darkness, and the witness borne by the Baptist, that greatest of the sons of Israel."[5] Thus, as Barrett perceptively points out, "The Prologue is not a jig-saw puzzle but one piece of solid theological writing."[6]

As students of the Fourth Gospel uniformly point out, one of the keys to understanding this gospel depends on recognizing the vital relationship of the Prologue to the rest of the Gospel narrative. Ever since Adolf von Harnack's significant question in 1892,[7] Johannine scholars have been challenged to seriously consider the profound relationship between the Johannine Prologue and the rest of the Gospel.[8] Although many proposals have been made regarding this significant relationship, the Prologue's invaluable role can be summarized in two aspects: literary and theological purposes. Literarily, the Prologue plays a strategic role in the Gospel by being positioned in a strategic place.[9] As Francis Moloney insightfully points out, one of the significant purposes the Prologue plays in the Gospel is to create a literary tension for the reader.[10] Bultmann similarly describes the Prologue's strategic position this way: "He (the reader) cannot yet fully understand them (motifs in the prologue), but they are half comprehensible, half mysterious, they arouse the tension, and awaken the question which is essential if he is to understand what is going to be said."[11] George Beasley-Murray's description of the Prologue's literary purpose is concise but as good as any: "He (the Evangelist) prepares for the story by describing the Son of God in terms that rivet the attention of his readers, and so encourages them to read the story for themselves."[12] In short, the Prologue serves an important

5. Morris, *Gospel According to John*, 71.

6. Barrett, "Dialectical Theology," 48.

7. Von Harnack, "Über das Verhältnis des Prologs des vierten Evangeliums zum ganzen Werke," 189–231. ("The Relationship of the Prologue in the Fourth Gospel to the Work as a Whole.")

8. For a survey of the modern discussion on this subject, see E. Harris's work, *Prologue and Gospel*, 9–25.

9. Moloney, *Belief in the Word*, 23–24.

10. Ibid.

11. Bultmann, *Gospel of John*, 13.

12. Beasley-Murray, *John*, 5.

literary purpose by setting the stage for the reader to anticipate the rest of the Gospel narrative.

The other important function the Prologue plays in the Fourth Gospel is theological, in that it introduces the main themes of the Gospel that will be developed later in the narrative. Central themes of the Gospel such as Jesus' eternality and His deity are stated in clear terms that will be demonstrated later through the Gospel narrative. Furthermore, key concepts such as life and light are also presented as having their origin in the divine λόγος. These are also demonstrated later throughout the Gospel, especially in Jesus' self-declaration as the "Resurrection and the Life" and as the "Light of the World." Additionally, significant reactions are predicted in the Prologue such as the rejection of the Messiah by the Jewish leadership, which is later demonstrated throughout the Gospel narrative and climaxes at the cross. Carson's table is helpful in visually seeing the many close connections between the Prologue and the rest of the Fourth Gospel:[13]

	Prologue	Gospel
the preexistence of the Logos or Son	1:1–2	17:5
in him was life	1:4	5:26
life is light	1:4	8:12
light rejected by darkness	1:5	3:19
yet not quenched by it	1:5	12:35
light coming into the world	1:9	3:19; 12:46
Christ not being received by his own	1:11	4:44
being born to God and not of flesh	1:13	3:6; 8:41–2
seeing his glory	1:14	12:41
the "one and only" Son	1:14, 18	3:16
truth in Jesus Christ	1:17	14:6
no one has seen God, except the one who comes from God's side	1:18	6:46

Carson's summary of the relationship between the Johannine Prologue and the rest of the Gospel narrative is insightful: "The Prologue summarizes how the 'Word' which was with God in the very beginning came into the sphere of time, history, tangibility—in other words, how

---

13. Carson, *The Gospel According to John*, 111.

the Son of God was sent into the world to become the Jesus of history, so that the glory and grace of God might be uniquely and perfectly disclosed. The rest of the book is nothing other than an expansion of this theme."[14] Thus, as Moloney aptly puts it, "The prologue is the 'telling' while the narrative is the 'showing.'"[15]

THE SUBJECT OF THE PROLOGUE

The subject of the Johannine Prologue is obviously the λόγος (the Word) of God. Although there is a consensus of opinions that the λόγος is the subject of the Prologue, there is hardly such a consensus concerning the antecedent or background of the λόγος. The various proposals for the conceptual background of the Johannine λόγος can be broadly classified into three sources: (1) Greek philosophy (Stoicism & Philo)[16];

14. Ibid.

15. Moloney, *Belief in the Word*, 24.

16. For a good discussion on the background of the Stoics and their teaching during the Hellenistic period, including the first centuries AD, see Bromiley, "Stoics," 4:621–22. In Stoic thought, Logos was Reason, the impersonal rational principle governing the universe. This principle was thought to pervade the entire universe and, according to Stoicism, human beings must live in keeping with this Reason. However, in spite of the parallel terminology to the Johannine Logos, Stoicism differs from the Christian doctrine in the essential points. Bromiley explains this way: "It (Stoicism) has no concept of a personal God, no radical view of sin, no place for historical divine acts culminating in the incarnation, no idea of ethical renewal through the ministry of the Word and Spirit, and no hope of the resurrection and eternal fellowship with God in His kingdom."

(2) the "Word" as the personification of Wisdom in Jewish wisdom literature (*sophia*)[17]; and (3) the Word of God in the Old Testament.[18]

Although it is clear that the Evangelist's primary antecedent for the λόγος is the Old Testament and the Hebrew term rbd, he may have used this particular word to effectively communicate to a wider audience. As

17. The personification of wisdom in Jewish wisdom literature is often proposed as the antecedent of the Johannine Logos. For instance, the personalization of wisdom in Prov 8:22–31 is explained: "The LORD brought me forth as the first of his works, before his deeds of old. I was appointed from eternity, from the beginning, before the world began.... when he marked out the foundations of the earth. Then I was the craftsman at his side. I was filled with delight day after day, rejoicing always in his presence, rejoicing in his whole world and delighting in mankind." In addition, the apocryphal literature also expresses Wisdom to have been at God's side at creation (cf. Sir 1:1–10; Wis Sol).

In spite of the close parallels between the Jewish wisdom literature and the Johannine Prologue concerning the Logos, there are also significant differences. Köstenberger summarizes these differences into three points: (1) wisdom literature does not present Wisdom as a second person of the Godhead but merely as a divine attribute already present at creation; Jesus, on the other hand, is portrayed not merely as "with God" (1:1, 2), but as himself God (1:1); (2) Wisdom is not really cast as a person—it is merely a concept that is *personified*, a common literary device; but in John, the exact opposite procedure is at work: Jesus, *a real person*, is presented in *conceptual terms* as the Word; (3) the stubborn fact remains that John does not use the term "wisdom" (*sophia*) but the expression "the Word" (*logos*). Köstenberger, *Encountering John*, 53.

18. With the shifting of consensus in the Johannine scholarship in regards to the historical milieu or background of the Fourth Gospel from being understood as essentially Hellenistic to being primarily Hebraic or Jewish, the Old Testament has been viewed as the primary background of the Prologue as well. Although various proposals have been given concerning the origin of the λόγος, its nearest and most logical antecedent is the Old Testament and the Hebrew term דבר. The use of the word λόγος in John 1:1 ties itself to Gen 1:3, where it describes God's creative acts by the simple yet powerful command of His Word. This is affirmed also in Ps 33:6: "By the word of the Lord were the heavens made, and all the host of them by the breath of His mouth." It is also often repeated in the OT Prophets, where their writings often begin with the familiar words, "The Word of the LORD came to...." (cf. Jer 1:4; Ezek 1:3; Hos 1:1; Joel 1:1; Amos 3:1; Jonah 1:1; Mic 1:1; Zeph 1:1; Hag 1:1; Zech 1:1; Mal 1:1).

Isaiah 55 has also been proposed as the background of the Johannine λόγος. Verses 9–11 state: "As the heavens are higher than the earth, so are my ways higher than your ways and my thoughts than your thoughts. As the rain and the snow come down from heaven, and do not return to it without watering the earth and making it bud and flourish, so that it yields seed for the sower and bread for the eater, so is my word that goes out from my mouth: it will not return to me empty, but will accomplish what I desire and achieve the purpose for which I sent it." According to Köstenberger, this passage is God's personified Word (not Wisdom), and thus draw parallels between these passages on three levels: (1) it is sent by God in order to accomplish a particular divine purpose; (2) it unfailingly accomplishes this purpose; (3) and it returns to God who sent it after accomplishing its mission. *Encountering John*, 54.

Köstenberger explains, however, a distinction must be kept in mind between John's conceptual background and his desire to contextualize his message to a particular audience.[19] He elaborates thusly: "This desire to contextualize his message may have led John to use a term that had currency among his readers in order to persuade them of the relevance of his gospel. Yet even if John used the term 'Word' because it served his purpose of communicating to a Hellenistic audience, this does not mean that he used the expression in the way in which it was commonly used in the world of his day; the background for this term may rather lie in John's own thought world."[20] W. Hall Harris's clarification is also insightful:

> Why did John choose to call Jesus the Logos in the prologue to his gospel, and what did he mean by it? As to why the term was used, the answer probably lies with John's audience. John gave no explanation of the Logos, apparently assuming his readers would understand the idea. Greek readers would probably think he was referring to the rational principle that guided the universe and would be shocked to find that this Logos had become not only personalized but incarnate (1:1–14). Jewish readers would be more prepared for some sort of personalized preexistent Wisdom, but they too would be amazed at the idea of incarnation. John presented Jesus as the true Logos as preparation for his own presentation of Jesus as the Son of God.[21]

In short, then, although the Evangelist uses a term that a wide audience would have understood in their respective cultures, his presentation of the λόγος is the preexistent Christ, the eternal Son of God who is now incarnate as Jesus of Nazareth. Perhaps Moloney's suggestion that the Johannine Logos is essentially about communication best describes the purpose of the Evangelist's choice of the word λόγος: "But the choice of the Greek expression ὁ λόγος, whatever its background, allows the author to hint to the reader that from the intimacy between the Word and God which has been described, 'the Word' will be spoken. A word is essentially about communication. The modality of that communica-

19. Ibid., 51.
20. Ibid.
21. W. H. Harris, "Theology of John's Writings," 191.

tion has not been indicated, but if there is the Word, then it exists to say something."[22]

THE STRUCTURE OF THE PROLOGUE

The Prologue in the Fourth Gospel (1:1–18) is a difficult passage to outline and, as a result, enjoys very little consensus about its structure. One of the reasons that make it difficult to outline is the apparent scattering of subjects throughout the passage. For instance, John the Baptist appears first towards the beginning of the passage (vv. 6–8), and yet appears again towards the end (v. 15). However, solutions have been offered to explain such lack of coherence within the passage. One of the significant proposals that demand a serious look is that the Johannine Prologue is structured in literary chiasm.[23] According to R. Alan Culpepper, if one begins with both ends of the Prologue and works toward the middle, then at certain levels 1:1–2 parallels 1:18, 1:3 parallels 1:17, 1:4–5 parallels 1:16, 1:6–8 parallels 1:15, 1:9–10 parallels 1:14, 1:11 parallels 1:13, and 1:12a parallels 1:12c, making 1:12b the "pivot" on which the chiasm turns, the center of attention.[24] This may explain why, for example, John the Baptist appears in two separate references within the passage (vv. 6–8, 15). In other words, they are not placed randomly or accidentally but intentionally for a literary purpose.

There are other proposals of chiastic structure that climaxes at a different point. Köstenberger, for example, suggests a chiasm of the Prologue with a different climactic point:[25]

A   The Word's activity in creation (1:1–5)
    B   John's witness concerning the light (1:6–9)
        C   The incarnation of the Word (1:10–14)
    B'   John's witness concerning the Word's preeminence (1:15)
A'   The final revelation brought by Jesus Christ (1:16–18)

---

22. Moloney, *Belief in the Word*, 30.

23. Although scholars such as N. W. Lund, M. E. Boismard, P. Lamarche, A. Feuillet, P. Borgen, and M. Hooker have proposed various forms of chiasms, the one proposed by Culpepper seems to be most thorough and thus serves as a good model for discussion. For a brief survey and critique of these works mentioned, see Culpepper's article, "Pivot of John's Prologue," 1–31.

24. Ibid., 9–17.

25. Köstenberger, *Encountering John*, 57.

Thus, Köstenberger sees the theme of the Word's incarnation as being the pivot point of the Prologue.

Although it is probable that the Evangelist, given his literary mastery, designed some sort of chiastic structure, the following outline will be proposed for the sake of dividing the passage for a thematic analysis.

I.   The origin and nature of the Logos (1:1–5)
II.   The witness to the Logos (1:6–8)
III.   The manifestation of the Logos (1:9–13)
IV.   The revelation of the Logos (1:14–18)

THE SIGNIFICANCE OF THE PROLOGUE

The Johannine Prologue, like the rest of the Fourth Gospel, is immersed in Old Testament theology. And, this particular section will analyze the different sections of the Prologue that draw its theology from the rich reservoir of the Hebrew Scriptures. In other words, the Prologue provides significant revelations about the one to whom the sign-miracles bear witness and thus sets the stage for the Gospel narrative. Further, the revelations that the Evangelist provides through the Prologue derive their significance from the Old Testament Scriptures.

The Origin and Nature of the Logos (1:1–5)

The opening words of the Johannine Prologue make an unmistakable and intentional reference to the opening words of Genesis. Emphasizing the eternality and deity of Jesus Christ, the Evangelist begins with the familiar words, "In the beginning was the Word, and the Word was with God, and the Word was God. He was with God in the beginning" (John 1:1). These words scream for a comparison to the opening words of the Hebrew Bible, "In the beginning God created the heavens and the earth" (Gen 1:1). The conceptual parallels between the two chapters are startling.[26] However, the Evangelist does not merely refer to the opening chapter of the Old Testament Scriptures, but he adds invaluable revela-

---

26. Evans, *Word and Glory*, 77–78. Evans shows the close parallel between the two passages by laying them side by side, using the Septuagint (LXX) for the Gen passage. The parallel concepts between the two passages are clearly seen by the identical Greek words used. The following are examples of commonly used words in both passages of Gen 1 and John 1: In the beginning (ἐν ἀρχῇ); God (θεός); came into being (ἐγένετο); light (φῶς); darkness (σκοτίᾳ); shines (φαίνει); life (ζωή); man (ἀνθρώπων).

tions concerning the eternal Logos. For instance, the beginning words of the Fourth Gospel shed further light on the creation account of Genesis 1, namely, that God the Father created the world through the Son (cf. Col 1:16–17; Heb 1:2). Thus, God the Son, the eternal Word who was coexistent with the Father in the beginning, is also revealed to be the Creator. This connection is summarized well by Waltke: "The creation account of the Old Testament finds its full explication in Jesus of Nazareth, the God-man. As He is the Creator, the One full of light, life, wisdom, and goodness. As man, He is the One who is bringing the earth under His dominion. . . . John wrote about Him as the Creator."[27] Another instance where the Evangelist supercedes the meaning of Genesis is when his reference to the beginning even goes beyond the beginning of time in Genesis 1. John's reference to the beginning goes back to eternity past. [28] In short, John's emphasis of the eternal Logos in these verses is that, as the Creator, He is distinct from all creation.

The opening verses of the Prologue also reveal that life exists in the eternal Logos.[29] Although the Evangelist could be referring to physical life generally, it is probable that he is also referring to eternal life specifically. Raymond B. Brown's description of the Johannine usage of life is insightful: "All created life is an expression of that life-giving power eternally existent in the Logos. Life, in John's mind, means the existence that is characteristic of God Himself. It is God's life."[30] The fact that the Evangelist is referring to more than just the physical life can be seen in the words that follow, namely, that "life was the light of men." In joining these two significant concepts of life and light, John must have had this familiar Old Testament verse in mind: "For with you is the fountain of life; in your light we see light" (Ps 36:9).[31]

The concept of light is also a significant theme in the Johannine writings that first find their antecedent from Hebrew Scripture.[32] Light

---

27. Waltke, "Creation Account in Genesis 1:1-3—Part IV," 28–41.

28. R. B. Brown, "Prologue of the Gospel of John," 430–31.

29. The Evangelist uses ζωή thirty-seven times in the Fourth Gospel: seventeen times it occurs with αἰώνιος, but it is clear from the context that the other occurrences also refer to eternal life.

30. R. B. Brown, "Prologue of the Gospel of John," 432.

31. The relationship between life and light are also found in later Jewish writings such as 1 Bar 4:2.

32. For a good discussion on the concept of light being derived primarily from the Hebrew Scriptures and its messianic significance, see Allen's article, "Light of the Coming One," 30–33.

characterizes the nature of God. As the apostle John describes in his first epistle, "God is light; in him there is no darkness at all" (1 John 1:5). For instance, the psalmist praises the Lord as both light and salvation (Ps 27:1). The prophet Isaiah also hopes for the day when the Messiah will bring light to people living in darkness (Isa 9:2). Borchert aptly explains concerning John's use of light, "Light, according to the Prologue, does not belong naturally to humanity. It is a gift or a power from outside the human situation that confronts the world."[33] These important characteristics of life and light that describe the divine Logos, are also characteristics that Jesus attributes of Himself and are illustrated through His miracles.

The last verse of the opening section of the Prologue, however, introduces the significant opposition to the Person and works of the Logos (John 1:5). Although the light of the Logos shines in the sphere of this darkened world, the world will oppose the light. As Brown aptly describes the Evangelist's use of darkness, "Darkness in the thought of John is not merely lack of knowledge or illumination, it is a symbol of rebellion, conflict, and hostility. It signals an existence both external and internal that opposes God."[34] In other words, the darkness that the Evangelist mentions is not merely a passive state that is absent of God's light, but rather an active opposition and rebellion to the things of God. This is a theme that will characterize Jesus' ministry in this Gospel.

In sum, then, the opening verses of the Johannine Prologue describe the origin and nature of the Logos as the eternal and divine Word who exists with God the Father from eternity past. He not only was present when the universe began (Gen 1:1), He Himself was the one who created all things. Furthermore, the Logos is the source of all life, particularly the kind of life that He possesses. And, it is He who penetrates the world of humanity that is characterized by spiritual darkness with His light. It is no accident that the qualities that characterize the divine Logos in the Prologue are also found to be true in Jesus in the sign-miracles recorded in the Gospel narrative. For instance, Jesus is demonstrated to be the Creator through the miracle of turning water into wine at the wedding in Cana of Galilee (2:1–11). And, Jesus is also demonstrated to be the source of life through the miracle of feeding of the five thousand (6:1–15) and His self-declaration as the Bread of Life (6:48). Furthermore,

33. Borchert, *John 1–11*, 108–9.
34. R. B. Brown, "Prologue of the Gospel of John," 433.

that Jesus is the source of life is also demonstrated through the miracle of raising of Lazarus from the dead (11:1–44) and His self-declaration as the Resurrection and the Life (11:25). And, Jesus is also demonstrated to be the source of light through the miracle of healing the man born blind (9:1–41) and His self-declaration as the Light of the World (8:12).

The Witness to the Logos (1:6–8)

These three verses in the middle of the Prologue apparently seem somewhat out of place literarily. As Borchert observes, "In the midst of the poetic section of the Prologue, the next three verses (vv. 6–8) appear as a prose section."[35] Moloney's description of these verses is even more dramatic: "The speculations of vv. 1–5 come to a halt as the reader is drawn quite rudely into history with the first words of v. 6: ἐγένετο ἄνθρωπος, 'a man appeared'. . . . The reader encounters a historical person. He is given a name: 'his name was John.'"[36] However, a careful reading of these verses in their context reveals an appropriate fitting. In these verses, John the Baptist is set in contrast to the Logos. Although John the Baptist is also sent from God, he is a mere witness to the Logos who is the light. Thus, literarily these verses are fitting since they contrast the coming of John the Baptist with another who has also come from God, the eternal Logos. However, whereas the Logos is the substance of God's revelation to the world, John the Baptist is merely a witness of Him.

The introduction of John the Baptist as a witness of the Logos also establishes a theological significance, a theme that will be repeated in the Gospel narrative. The theme of witness (μαρτυρία) in the Fourth Gospel is significant since witnesses establish the legitimacy of another's testimony, a principle that was emphasized in the Old Testament.[37] Where there is a need for a verifiable testimony, it is necessary that there be the presence of two or three witnesses to corroborate the matter (cf. Deut 19:15–21). Jesus accepted this principle (Matt 18:16; John 8:17), as did the apostles in the New Testament (cf. 2 Cor 13:1). Thus, for the Evangelist, John the Baptist's witness was significant to the testimony of the Logos, a fact reiterated by Jesus Himself concerning John the Baptist's testimony (John 5:33–35; cf. 10:41). In sum, then, these verses in

---

35. Borchert, *John 1–11*, 111.

36. Moloney, *Belief in the Word*, 34.

37. This particular theme will be discussed in more detail in chapter 7 of the book, since this theme is developed in John 5.

the Prologue that seem to stick out like a sore thumb, play an important role both literarily and theologically concerning the significant witness of John the Baptist.

The Manifestation of the Logos (1:9–13)

Although these verses continue the theme of the Logos as the true light who is coming into the world of men, their main emphasis is the world's rejection of Him. The concept of "the coming one" (ὁ ἐρχόμενος) is an idea that is deeply rooted in Jewish messianic expectations, and it is a phrase that is repeated later in the Gospel narrative.[38] For instance, even the Samaritan woman understood the concept of the coming Messiah (4:25; cf. 1:30; 7:27–31; 12:15). The Jewish expectations of the coming Messiah are surely derived from the Hebrew Scriptures, such as Psalm 118:26 where it states: "Blessed is he who comes in the name of the LORD." Furthermore, the Evangelist records the crowd quoting the familiar messianic verse at Jesus' triumphal entry (John 12:15): "Rejoice greatly, O Daughter of Zion! Shout, Daughter of Jerusalem! See, your king comes to you, righteous and having salvation, gentle and riding on a donkey, on a colt, the foal of a donkey" (Zech 9:9). Thus, the Evangelist is equating the coming of the Logos into the world with the advent of the Messiah, and thereby preparing the reader for the revelations concerning Jesus.

The Evangelist also emphasizes the theme that the coming of the Messiah (Logos) will be predominantly met with intense opposition. These verses reiterate the previous statement that "the light shines in the darkness, but the darkness has not understood/overcome it" (John 1:5).[39] The Logos, the true light, has come into the world of men, but the world rejects the light because it is characterized by darkness. Thus, in the Evangelist's words, the Creator has drawn near to His creation, but they did not receive Him. This rejection motif is one of the central themes of the Fourth Gospel. However, what is even more mind-boggling to the Evangelist is that even the Jews reject the promised Messiah: "He came to that which was his own (ἴδια) but his own did not receive him" (1:11).

---

38. Borchert, *John 1–11*, 113.

39. The Greek verb κατέλαβεν can be translated here as either "comprehended it," or "overcome it." It is probably one of John's many double meanings in the Fourth Gospel. For an excellent study of John's double meanings in the Fourth Gospel, see Hamidkhani's master's thesis, "Johannine Expressions of Double Meaning."

The rejection of the Messiah by His own people is a central theme of the Fourth Gospel, as it characterizes the public ministry of Jesus and finally climaxes at the cross.

The theme of the Messiah being rejected by His own people also finds its antecedent in the prophetic parts of the Hebrew Bible. This rejection-motif of the Messiah by His own people is foreseen in the commissioning of the prophet Isaiah, where God warns the prophet that rejection of God's messengers will be the characteristic of the nation Israel (Isa 6:1–13; cf. John 12). The psalmist also predicted such rejection of the Messiah: "The stone the builders rejected has become the capstone" (Ps 118:22). Furthermore, this same theme of Israel rejecting the prophets of God is also foretold by Jesus Himself through the parable of the Tenants, where the nation Israel will not only reject the prophets of God but will ultimately kill the son (Mark 12:1–12; cf. Matt 21:33–44; Luke 20:9–19).

The Revelation of the Logos (1:14–18)

The Johannine Prologue reaches its climax with the incarnation of the Logos. The divine Logos, who exists eternally with God the Father, has now taken on humanity in Jesus Christ. The theme of the incarnation of the divine Logos is the main emphasis of these closing verses of the Prologue. The eternal Logos has revealed Himself fully through His incarnation in Jesus. It is clear that the Evangelist's thought in these verses is immersed in the background of the Old Testament, particularly Exodus 33–34.[40] Köstenberger's helpful chart of paralleling the two passages highlights the connection between the two:[41]

---

40. A large number of the Johannine scholars recognize this significant connection between Exod 33–34 and John 1:14–18. R. E. Brown, *Gospel According to John (I–XII)*, 36; Beasley-Murray, *John*, 14–15; Carson, *Gospel According to John*, 129, 134; Evans, *Word and Glory*, 79–83; Glasson, *Moses in the Fourth Gospel*; Hanson, "John 1:14–18 and Exodus 34," 90–101; Koester, *Dwelling of God*, 100–15; Köstenberger, *Encountering John*, 52; Moloney, *Belief in the Word*, 34–52.

41. Köstenberger, *Encountering John*, 52.

Exodus 33–34	John 1:14–18
Israel finds grace in Yahweh's sight (33:14)	disciples receive "grace instead grace"(1:16)
no one can see Yahweh's face and live (33:20)	no one has seen God at any time (1:18)
Yahweh's glory passes by Moses (33:23; 34:6–7)	the disciples beheld the Word's glory (1:14)
Yahweh abounds in lovingkindness and truth (34:6)	Jesus is full of grace and truth (1:14, 17)
Yahweh dwelt in a tent (33:7)	the Word "tented" among the disciples (1:14)
Moses was given the law (34:27–28)	the law was given through Moses (1:17)
Moses, mediator between Yahweh, Israel (34:32–35)	Jesus, the mediator between God and man (1:17–18)

The expression of the incarnation of the divine Logos in these verses (John 1:14–18) is communicated powerfully through the familiar Old Testament imagery of God dwelling in the midst of His people through the tabernacle in the book of Exodus. Craig A. Evans even asserts that the incarnation of the Logos must be understood in the proper background with Moses and the Sinai covenant.[42] He explains the connection this way:

> Prior to the second giving of the covenant, God had been giving Moses instructions for the building of the tabernacle (Exod 26–31). After the calf incident (chap. 32) and the renewal of the covenant (chaps. 33–34), the tabernacle is built (chaps. 35–40). When it is completed and consecrated, "the cloud covered the tent of meeting, and the glory (כָּבוֹד/δόξα) of the Lord filled the tabernacle (מִשְׁכָּן/σκηνή)" (Exod 40:34). In essence, then, the second half of the Johannine Prologue presupposes the second half of the Book of Exodus (chaps. 20–40), which tells of Israel's meeting God at Sinai. The balance of the Fourth Gospel

42. Evans, *Word and Glory*, 81–82.

bears this out, as we find several comparisons between Jesus, Moses and various aspects of the wilderness story.[43]

Such connection of the tabernacle imagery in the Old Testament with the incarnation of the Logos in the Johannine Prologue seems valid, since the tabernacle (tent of meeting) is the place where God spoke to Moses (Exod 33:9) and it is where God revealed His glory to His people (Exod 40:34).[44] Thus, Craig R. Koester is correct when he says that "the tabernacle imagery is uniquely able to portray the person of Jesus as the locus of God's Word and glory among humankind."[45]

These closing verses (John 1:14–18) and the Johannine Prologue as a whole (vv. 1–18) reveal the main purpose of the incarnation of the divine Logos according to the Evangelist, that is, to reveal God through the Person and works of Jesus Christ. As the unique Son of God, only Jesus is able to truly reveal Him (cf. John 14:9).[46] Thus, as Allen correctly concludes, "In John 1, the apostle deliberately built on Hebrew words and phrases because Jesus Christ is clearly linked to the revelations of Yahweh in the Hebrew Bible."[47] Therefore, Jesus could confidently say to His critics, "I and the Father are one" (10:30, 38).

To summarize, the Johannine Prologue plays a significant role in the Fourth Gospel, both literarily and theologically. Literarily, the Prologue prepares the reader in advance by setting the stage, so that the Gospel narrative can be approached with knowledgeable anticipation. Theologically, the Prologue introduces the main themes of the Gospel that will be developed later in the narrative. Carson's summary aptly highlights both the literary and theological emphases of the Johannine Prologue, when he likens it to "a foyer to the rest of the Fourth Gospel, simultaneously drawing the reader in and introducing the major themes."[48]

43. Ibid.

44. Koester, *Dwelling of God*, 102.

45. Ibid.

46. The uniqueness of the Logos is highlighted through the use of the word μονογενής. Its Hebrew counterpart יחיד is used to describe Abraham's son, Isaac. The idea does not connote that Isaac is the only son, since Abraham had other sons, but that he is a "one-of-a-kind" son since he is the child of the promise (cf. Heb 11:17). For a good discussion of the significance of the word μονογενής, see De Kruijf, "Glory of the Only Son," 111–23.

47. Allen, "Affirming Right-of-Way," 10.

48. Carson, *Gospel According to John*, 111.

4

The Testimonium (1:19–51)

INTRODUCTION

THE FIRST CHAPTER OF the Fourth Gospel has significant literary and theological roles within the book. It prepares the reader for the rest of the book by introducing key concepts and themes that are developed later in the book. The first chapter provides a foretaste of the kind of revelations to come in the Gospel narrative concerning its main character, Jesus Christ. Since they are sandwiched between the Prologue (1:1–18) and the rest of the Gospel narrative, the significance of the remaining verses in the chapter (vv. 19–51), commonly known as the "Testimonium," is often overlooked. However, what these verses lack in exposure, they certainly make up for it in their importance within the Fourth Gospel. These verses bring an invaluable "piece of the puzzle" to the understanding of this Gospel. This significant portion of John's Gospel contains proclamations by John the Baptist and the disciples concerning Jesus' identity as the promised Messiah of the Old Testament Scriptures and the divine Son of God, who is the main subject in the remaining chapters (cf. 20:30–31).[1]

---

1. In his purpose statement (20:30–31) John noted that the aim of his Gospel is to present Jesus as the promised Messiah and the unique Son of God. And his primary means of revealing Jesus as the Messiah are the sign-miracles (σημεῖα) and attendant contexts with discourses and narratives, all of which are recorded in the first twelve chapters of the Gospel, commonly referred to as the "Book of Signs" (chaps. 2–12). The term Book of Signs, now widely accepted by most Johannine scholars, is usually associated with Dodd (*Interpretation of the Fourth Gospel*, x) and R. E. Brown (*Gospel according to John [I–XII]*, cxxxviii). John 1–12 records the public ministry of Jesus, the second section (chaps. 13–17) records Jesus' Farewell Discourse with His disciples, and the third section (chaps. 18–20) is the Passion Narrative. Dodd calls the entire latter section (chaps. 13–20) the "Book of Passion," and Brown calls it the "Book of Glory."

Although the Johannine Testimonium is often placed within the Book of Signs as being part of the first major literary unit within the Fourth Gospel,[2] it seems more fitting both literarily and theologically to place it along with the Prologue as an introduction to the Book of Signs, or the whole Gospel, for that matter.[3] Smalley is correct in seeing the entire first chapter as an introduction to the Gospel: "Die beiden Hälften des ersten Kapitels gehören zusammen, und sie stehen in enger Verbindung nicht nur miteinander, sondern auch mit Joh 2–21."[4] Or, as Beasley-Murray says, "the prologue of the Gospel ends not with v 18 but with the Christological utterance of v 51."[5] He further advocates the unity between the Johannine Prologue and the Testimonium this way: "Certainly 1:19–51 is closely linked with the prologue through its expansion of the theme of John's witness to Jesus (cf. 6–8, 15) and its Christological declarations."[6] Culpepper even characterizes the Testimonium as "a second, narrative introduction" to the Fourth Gospel.[7] He says, "Just as the Gospel seems to have two conclusions (at the end of John 20 and at the end of John 21), so it has two beginnings."[8] In short, the Johannine Prologue (1:1–18) and the Testimonium (1:19–51) seem to form a literary unity, in that they prepare the reader for the revelations to come in the Gospel narrative through the sign-miracles and their attendant contexts. It lays the groundwork, so to speak, for the revelations to come concerning Jesus Christ.

2. R. E. Brown, for example, includes the Testimonium within the Book of Signs (1:19–12:50), *Gospel According to John (I–XII)*, XI–XII. Köstenberger does the same. *John*, 51–88.

3. Dodd, for instance, places the Prologue (1:1–18) and the Testimony (1:19–51) together as a unit, calling the entire first chapter of the Fourth Gospel a Proem. *Interpretation of the Fourth Gospel*, 289–96.

4. Smalley, "Johannes 1, 51," 300–13, esp. p. 300. ("The two halves of the chapter belong together, so that they stand in a relationship not only with each other but also with John 2–21.")

5. Beasley-Murray, *John*, 18.

6. Ibid.

7. Culpepper, *Gospel and Letters of John*, 120.

8. Ibid.

THE STRUCTURE OF THE TESTIMONIUM

The Testimonium (1:19–51) begins the prose narrative of the Fourth Gospel by means of a "poetic narrative."[9] This poetic narrative section of John's Gospel includes the testimonies by John the Baptist and Jesus' first disciples. However, this invaluable section of the Gospel has been structured variously depending on different thematic outlooks.[10] For instance, Culpepper outlines this section in two parts, following two significant elements: first, the trial motif of John the Baptist (vv. 19–28); and second, the fulfillment of messianic expectations (vv. 29–51).[11] Borchert's outline is similar to Culpepper's, with slightly different yet interesting subsections: first, the Baptizer's model (vv. 19–28); and second, the three cameos of witness (vv. 29–51). According to Borchert, the three subsections in the second section (vv. 29–34, 35–42, 43–51) are like "three beautiful cameos that reveal a series of fascinating confessional identifications of Jesus."[12] Beasley-Murray's outline, on the other hand, follows a slightly different structure. His outline is determined by the "witness" theme of John the Baptist already announced in vv. 6–8, 15 of the Prologue.[13] He divides the section this way: (1) the witness of John to Jewish leaders (vv. 19–28), first negatively (vv. 19–24), then positively (vv. 25–28); (2) the witness of John to people who came to hear him (vv. 29–34); (3) the witness of John to certain disciples, resulting in their following Jesus and the call of others through their witness, the whole providing a chain of testimonies concerning Jesus (vv. 35–50); and (4) a concluding

9. Moloney, *Belief in the Word*, 53.

10. Although the Johannine Testimonium (1:19–51) enjoys no uniformity in its structure among the Johannine scholars, there is a basic structure that runs through most of them. It may be helpful to discuss the christological titles of Jesus in this section in light of their context.

11. Culpepper, *Gospel and Letters of John*, 120–28. The second section of Culpepper's division (vv. 29–51) is divided into three subdivisions: John's witness to Jesus (vv. 29–34); the first disciples of Jesus (vv. 35–42); and the calling of Nathanael by Jesus (vv. 43–51).

12. Borchert, *John 1–11*, 125–50. Borchert's three "cameos of witness" (vv. 29–51) is subdivided under these titles: John's witness in proclamation (vv. 29–34); John's witness and the coming of the first disciples (vv. 35–42); Philip's witness to Nathanael (vv. 43–51).

13. Beasley-Murray, *John*, 22.

statement, which, though addressed to Nathanael, it is also addressed in the plural to the disciple group (v. 51).[14]

Although the various ways of outlining this section of the Gospel are helpful in their own ways, the simplest and most effective means of structuring these verses may be according to the temporal indicators within the text. The passage is marked by a series of days, indicated by the Evangelist: "the next day" (v. 29), "the next day" (v. 35), and "the next day" (v. 43). Thus, as Moloney concludes, "John 1:19–51 tells a story about a succession of events that took place over a period of four days."[15] Moloney thus outlines the passage accordingly:[16]

> I.   Day One (vv. 19–28)
> II.   Day Two (vv. 29–34)
> III.   Day Three (vv. 35–42)
> IV.   Day Four (vv. 43–51)

THE SIGNIFICANT TITLES WITHIN THE TESTIMONIUM

The Johannine Testimonium (1:19–51), along with the Prologue, prepares the reader for the christological and messianic revelations concerning Jesus in the Gospel narrative. Through this section the Evangelist introduces many of the revelations that will be developed and demonstrated through the sign-miracles and their contexts, in the form of narratives and discourses. There are seven christological/messianic titles that are highlighted in the Testimonium, and they all contribute in portraying Jesus to be the promised Messiah of the Hebrew Bible, and the divine Son of God (cf. John 20:30–31).

---

14. Ibid. Beasley-Murray then compares the division of the Johannine Testimonium to the references to John the Baptist in the Prologue. He says: "The relation of the section to references to John in the prologue is clear: 'He came for witness' (7a) governs the whole passage; 'he was not that light' (8a) is elaborated in 19–28, 'he came to bear witness about the light' (8b) in 29–34, 'that all might believe through him' (7c) in 35–50."

15. Moloney, *Belief in the Word*, 53. Some scholars have proposed various theological significance to the "days" in these verses. For example, see Barrosse's article, "Seven Days of the New Creation," 507–16; also, Trudinger, "Seven Days of the New Creation," 154–58.

16. Moloney, *Belief in the Word*, 53–54. Moloney's outline will be used here only because of its simplicity. Although various scholars assign different thematic titles to their outlines, the common breakdown of the passage generally follows thusly: (1) vv. 19–28; (2) vv. 29–34; (3) vv. 35–42; (4) vv. 43–51.

Day One (vv. 19–28)

Although the opening verses of the Johannine Testimonium center around John the Baptist and thus contain no christological titles of Jesus, they nevertheless make a significant contribution to the Fourth Gospel both literarily and theologically. Literarily, they connect the Testimonium with the Prologue by authenticating the claims made in the Prologue concerning the role of John the Baptist.[17] What the Evangelist describes in the Prologue concerning John the Baptist (vv. 6–8, 15), the Baptist himself reiterates in these verses, namely, that he is merely a witness to the eternal Logos. Theologically, by the negative witness ("I am not," vv. 20, 21, and 27) the Baptist gives to the Jewish religious leaders when interrogated by them, as to whether or not he was the promised Christ, a contrast is drawn to the following verses that highlight christological titles (vv. 29–51). In other words, as John the Baptist denies any messianic claims in no uncertain terms (οὐκ εἰμὶ), it draws a stark contrast to the one who alone can claim, "I am he" (ἐγώ εἰμι).[18] Furthermore, the Baptist's denial of any messianic titles builds anticipation for the one of whom the sign-miracles and the discourses reveal as the promised Messiah.

Day Two (vv. 29–34)

The second day of testimony is indicated by the phrase "the next day" (v. 29). These verses are also devoted to John the Baptist's testimony, but whereas the preceding passage consists of his negative witness concerning himself, this passage includes affirmative testimonies concerning Jesus' messianic identity. The Baptist heralds two significant messianic titles in these verses: the Lamb of God (v. 29), and the chosen One of God (v. 34).

THE LAMB OF GOD (1:29, 36)

The first title attributed to Jesus in the Johannine Testimonium is the Lamb of God (ὁ ἀμνὸς τοῦ θεοῦ). Although there are numerous proposals concerning the Old Testament background or antecedent to this

---

17. Beasley-Murray, *John*, 18.

18. Moloney, *Belief in the Word*, 61. For a more thorough treatment of this theory, see E. D. Freed's article "Ἐγώ εἰμι in John 1:20 and 4:25," 288–91.

significant messianic term,[19] there are three principal suggestions that are commonly found among the Johannine scholars: (1) the Lamb as the apocalyptic lamb; (2) the Lamb as the suffering servant; (3) the Lamb as the pascal lamb.[20] Each of these will be discussed briefly.

The first of these suggestions describes an eschatological figure, like the Lamb in many passages of the Johannine Apocalypse, who, as the victorious leader of his people, will put away sin from among them and overcome the powers of evil.[21] Dodd succinctly explains this position: "That the evangelist understood 'The Lamb of God' to be a synonym for 'The Messiah' appears from the context. The Baptist says, 'Behold the Lamb of God.' Andrew hears him, and says to his brother Simon Peter, 'We have found the Messiah.' Moreover the idea of the Messiah as 'King of Israel,' which is suggested by the horned lamb or young wether as leader of the flock, is, as we have seen, one that John accepts, and interprets in his own way.... To make an end of sin is a function of the Jewish Messiah, quite apart from any thought of a redemptive death."[22]

However, there are some legitimate objections to this view. The first objection is one that is raised by Dodd himself, and that is, the chief difficulty of comparing the Lamb of God in the Fourth Gospel to the eschatological victorious Lamb of the Apocalypse due to the vocabulary difference between their descriptions of the Lamb. The term that the apostle John uses in the Apocalypse for the Lamb is not ἀμνὸς but ἀρνίον. The second objection to this view is based on the clause that describes the Lamb in this verse, namely, that He takes away the world's sin (ὁ αἴρων τὴν ἁμαρτίαν τοῦ κόσμου).[23] As R. E. Brown explains, "Understood against the background of the salvific actions of Jesus, such a description scarcely seems to fit the synoptic picture of John the

---

19. Morris lists nine possible antecedents that have been raised: (1) the Passover lamb; (2) the lamb that is led to the slaughter in Isa 53; (3) the Servant of the Lord in Isa 53; (4) the lamb of the daily sacrifice; (5) the "gentle lamb" of Jer 11:19; (6) the scapegoat; (7) the triumphant Lamb of the Apocalypse; (8) the God-provided lamb of Gen 22:8; (9) a guilt-offering. *Gospel According to John*, 145–47.

20. For a good survey of these three views, see R. E. Brown's commentary, *Gospel According to John (I–XII)*, 58–63.

21. A strong proponent of this view is Dodd, whose view is explained in detail in his book, *Interpretation of the Fourth Gospel*, 230–38.

22. Ibid., 236–37.

23. R. E. Brown, *Gospel According to John (I–XII)*, 59–60.

Baptist's preaching where the one to come is to destroy the evildoer."[24] In other words, the clarifying statement concerning the mission of the Lamb seems to indicate that His mission is primarily redemptive. And, as W. H. Harris perceptively points out, the redemptive mission of the Lamb accords well with other statements elsewhere in the Fourth Gospel: "For God did not send his Son into the world to condemn the world, but to save the world through him" (3:17); and "Now we have heard for ourselves, and we know that this man really is the Savior of the world" (4:42).[25] In short, then, although it is possible that John the Baptist has in mind the conquering and victorious Lamb of the eschaton, it is more probable that the Lamb of God in the Fourth Gospel points rather to the redemptive work of Christ.

The second principal suggestion for the possible antecedent of the lamb imagery is derived from the "suffering servant" passages in the book of Isaiah, where the Messiah is likened to a lamb "who was led to the slaughter" on behalf of His people.[26] There seems to be strong evidences that support this view.[27] First, based on the Evangelist's ample references to the book of Isaiah throughout his Gospel, particularly the second half of the book or "Deutero-Isaiah" (chaps. 40–66), it seems reasonable to assume that he is also referring to Isaiah's prophecy concerning the suffering servant. For instance, John the Baptist quotes from Isaiah (40:3) in the immediately preceding passage concerning his mission (1:23). Furthermore, the Evangelist also relates Jesus with the suffering servant by quoting Isaiah 53:1 (12:38). Second, the reference of the Isaianic suffering servant is attributed to Jesus in other places of the New Testament (Acts 8:32; cf. Matt 8:17). Thus, there are strong evidences that the Isaianic suffering servant was at the forefront of John the Baptist's mind when he referred to Jesus as the Lamb of God, who takes away the sin of the world.

24. Ibid., 60.

25. W. H. Harris, "Theology of John's Writings," 192.

26. The prophecies of the "suffering servant" appear in Isa 40–55 generally and 53:7 specifically. Incidentally, the Greek word for "lamb" used in Isa 53:7 in the Septuagint (LXX) is the same word as the word used in John 1:29, 36 (ἀμνός). W. H. Harris, "Theology of John's Writings," 192–93.

27. For a good support of this view, see R. E. Brown, *Gospel According to John (I–XII)*, 60–61.

The third principal suggestion for the possible antecedent of the lamb imagery is the Passover lamb.[28] According to R. E. Brown, this view was favored by many of the Western Fathers while the Eastern Fathers favored the suffering servant imagery in referring to the Lamb of God.[29] This view, like the second view, also has much to commend it.[30] First, the Passover lamb motif is entirely possible since the Passover symbolism is significantly highlighted throughout the Fourth Gospel, climaxing in the death of Christ.[31] And, as Brown correctly points out, John 19:4 clearly indicates that Jesus was condemned to die at noon on the day before the Passover, at the very time the priests began to slay the paschal lambs in the Jerusalem temple.[32] Second, the imagery of Christ as the Passover lamb is also used elsewhere in the New Testament. For instance, the apostle Paul refers to Jesus as "Christ, our Passover lamb" (1 Cor 5:7). The apostle Peter also alludes to the Passover imagery when he refers to Christ as a lamb (1 Pet 1:18–19), although not as explicitly as the apostle Paul. In sum, then, the imagery of the Passover lamb is also very plausible background behind the Lamb of God title for Jesus.

The Genesis passage of Abraham being commanded to sacrifice his son Isaac (chap. 22) is another frequently mentioned passage that may serve as an antecedent to the Lamb of God in referring to Jesus. When asked by Isaac where the lamb was for the burnt offering, Abraham answered, "God himself will provide the lamb for the burnt offering, my

---

28. A strong proponent of this view is Barrett, "Lamb of God," 210–18.

29. R. E. Brown, *Gospel According to John (I–XII)*, 61.

30. Many scholars see both the suffering servant background of Isa 53 and the Passover lamb imagery from Exod 12 as the background of John the Baptist's designation of Jesus as "the Lamb of God." For instance, see Gryglewicz's article, "Das Lamm Gottes," 133–46. He explains: "Die doppeldeutige Wörter 'Lamm' und 'hinwegnimmt' sprechen über Christum als über den Knecht Jahwes und das Paschalamm, und gleichzeitig über Tragen und Hinwegnehmen der Sünden der Menschheit." (The two words "Lamb" and "who takes away" speak of Christ as both the Servant of the Lord and the Paschal Lamb, and likewise as the One who bears and the One who takes away the sins of men).

31. Borchert, *John 1–11*, 134. Cf. idem, "Passover and the Narrative Cycles," 303–16.

32. R. E. Brown, *Gospel According to John (I–XII)*, 62. He also draws further parallel ideas between Christ's death and the Passover event of Exod 12. For instance, the hyssop that was used to give Jesus a sponge of wine while He was on the cross (John 19:20) is compared to the hyssop that was used to smear the blood of the Passover lamb on the doorposts (Exod 12:22). Further, John 19:36 sees a fulfillment of Old Testament Scripture in that none of Jesus' bones was broken, and this is paralleled with Exod 12:46 where no bone of the Passover lamb was to be broken.

son" (22:8). Köstenberger supports the legitimacy of the view when he perceptively compares the possible allusion of John 3:16 to the patriarchal scene: "This is especially suggestive since John 3:16 probably alludes to this scene, highlighting one important difference: what Abraham was spared from doing at the last minute, God actually did—he gave his unique son."[33] The apostle Paul also echoes a similar picture of God's sacrifice: "He who did not spare his own Son, but gave him up for us all—how will he not also, along with him, graciously give us all things?" (Rom 8:32). Thus, the Genesis passage is also a viable option for the background behind the Lamb of God imagery.

In conclusion, then, having viewed the oft-mentioned proposals for the antecedent or background behind the Lamb of God imagery, it is reasonable to conclude that no single Old Testament allusion is sufficient to account for it.[34] Each view has some strengths and weaknesses, although some views are more probable than others, of course. The most likely background behind the Lamb of God imagery of John the Baptist is probably a combination of the suffering servant background in Isaiah 53, the Passover lamb imagery in Exodus 12, and the substitutionary lamb in Genesis 22. Or, perhaps, as Moloney suggests, the lamb imagery points "to the whole of the ritual practice of Israel, where the lamb was used both for the sacrificial rites of communion and reconciliation after sin."[35] Morris is even more hesitant to pinpoint the reference to a specific passage in the Old Testament:

> From all this it is clear that there is no agreement (though many would be found to accept one or other of two or three of those views). The fact is that a lamb taking away sin, even if it is distinguished as God's Lamb, is too indefinite a description for us to pin-point the reference. If the writer really had in mind an allusion to one particular offering we are not able any longer to detect it with certainty. But it seems more probable that of set purpose he used an expression which cannot be confined to any one view. He is making a general allusion to sacrifice. The lamb figure may well be intended to be composite, evoking memories of several, perhaps all, of the suggestions we have canvassed.

33. Köstenberger, *Encountering John*, 70.

34. Barrett, "Lamb of God," 210–18.

35. Moloney, *Belief in the Word*, 65.

All that the ancient sacrifices foreshadowed was perfectly fulfilled in the sacrifice of Christ.[36]

Morris's conclusion is not entirely out of the question since the Evangelist's use of the Hebrew Scriptures is often not characterized by specific references to specific passages, but rather it is often a general allusion to the overall theology of the Old Testament.

THE CHOSEN ONE OF GOD (1:34)[37]

This verse brings the reader to the climax of John the Baptist's testimony concerning Jesus as the promised Messiah of the Scriptures. The context of John the Baptist's testimony (vv. 19–28, 29–34) certainly reflects the Evangelist's stated purpose (20:30–31), namely, to present Jesus as the promised Christ, the Son of God. The immediately preceding verses of the Baptist's testimony concerning Jesus' possession of the Spirit (v. 32) and baptizing of others with the Spirit (v. 33) certainly signals the imminent commencement of the long-awaited messianic age (cf. Isa 11:1–2, 42:1, 61:1–2; Ezek 36:25–27; Joel 2:28–32).[38] If the variant reading of "The Chosen One of God" is correct, then the theme of the Servant Songs of Isaiah (42:1–9; 49:1–9; 50:4–11; 52:13; 53:12), particularly the

36. Morris, *Gospel According to John*, 147–48.

37. This verse involves a significant textual critical issue. The debate concerns what John the Baptist declared concerning Jesus Christ. Did he say, "This is the Son of God" (οὗτός ἐστιν ὁ υἱὸς τοῦ θεοῦ), or "This is the Chosen One of God" (οὗτός ἐστιν ὁ ἐκλεκτός θεοῦ). The external evidence favors the "This is the Son of God" reading because of age and diversity of witnesses, see Metzer, *Textual Commentary*, 200. However, although the evidence for ἐκλεκτός is not nearly as impressive as that for υἱός, the reading is found in early Alexandrian and Western witnesses, see NET Bible, NT ed., 275 n. 12.

The internal evidence, however, seems to favor the "This is the Chosen One of God" reading. Since the expression "Son of God" is a common expression of the Fourth Evangelist (cf. 1:49; 3:18; 5:25; 10:36; 11:4, 27; 19:7; 20:31), it is not difficult to imagine the situation where the scribes would be naturally motivated to change ἐκλεκτός to ui9o\j. As R. E. Brown describes, "It is difficult to imagine that Christian scribes would change 'the Son of God' to 'God's Chosen One,' while a change in the opposite direction would be quite plausible." *Gospel According to John (I–XII)*, 57. Schnackenburg also echoes this view when he describes, "The title (God's Chosen One) occurs only here in John and elsewhere only in Lk 23:35 (cf. also Lk 9:35, ὁ ἐκλελεγμένος). It is easy to understand the alteration from this unusual and peculiar title to the ordinary 'Son of God.'" *The Gospel According to St. John*, 1:305–6. Therefore, despite the weaker external support of the manuscripts, based on the internal evidence, the "This is the Chosen One of God" reading is preferred here.

38. Laney, *John*, 53.

first song, where the Servant is designated as the "elect" or "chosen" one who delights God and in whom God has placed His spirit, is foremost in the Baptist's mind.[39] Thus, this title along with "the Lamb of God" title, are messianic proclamations concerning Jesus by John the Baptist. R. E. Brown's summary of John the Baptist's testimony in these verses ties the two passages (vv. 19–28 and 29–34) in literary unity: "Verse 34 ends this two-part scene of the testimony of John the Baptist in vss. 19–28 and 29–34. As often, John signifies this by an inclusion: vs. 19 began, 'This is the testimony John gave . . . ,' and v. 34 ends when John the Baptist says, 'I have testified. . . .' When we look back on the wealth and depth of the material contained in the intervening verses, we appreciate John's genius at incorporating a whole Christology into one brief scene."[40]

Day Three (vv. 35–42)

The third day of testimony is also indicated by the phrase "the next day" (v. 35). These verses describe the calling of Jesus' first disciples, as John the Baptist pointed their way to the one whom he recently proclaimed as "the Lamb of God" (v. 29) and "the Chosen One of God" (v. 34). On this day, the Baptist again points to Jesus as "the Lamb of God" (v. 36), as if to say, "Look, there is the one about whom I've been testifying, follow Him!" This testimony of Jesus as the Lamb of God is followed by the testimony of Andrew, whom he refers to as the Messiah (v. 41).[41]

THE MESSIAH (v. 41)

The third title attributed to Jesus in the Johannine Testimonium is "the Messiah" (τὸν Μεσσίαν). In the four Gospels, only the Fourth Evangelist uses the transliterated form of the Hebrew or Aramaic term for Messiah, once here by Andrew (v. 41), and later by the Samaritan woman (4:25). Interestingly, however, both times he gave a Greek translation (Χριστός), which may give an indication regarding the recipients' predominant identity. In contrast to the Hebrew or Aramaic term τὸν

39. Carson, *Gospel According to John*, 152–53. Carson especially points to Isa 42:1, where God promises to pour out his Spirit on his servant, his "chosen one" which, in the Septuagint (LXX) reads ὁ ἐκλεκτός.

40. R. E. Brown, *The Gospel According to John (I–XII)*, 67.

41. By the way, Andrew's testimony of Jesus as "the Messiah" in verse 41 also affirms John the Baptist's proclamation of Jesus as "the Lamb of God" to be primarily messianic. Verse 40 describes that Andrew was one of the disciples who followed Jesus because he heard what John the Baptist had said about Him (vv. 35, 40, 41).

Μεσσίαν, however, the Evangelist uses the Greek term Χριστός seventeen times. As the Evangelist's own purpose statement of the Gospel indicates (20:30–31), the messianic identity of Jesus is the central thrust throughout the book.

The question of Jesus' messiahship thus comes up repeatedly in the Fourth Gospel. For instance, from John the Baptist's denial that he was the Christ (1:20, 3:28), to the disciples' confession that Jesus was the Messiah (1:41), to the Jewish leaders' discussion of Jesus' messiahship (7:52), to the people's confusion regarding Jesus' messianic identity (7:25–31, 40–43; 12:34), and even to the Samaritans' perplexity concerning Jesus' messiahship (4:29–30), the Evangelist intentionally raises questions regarding Jesus' messianic identity. Morris clearly explains the Evangelist's intentions thusly: "It was easy to call Jesus 'Messiah.' It was quite another thing to understand what this should mean as He interpreted His vocation. Part of John's purpose appears to be to refute erroneous ideas about messiahship. It would be quite in accordance with this that he should record the disciples' first inadequate recognition of Jesus as Messiah, preparatory to unfolding in his Gospel the true meaning of the messianic office. Messiahship means a good deal to John. He writes his whole Gospel to make us see that Jesus is the Messiah."[42] Furthermore, the Evangelist also paints a picture of contemporary Jewish messianic expectations, which he rejects through the messianic revelations given throughout the Gospel.[43] And, as W. H. Harris points out, "John evidently included these (mistaken) insights to show that Jesus was not the Messiah the common people were expecting, and thus it is not surprising that they rejected Him (cf. 1:11–12)."[44] While the people expected a political Messiah who

---

42. Morris, *Gospel According to John*, 147–48.

43. W. H. Harris, "Theology of John's Writings," 187–88. Apparently, some believed the Messiah would appear suddenly from an unknown origin (7:27), and some apparently believed that the Messiah would perform miraculous signs (7:31). Others apparently thought that when the Messiah came, He would remain forever (12:34).

44. Ibid., 188. W. H. Harris explains the people's common messianic misconceptions this way: "The belief that the Messiah would appear from a secret place excluded Jesus because His (supposed) origin was known (Nazareth). The belief that the Messiah would remain forever excluded Jesus because He predicted His departure (i.e., His approaching death on the cross). In both of these dialogues John showed that Jesus really is the Messiah and that the expectations of the people were mistaken. In 7:29 Jesus answered the question of origin by appealing to His heavenly origin, which really was unknown. In 12:35–36 Jesus pointed out that spiritual enlightenment (which He Himself provides) is needed to understand a suffering and dying Messiah."

would deliver them and provide messianic blessings for them in His kingdom, Jesus shows that He must first be a suffering Messiah, whose kingdom and messianic blessings must come through the cross. The sign-miracles and their attendant contexts, in the form of discourses and narratives, will clearly reveal the true nature of Jesus' messiahship.

Day Four (vv. 43–51)

The fourth day of testimony is once again indicated by the phrase "the next day" (v. 43). In terms of the "days" within the Johannine Testimonium (1:19–51), these verses describe the fourth and last day of testimonies. This section, along with the previous section (vv. 35–42), describes the calling of Jesus' first disciples as well as the disciples' testimonies about Him. These closing verses of the Testimonium possess four significant messianic titles of Jesus: the One about whom the Scriptures spoke (v. 45); the Son of God (v. 49); the King of Israel (v. 49); and the Son of Man (v. 51).

The One about Whom the Scriptures Spoke (1:45)

Philip, in describing Jesus to Nathanael, utters the fourth messianic title of Jesus in the Johannine Testimonium: "We have found the one Moses wrote about in the Law, and about whom the prophets also wrote" (Ὃν ἔγραψεν Μωϋσῆς ἐν τῷ νόμῳ καὶ οἱ προφῆται) (v. 45). As R. E. Brown observes correctly, "the identification of Jesus as the very 'one described in the Mosaic Law and the prophets' is probably a general statement that Jesus is the fulfillment of the whole OT."[45] That the Scriptures bear witness to Jesus is, of course, a theme that is repeated throughout this Gospel (e.g., 5:39–40, 19:36).[46] Carson's explanation of this point is helpful:

> Philip's witness is of a piece with Andrew's (v. 41), except that he does not call Jesus the Messiah but *the one Moses wrote about in the Law, and about whom the prophets also wrote*. That is the stance of this entire Gospel: Jesus fulfils the Old Testament Scriptures (cf. 5:39). The earliest disciples could not have identified Jesus as the promised Coming One, the Messiah, without believing that the Scriptures pointed to him, for that was part of the common stock of Jewish messianic hope. In this stream of thought, not only the

---

45. R. E. Brown, *Gospel According to John (I–XII)*, 86.
46. Borchert, *John 1–11*, 146.

prophets but even "the Law"—i.e., the Pentateuch—anticipated the coming of the Messiah. Philip refers to no specific passage, but in this chapter Deuteronomy 18:15–19 and Genesis 28 are alluded to (in v. 21 and v. 51 respectively). To this must be added the large stock of material from the rest of the Old Testament, here lumped together as what "the prophets" wrote.[47]

In fact, this is precisely the point Jesus makes to His disciples on the road to Emmaus during His post-resurrection ministry: "This is what I told you while I was still with you: Everything must be fulfilled that is written about me in the Law of Moses, the Prophets and the Psalms" (Luke 24:44). In short, by Philip's description of Jesus as the object of Old Testament prophecy, he was in essence pointing to Jesus as the promised Messiah.[48]

The Son of God (1:49)

The following three significant messianic titles all involve Nathanael and Jesus, and they are also all connected with the previous confession made by Philip, that Jesus is the one who fulfills the messianic prophecies of the Hebrew Scriptures. In other words, all four messianic titles heralded in these verses (vv. 43–51) are closely related. And, since these remaining three titles are all declared in the midst of the exchange between Nathanael and Jesus, the understanding of their enigmatic dialogue concerning the fig tree may shed some light on these significant messianic titles.

When Nathanael came to see Jesus for himself at the urging of Philip, Jesus said to him, "Here is a true Israelite, in whom there is nothing false," to which Nathanael responded by asking incredulously, "How do you know me?" Jesus answered, "I saw you while you were still under the fig tree before Philip called you." Nathanael then declared the significant titles, "Rabbi, you are the Son of God, you are the King of Israel" (v. 49). What was the significance of Jesus' statement that prompted Nathanael to declare such grand titles upon Him? Some interpret that the point of Jesus' statement simply reveals His supernatural knowledge.[49] The dif-

---

47. Carson, *Gospel According to John*, 159.

48. Laney lists a few OT verses to illustrate the richness of messianic prophecy throughout the Hebrew Scriptures: Moses (cf. Gen 3:15; 22:8; 28:12; 49:10; Num 21:9; 24:17); the prophets (Isa 7:14; 9:6; 52:13–53:12; Mic 5:2; Zech 9:9). *John*, 57.

49. See for instance, Beasley-Murray, *John*, 27. Beasley-Murray surprisingly sees no symbolic significance of the fig tree: "There is no hidden subtlety here, just a statement

ficulty with this interpretation is that it does not provide an adequate explanation between Jesus' comment and the royal titles Nathanael immediately bestowed on Him.[50]

The key to understanding the import of this passage and the royal titles that are attributed to Jesus by Nathanael, may lay in grasping the symbolic significance of the fig tree and Nathanael's activity under the fig tree. J. Duncan M. Derrett correctly points out that throughout both the Old and New Testaments, the fig tree is often a symbol for the dawn of the messianic age.[51] Jesus often used the fig tree as an illustration for a sign of the coming eschatological kingdom (Mark 13:28–32; cf. Luke 21:29–33). The Old Testament Scriptures also often used the fig tree as a symbol for messianic peace and plenty in the promised kingdom (1 Kgs 4:25; Mic 4:4; Zech 3:10; cf. 1 Macc 14:12), and it is associated with the coming of a messianic figure called the "Branch" in Zechariah 3:8–10.[52]

Although what Nathanael might have been doing under the fig tree is speculative, given the messianic contexts of the fig tree in the Hebrew Scriptures, it is entirely possible that a devout Jew like Nathanael may have been contemplating the coming of the Messiah and the nature of His promised kingdom. L. Paul Trudinger's suggestion is imaginatively perceptive: "Nathanael, we suggest, is contemplating the fulfillment of Israel's history and thinking in particular about the patriarch Jacob who was privileged to be brought to the very gate of heaven. We have suggested further that Nathanael is reflecting upon the fact that when Messiah does come he will lead Israel into the kingdom of heaven, but that Israel would need to be cleansed of every trace of deceit (Jacob) before Messiah could appear. Israel would 'see God' when she is 'pure in

---

of place where the two met." Carson also misses the significance of the fig tree and its Old Testament context by concluding, "But John's chief point here is Jesus' supernatural knowledge, not Nathanael's activity." *Gospel According to John*, 161. See also Michaels's article, "Nathanael Under the Fig Tree," 182–83. Michaels also misses the messianic significance of the setting.

50. For messianic significance of this passage, see Koester's excellent article, "Messianic Exegesis," 23–34.

51. For a good survey of fig trees in the Bible, see Derrett's article, "Fig trees in the New Testament," 249–65.

52. For the messianic significance of this passage see Koester, "Messianic Exegesis," 24.

heart,' without guile. Nathanael could only think of Messiah in glorious, grand terms."[53]

Based on both the symbolic significance of the fig tree and Nathanael's possible meditation on the messianic texts of the Hebrew Bible, it is reasonable to assume that the two titles bestowed on Jesus by Nathanael are messianic titles. Thus, the Son of God title probably has strong allusions to messianic passages such as Psalm 2:6–7, 2 Samuel

---

53. Trudinger, "Israelite in whom there is no Guile," 117–20. Trudinger's lengthy comment on Jesus' statement concerning Nathanael as "an Israelite in whom there is no guile" is also insightful and highlights its messianic context: "It is easy to miss in the English translation the probable word-play originally involved in Jesus' greeting. Its thrust is lost until we recall that the name of Jacob, in the traditional story of Jacob and Esau, had become virtually a synonym for 'deceit.' In Gen 27:36, Esau laments: 'Has he not rightly been called Jacob, because he has cheated me these two times?' This very same deceitful Jacob, however, is a key figure in God's plan for humankind's salvation and later in the story is re-named 'Israel' by God. Jesus' greeting could thus be expressed, 'Look, Israel without a trace of Jacob left in him!' It is this that startles Nathanael who, I suggest, was a devout and sincere Jew (historically as an individual, if you will, but perhaps functioning in John as a representative figure), who spent much time in the privacy of his own thoughts and reflections (the surface meaning, perhaps, of 'under the fig tree') meditating upon his race, its patriarchs, and the promises God had made to them about the coming salvation. I suggest further that the character of Jacob was somewhat of an embarrassment and a perplexity to many a devout Jew. How was it possible that God should work his will through such morally dubious persons? Why should such a deceiver as Jacob be the recipient of such blessings and of such a revelation as he had at Bethel, with the attendant promises made to him on that occasion (Gen 28:12–16)?

"Nathanael and other devout Jews like him (as, for example, Simeon in Luke 2:25ff.) who were waiting for the 'consolation of Israel' must often have pondered over the wonder of God's ways in human history. How could Israel's salvation be revealed while so much of the old 'Jacob' was still evident in the nation's life? One of John's aims seems to be to convey the scene that Jesus had a sensitivity, a psychic insight that made him fully aware of what was going on in Nathanael's innermost thoughts and longings concerning Israel's salvation. 'How do you know me?', Nathanael says with surprise! Jesus replies, 'When you were under the fig tree I saw you.' Again, John is using a multi-faceted, many-splendored metaphor. At its most obvious level, 'under one's fig tree' meant at home (1 Kgs 4:25), with one's own thoughts. On a deeper level of meaning, however, 'under the fig tree' may mean 'when the fulfillment of Israel's history is revealed,' that is, when Messiah comes. For not only is the fig tree a symbol for Israel, but as the synoptic references to it indicate (Luke 13:6–9; Matt 21:14ff.), it is spoken of with references to Israel's fruitfulness in the New Age. The prophet Micah also so describes Israel in the day of salvation, when every man beneath his vine and fig tree shall live in peace (Mic 4:4). A further meaning of the phrase, quite possibly known to John, and if so most applicable to Jesus' encounter with Nathanael, is set forth in the later rabbinic literature, where 'under the fig tree' is the recommended place for the devout Jew to study the Torah."

7:14, and Psalm 89:26–27, linking sonship with Davidic royalty.[54] This is also supported by its linkage with the following title of Jesus as "the King of Israel." (cf. Ps 2:1–6).[55]

THE KING OF ISRAEL (1:49)

This royal title attributed to Jesus as "the King of Israel" (ὁ βασιλεὺς τοῦ Ἰσραήλ), along with the previous title "the Son of God," portray Him as the promised Messiah of the Scriptures.[56] This unusual expression is used only three other times in the New Testament (Matt 27:42; Mark 15:32; John 12:13).[57] Whereas the Synoptic Gospels record the expression as a mockery by the crowd at Jesus' crucifixion, the Fourth Evangelist records Nathanael's expression as a genuine messianic title. The crowd also hails this expression at Jesus' triumphal entry into Jerusalem preceding His death (John 12:13). "Blessed is he who comes in the name of the Lord! Blessed is the King of Israel!" The citation of this messianic psalm (Ps 118) by the crowd is followed immediately by a quotation of another messianic passage in the Old Testament (Zech 9:9), the same prophetic passage quoted by Matthew in connection with Jesus' Davidic kingship (Matt 21:4–9). Thus, as W. H. Harris perceptively points out, "It seems clear that the title "King of Israel" for John carries connotations of Davidic kingship and that Jesus is understood to be the heir and successor to the Davidic throne."[58] Furthermore, in John 18–19 the similar expression "King of the Jews" occurs several times, where, although Pilate and others used them in mockery of Jesus, the Evangelist uses it to fittingly portray Him as the promised Messiah.[59]

---

54. Carson, *Gospel According to John*, 162. However, knowing the Evangelist's affinity with double meanings throughout his Gospel, he could also be emphasizing Jesus' divine sonship.

55. Borchert, *John 1–11*, 148.

56. According to Beasley-Murray, these two titles are virtually synonymous. *John*, 27.

57. Morris, *Gospel According to John*, 168. In Matt 27:42 Jesus is mockingly saluted as "king of Israel" and invited to come down from the cross. In the Markan passage (15:32), the expression "the King of Israel" is used synonymously with "the Christ," and the crowd that witnessed the crucifixion also used it mockingly.

58. W. H. Harris, "Theology of John's Writings," 189.

59. See Berger's helpful article, "Die Königlichen Messiastraditionen," 1–44, especially under the section, "Königliche Messiastraditionen Bei Johannes," 41–43.

In sum, then, these two titles of Jesus as "the Son of God" and "the King of Israel," portray Him as the Davidic King, the promised Messiah of the Old Testament Scriptures. However, in the Old Testament God Himself is also attributed to be the King of His people (i.e., Pss 44–45). The prophet Zephaniah also declares, for example, "The LORD has taken away your punishment, he has turned back your enemy. The LORD, the King of Israel, is with you; never again will you fear any harm" (3:15). Thus, as R. E. Brown concludes perceptively, that in the Fourth Gospel the Evangelist intends to give these titles a more profound meaning, also emphasizing His divinity.[60] Therefore, as J. Carl Laney correctly concludes, "Nathanael was recognizing Jesus as the divine Messiah who had a right to the royal throne of David (cf. 2 Sam 7:12–16). He realized that the promised ruler had come. He could be expected to assume His rightful, royal office."[61]

THE SON OF MAN (1:51)

The seventh and last title attributed to Jesus in the Johannine Testimonium (1:19–51) is "the Son of Man" (τὸν υἱὸν τοῦ ἀνθρώπου), which is Jesus' favorite self-designation in the Gospels. Although the title "Son of Man" is more prominent in the Synoptic Gospels than in the Fourth Gospel, the title is nonetheless used quite frequently in John's Gospel (1:51; 3:13, 14; 5:27; 6:27, 53, 62; 8:28; 9:35; 12:23, 34c, 34d; 13:31).[62] There is considerable debate among interpreters regarding the origin or the background of the term, whether, for instance, Jesus drew upon Ezekiel's use of the term (Ezek 2:1–3) to emphasize His humanity or upon Daniel's use of the term (Dan 7:13) to emphasize His divine messiahship.[63] Judging from the context of this verse and the Fourth Gospel as a whole, it seems without question that the Evangelist is emphasizing Jesus' messiahship.

---

60. R. E. Brown, *Gospel According to John (I–XII)*, 88.

61. Laney, *John*, 58.

62. Schnackenburg, "Der Menschensohn im Johannesevangelium," 123–37. According to Schnackenberg, the title "Son of Man" appears thirteen times in the Fourth Gospel.

63. For a detailed study on the background of the title "Son of Man," see Burkett's fine work, *Son of Man*. In it he surveys diverse backgrounds such as the Jewish apocalyptic literature (i.e., Dan 7:13) and the non apocalyptic uses like the "Son of Man" in Ezek, and so on. See also Moloney's detailed book for background of the term "Son of Man," in his *Johannine Son of Man*, 23–41.

What aspect of Jesus' messiahship is revealed, however, by the title "Son of Man" in these verses? An important aspect of the "Son of Man" theme found in the Fourth Gospel is an emphasis on the descent and ascent of the Son of Man, which, according to W. H. Harris, implies both His preexistence and exaltation.[64] In 1:51 Jesus speaks of angels ascending and descending on the Son of Man, which most interpreters recognize as an allusion to Jacob's dream in Genesis 28.[65] When Jacob awoke from his apocalyptic dream, he exclaimed, "Surely the LORD is in this place, and I was not aware of it." He was afraid and said, "How awesome is this place! This is none other than the house of God; this is the gate of heaven" (Gen 28:16–17). By alluding to this patriarchal story, what Jesus discloses to Nathanael, then, is that He Himself will be the place of much greater divine revelation.[66] Or, as Laney puts it succinctly, "The divine Messiah is the ladder, the bridge, the mediator between heaven and earth (1 Tim 2:5). He is the one through whom man can have access to and fellowship with God."[67] Moloney says, "In Jesus, the Son of Man, God will be revealed."[68] W. H. Harris's comment on these verses is perhaps the most helpful in light of the Genesis passage:

> In John 1:51 Jesus alluded to this incident in Jacob's life, drawing a parallel between Himself and Jacob as recipients of God's revelation. Jesus thereby assured the disciples that they would receive divine confirmation that He really is the Messiah sent from God. No longer is Bethel the place of God's revelation, as it was for Jacob. Now Jesus Himself is the "place" of God's revelation, just as later in John's gospel Jesus replaced the temple in Jerusalem (2:19–22) and Mount Gerizim in Samaria (4:20–24). The fulfillment of Jesus' promise to the disciples takes place in the remainder of the fourth Gospel, especially in Jesus' death, resurrection, ascension, and exaltation through which He accomplished His return to the Father.[69]

---

64. W. H. Harris, "Theology of John's Writings," 186. For a good discussion on the divine emphasis of the "Son of Man," see Kim's work, *"Son of Man,"* 5, 82–86. For a similar idea, see also Dodd's detailed work, *Interpretation of the Fourth Gospel*, 241–49.

65. Carson, *Gospel According to John*, 162–64.

66. Köstenberger, *Encountering John*, 71.

67. Laney, *John*, 59.

68. Moloney, *Belief in the Word*, 74.

69. W. H. Harris, "Theology of John's Writings," 186.

In other words, Jesus' clear reference to Jacob's dream and his encounter with heaven (Gen 28) reveals that He, as the Son of Man (Dan 7:13), is the essence and embodiment of the coming messianic revelations (v. 51).

To summarize, then, as the divine "Son of Man" (Dan 7:13; cf. Rev 1:7) Jesus will open the "gates of heaven" and reveal heavenly or spiritual truths to not only Nathanael but to all the disciples.[70] More specifically, however, the "greater revelations" can be referring to the sign-miracles of Jesus that are recorded in the following chapters, commonly known as the Book of Signs (John 2–12). Literarily, the Evangelist has ingeniously placed the last verse of the Testimonium (v. 51) precisely, in order to link the Testimonium with the Book of Signs and also with the whole Gospel.

In conclusion, the Johannine Testimonium (1:19–51) prepares the reader for the messianic revelations concerning Jesus in the Gospel narrative, particularly the sign-miracles in the Book of Signs (chaps. 2–12) and their attendant contexts. There are seven messianic titles that are highlighted in the Testimonium: Jesus is the Lamb of God (1:19, 36), the Chosen One of God (1:34), the Messiah (1:41), the One about whom the Scriptures spoke (1:45), the Son of God (1:49), the King of Israel (1:49), and the Son of Man (1:51). These seven[71] titles portray Jesus to be the divine Messiah promised in the Old Testament Scriptures (cf. John 20:30–31). Literarily, the Testimonium (1:19–51), along with the Prologue (1:1–18), prepare the reader for the kind of revelations to come concerning Jesus Christ as they introduce Him in no uncertain messianic terms. The first chapter of John's Gospel serves as a sneak preview, so to speak, for the coming main attraction concerning Jesus Christ, the main character.

70. Moloney correctly points out that by shifting from His use of a singular "you" in v. 50 and "him" in v. 51a to a plural "you" in v. 51bc, Jesus is now addressing a wider group of disciples, including the readers of the Gospel. *Belief in the Word*, 74.

71. Is the number "seven" accidental here or does it symbolically represent completeness of messianic revelation? See chapter 2 of the book for a discussion on the symbolic meaning of the number "seven."

PART TWO

The Seven Sign-Miracles of Jesus in the Fourth Gospel

5

The First Sign: Changing Water into Wine (2:1–11)

INTRODUCTION

The chief clue to the interpretation of the Fourth Gospel, or any other book for that matter, is its structure.[1] Fortunately, in the Gospel of John, the book's structure can be identified in the Evangelist's purpose statement (20:30–31). According to these verses, although there were many other miracles that Jesus performed during His earthly ministry among His disciples, the Evangelist recorded these particular miracles for a definite purpose, namely, to present Jesus as the promised Messiah of the Old Testament Scriptures and the divine Son of God. The aim of his presentation of Jesus' Person is so that His disciples might continue to believe, thereby partaking in the divine life or, as John calls it, eternal life. And, these sign-miracles of Jesus are all recorded in the Book of Signs (2:1—12:50),[2] which describes our Lord's public ministry.[3]

The first two sign-miracles are included in the first four chapters of the Gospel that are often characterized as the "Cana Cycle" (2:1—4:54),[4] while the remaining sign-miracles are recorded in the following section

---

1. Tenney, *John*, 27.

2. Dodd refers to the first part of the Fourth Gospel as the "Book of Signs" (chaps. 2–12) and the second part of the Gospel as the "Book of Passion" (chaps. 13–20). *Interpretation of the Fourth Gospel*, x. R. E. Brown, on the other hand, entitles the second part of the Gospel as the "Book of Glory," while also referring to the first part as the "Book of Signs." *Gospel According to John (I–XII)*, 1:cxxxviii.

3. The first twelve chapters of the Fourth Gospel record the public ministry of Jesus, while the second section, particularly chapters 13–17, records the private Farewell Discourse with His disciples. Chapters 18–20 record the passion and resurrection of Jesus Christ, while chapter 21 serves as an "epilogue" to the Gospel. For a helpful structural layout, see Burge's book, *Interpreting the Gospel of John*, 75–82.

4. Moloney, *Gospel of John*, 63–65.

commonly known as the "Festival Cycle." The first two sign-miracles are generally distinguished from the others because they are both performed in Cana of Galilee, and thus they form a geographical inclusio in the early chapters of the Gospel.[5] These chapters also form a literary unit because they are not only bounded geographically but also thematically. Thematically, these chapters present Jesus as the divine Messiah who offers newness of life to those who believe. As Carson explains, "These three chapters are organized to convey what Paul says in 2 Corinthians 5:17: 'the old has gone, the new has come!'"[6] Beasley-Murray calls this section, "The revelation of the new order in Jesus."[7] Borchert thus summarizes, "The geographical settings here are clearly important to the evangelist's theological intention. Cana becomes the center for both the first and second signs."[8]

JESUS' FIRST SIGN-MIRACLE OF CHANGING WATER INTO WINE (2:1–11)

Although the Cana Cycle (chaps. 2–4) forms a separate literary unit from the opening chapter of the Fourth Gospel, it is obvious that these chapters are linked closely with the themes introduced in the Prologue (1:1–18) and the Testimonium (1:19–51). For instance, the theme of Christ's glory ($\delta\delta\xi\alpha$) that is central to the first miracle of Jesus' turning water into wine was first introduced in the Prologue (2:11; cf. 1:14). The Testimonium's linkage to the following chapter is even more obvious as the second chapter begins with the words, "On the third day" (2:1). It seems apparent that Jesus' promise to the disciples in 1:51 is given its first fulfillment in His miracle of turning water into wine.[9] Furthermore,

---

5. Moloney, "From Cana to Cana," 185–213. Borchert explains the geographical bounding of this section this way: "The five segments of the Gospel and two transitional statements (2:12, 23–25) that compose the Cana Cycle move the reader's attention from Cana (2:1–11) and Capernaum (2:12) through Jerusalem (2:13–24) to an unclear Jewish/Judean (?) context (3:1–36), then to Samaria (4:1–42) and back to Cana in Galilee (4:43–54)." *John 1–11*, 151.

6. Carson, *Gospel According to John*, 166.

7. Beasley-Murray, *John*, 5.

8. Borchert, *John 1–11*, 151.

9. Beasley-Murray, *John*, 31. He further explains: "But it is equally plain that the sign described in vv. 1–11 is the first of the series of signs incorporated in chaps. 2–12 as examples of the deeds of the Redeemer-Revealer, hence that a new start is being made at 2:1. It commences the account in this Gospel of the public ministry of Jesus."

as the Evangelist's purpose statement in 20:30–31 explicitly states, the sign-miracles are all designed to reveal the Person of Jesus; and the reason behind this revelation is so that the disciples would believe (or keep on believing) in Him.[10] And, the concluding verse of the first miracle states that through it Jesus revealed His glory and that His first disciples believed in Him (2:11). Thus, R. E. Brown is right to conclude "the first sign had the same purpose that all subsequent signs will have, namely, revelation about the person of Jesus."[11]

---

10. In using John 20:30–31 as the beginning place in determining the author's purpose, one is left with two options of interpretation because of the textual variant of the verb πιστεύω with the ἵνα clause. The verb can either be read as aorist subjunctive πιστεύσητε, or as present subjunctive πιστεύητε. The aorist subjunctive would indicate an evangelistic message that is directed to unbelievers, in order to convince them to believe. The present subjunctive, on the other hand, would indicate an edificatory or didactic message that addresses believers, in order to strengthen and confirm their faith. Most modern commentators seem to prefer the present subjunctive and thus translate the verse this way: "that you may *continue to believe.*" Textually, the evidence seems evenly balanced between the two, and thus cannot be conclusive. Besides, the outcome of the text-critical decision cannot be determinative concerning the Gospel's purpose, since there are examples of both the present subjunctive and aorist subjunctive that occur in both the context of coming to faith and in the context of continuing in faith. Carson, "Purpose of the Fourth Gospel," 640–41. Thus, the determining factor concerning the author's purpose statement in 20:31 is not textual evidence but the context of the book as a whole. Besides, it is also significant that for the apostle Paul, the process of believing is more a process than a point in time. Unlike the apostle Paul, John is not focusing on the point of justification.

Although the purpose statement in 20:30–31 may seem primarily evangelistic in its focus, the content of materials discussed in the Gospel itself seem instructive toward those who are already believers. See Borchert, *John 1–11*, 35–36. The Farewell Discourse in chapters 14–17, especially seems to be addressing those who are already believers rather than attempting to evangelize unbelievers. If the Fourth Gospel is addressed primarily for believers, then, what intention did the Evangelist have in mind when he penned his Gospel? The purpose statement of the apostle John seems to suggest that he intends to present Jesus to second and subsequent generations of believers, those who did not "see signs" but have the written account of them. Thompson, "John, Gospel of," 372. Jesus' remarks after Thomas's confession, "My Lord and My God" (20:28), may be a clue to John's primary audience. Jesus comments, "Because you have seen me, you have believed. Blessed are those who have not seen and yet have believed" (20:29). Thus, much content of the Gospel seems designed to encourage believers to persevere in the faith they already possess, even in the midst of the hostile world in which they live (15:18–25). In conclusion, then, although the Gospel story certainly can be used to bring unbelievers to a saving knowledge in Jesus Christ, the book as a whole seems to be written primarily with the aim of strengthening and instructing those who already possess eternal life.

11. R. E. Brown, *Gospel According to John (I–XII)*, 103–4.

THE SETTING

The setting of the story is described in the beginning verses of the passage: "On the third day a wedding took place at Cana of Galilee. Jesus' mother was there, and Jesus and his disciples had also been invited to the wedding" (2:1–2).[12] The miracle narrative begins with a temporal indicator, "On the third day,"[13] which significantly links this miracle with the Johannine Testimonium (1:19–51), both chronologically and theologically. Chronologically, this miracle occurred on the third day after the four days of testimonies by John the Baptist and the disciples (cf. 1:19–28, 29–34, 35–42, 43–51). More specifically, the miracle took place on the third day following the exchange between Jesus and Nathanael in the closing verses of chapter 1.[14] Theologically, this miracle is the initial fulfillment of the promise made by Jesus to Nathanael and the disciples, namely, that they will see greater revelation of the Son of Man than even the patriarch Jacob's apocalyptic vision (1:51). Furthermore, this miracle and the subsequent ones are demonstrations of Christ's mes-

---

12. For a good structure of this pericope, see Moloney's book, *Belief in the Word*, 78–79. He outlines the passage as follows: (1) verses 1–2: the setting of account; (2) verses 3–5: a verbal exchange; (3) verses 6–10: the main action of the miracle story; (4) verse 11: the narrator's comment; (5) verse 12: a final comment by the narrator. It is preferable to see the final verse as more of a transitional verse to the next pericope rather than a part of this miracle. Owings's structure of the pericope is simpler and thus more preferable to follow: (1) the setting of the marriage; (2) the draught of the wine; (3) the request of Mary; (4) the response of Jesus; (5) the belief of the disciples. "John 2:1–11," 533–37.

13. There have been a number of suggestions as to the meaning of the Evangelist's enigmatic temporal indicator, "On the third day." Many have attempted to read a symbolic meaning into it from the outset, often leading to unrestrained allegorisms. It seems fitting rather to see the time indicator with the "days" in the Testimonium (1:19–51) as literal time indicators. However, it is also possible to see a symbolic meaning along with the literal days. For instance, Dodd has proposed that "the third day" is an allusion to Easter: the miracle anticipating the manifestation of Christ's glory in the Resurrection. *Interpretation of the Fourth Gospel*, 300. Moloney, on the other hand, sees "the third day" as reflecting back to God's revelation to Israel at Mt. Sinai when Moses went up to meet with God and receive the gift of the law. See Exod 19:16. He explains, "The four days of 1:19–51 look forward to 'the third day.'" *Gospel of John*, 66. Moloney's proposition is more plausible contextually based upon Jesus' promise of greater revelation to His disciples in 1:50–51. Thus, the Fourth Evangelist is introducing Jesus as the "New Moses" who will reveal the new age. This is probably one of many instances where the Evangelist is using double meanings to indicate both the literal and symbolic (cf. 3:2; 13:30).

14. Köstenberger, *John*, 91.

sianic identity heralded by John the Baptist and Jesus' disciples in the Testimonium.

The first miracle of Jesus took place at a wedding in Cana of Galilee.[15] A Jewish wedding and its attendant wedding feast were the occasion for the miracle.[16] It was an occasion of great joy and festivity, and it was the culmination of a long process toward marriage. R. E. Brown explains the atmosphere of this joyous occasion: "The usual festivities consisted of a procession in which the bridegroom's friends brought the bride to the groom's house, and then a wedding supper; seemingly the festivities lasted seven days (Judg 14:12; cf. Tob 8:19; 11:18–19).[17] Laney adds, "The festivities could last one day or continue on for a week, depending on the resources of the husband.[18] Presents were given, and the hosts were expected to supply plenty of food and wine for the guests.[19] To run out of wine would have been a major embarrassment to the hosting family and, according to Morris, this social faux pas could even result in a lawsuit.[20] Thus, when the wine did run out the hosting family became desperate, including Jesus' mother who suggested that Jesus do something about it (John 2:3).[21] This desperate situation then set the stage for Jesus' miracle.

---

15. Cana is apparently a little known village because every time John refers to it he describes it as being "of Galilee" (2:1, 11; 4:46; 21:2). Furthermore, no other New Testament writer alludes to it. R. E. Brown, citing Josephus (*Life* 16), suggests Kihirbet Kana, which is located nine miles north of Nazareth, as the place of reference. *Gospel According to John (I–XII)*, 98. See also Laney's commentary for a detailed explanation of the same view, *John*, 58. The town is perhaps mentioned by the Evangelist to emphasize the "Cana Cycle" (2:1—4:54) as a literary unit.

16. Polhill, "John 1–4," 450.

17. R. E. Brown, *Gospel According to John (I–XII)*, 97–98.

18. Laney, *John*, 62.

19. For a discussion on the historical and cultural context of Jewish wedding feasts behind this story, see Derrett's article, "Water into Wine," 80–97. He explains the strong expectations of reciprocity in ancient Near Eastern weddings. Failure to provide adequate wine for the guests would have been a major social blunder for the hosts.

20. Morris, *Gospel According to John*, 179.

21. It is quite clear from the context that Mary expected Jesus to do some kind of a miracle, although He had not as yet performed any miracles (cf. 2:11). However, it is also true that she certainly had many evidences of His supernatural and messianic identity—His supernatural conception and the announcement by the angel Gabriel, the events preceding His birth such as Zechariah's Song, the events surrounding His birth such as the angel's announcement, and Jesus' presentation in the temple and Simeon's exultation (cf. Luke 1–2). In short, she had good reasons to believe in Jesus' messianic identity.

THE SIGN

The Evangelist sets the scene for the miracle with an important description of the stone jars of water: "Nearby stood six stone water jars, the
kind used by the Jews for ceremonial washing, each holding from twenty
to thirty gallons" (v. 6). The total amount of wine involved in the miracle
was between 120 and 180 gallons.[22] This was a miracle of no small measure! Jesus provided wine in "superabundance."[23] Verse 7 indicates that
Jesus instructed the servants to fill the stone jars with water, and the
Evangelist notes they were filled "to the brim." Jones is correct to point
out that John wanted to make certain there could be no mistake as to the
original contents of these vessels, that there was only water.[24] The closing
verses describe the happenings after the miracle had already taken place
(vv. 8–10). The transformation of the water into wine is not narrated,
but it is assumed to be understood. Jesus commanded the servants to
take the new wine to the master of the banquet (v. 8).[25] Although the
master of the banquet did not know where the wine had come from
(v. 9), he confirmed the authenticity of Jesus' miracle when he declared to
the bridegroom: "Everyone brings out the choice wine first and then the
cheaper wine after the guests have had too much to drink; but you have
saved the best till now" (v. 10). The wine Jesus provided was the best of
the wines in its quality (καλόν).[26]

THE SIGNIFICANCE

The point of this miracle story is brought together by the closing verse:
"This, the first of his miraculous signs, Jesus performed in Cana of
Galilee. He thus revealed his glory, and his disciples put their faith in him"
(v. 11). This verse also discloses the purpose of the first miracle: through

---

22. According to the Greek text, the capacity of water consisted of two to three
measures (μετρητὰς), with each measure being roughly between eight and nine gallons. Each stone jar therefore contained somewhere between sixteen and twenty-seven
gallons. Thus, the NIV's translation of "twenty to thirty gallons" is close (v. 6). For a good
discussion of this, see Villescas's article, "John 2:6," 447; see also R. B. Y. Scott, "Weights
and Measures in the Bible," 22–40, especially 29–32.

23. Moloney, *Gospel of John*, 68.

24. Jones, *Symbol of Water*, 60.

25. On the nature and content of wine in biblical times, see Keener, *Gospel of John*,
1:500–501. See also Watson's article, "Wine," 870–73.

26. See BAGD 504–5.

it Jesus revealed His glory (δόξα). Essentially, the purpose of the first sign-miracle is the same for all the sign-miracles, namely, to reveal the Person of Jesus. The Johannine Prologue (1:1–18) further reveals the purpose of Jesus' words and works in this gospel. First, Jesus' glory was revealed so that we might know that He came from the Father (v. 14). Furthermore, Jesus came to reveal the Father by manifesting Himself through the flesh (v. 18). Therefore, this dual-purpose of revealing His own Person and the Father during His earthly ministry is manifested in all the sign-miracles of Jesus. Schnackenburg is correct then to highlight the christological emphasis of the first miracle: "The most important for the evangelist is the revelation of Jesus' glory (v. 11) and any interpretation which departs from this Christological perspective loses sight of the central issue."[27]

On its most obvious level, the first miracle reveals Jesus as the Creator.[28] As the divine Son of God, Jesus shares with the Father one of the most significant divine attributes, namely, the work of creation. Edwin Blum explains how Jesus was involved in the miracle of creation through this act: "The sign points to Jesus as the Word in the flesh, who is the mighty Creator. Each year He turns water into wine in the agricultural and fermentation process. Here He simply did the process immediately."[29] In other words, by the mere command of His word Jesus was able to turn the jars of water into the finest of wines. The Evangelist could have been referring to the opening chapter of Genesis where God is said to have created the whole universe by the simple command of His word (Gen 1:1; cf. 1:3, 6, 9, 14, 20, 24). That Jesus was also involved in the work of creation in the beginning is emphasized first in the Prologue: "Through him all things were made; without him nothing was made that has been made" (John 1:3). The apostle Paul also describes Jesus as the Creator in defense of His deity to the church in Colossae: "For by him all things were created: things in heaven and on earth, visible and invisible, whether thrones or powers or rulers or authorities; all things were cre-

---

27. Schnackenburg, *Gospel According to John*, 1:337.

28. It is surprising that most of the major commentators such as R. E. Brown, Schnackenburg, Beasley-Murray, Carson, Morris, and others hardly mention this aspect of the miracle. Granted that this is not the major emphasis of the Evangelist either judging from his lack of emphasis on the miracle itself, it is surprising nevertheless that such an important aspect of Jesus' work is not highlighted more.

29. Blum, "John," 278.

ated by him and for him" (Col 1:16; cf. Heb 1:1–3). But, perhaps a more specific aim of this miracle is to reveal Jesus as the Creator of life, the kind of life that exists only in Him (cf. John 1:4). In short, through this miracle John reveals the Person of Jesus as the divine Son of God who is also the Creator of life, just as the Father Himself is (5:21).

This miracle reveals a deeper christological truth of Jesus' Person, however. By recording Jesus' miracle of turning water into wine at a wedding, the Evangelist reveals Jesus as the promised Messiah of the Old Testament Scriptures who is capable of ushering in the predicted kingdom. Three symbols in the narrative lead to this conclusion: the wedding, the water, and the wine. First, the setting of the miracle at a Jewish wedding clues the reader of its messianic message. In the Old Testament, wedding or marriage often symbolizes the messianic kingdom (Isa 54:1–8; 62:1–5).[30] Also, in the New Testament Jesus uses both the wedding and the banquet to portray His coming (Matt 8:11, 22:1–4; Luke 13:29, 14:15–24). The apostle John also uses the wedding as a symbol of messianic fulfillment at the Second Advent of Christ in his Apocalypse (Rev 19:9). Thus, Stanley Toussaint is correct when he observes, "The presence of the Lord at these marriage festivities at Cana graphically pictures the coming of the kingdom."[31]

Second, when Jesus transformed water into wine at the Cana wedding, the water He used to transform into wine may also carry a symbolic message in the miracle. The water Jesus used to transform into wine obviously is intended to stand in contrast to the wine. In other words, Jesus could have supplied the wine by creating it out of nothing. But He chose to perform the miracle using water from which to create the wine. Besides, water is a significant motif that runs through the whole Fourth Gospel. R. H. Lightfoot perceptively observes that "the theme of water runs like a silver thread through the early chapters of this Gospel."[32] Culpepper also notes, "The image of water appears surprisingly frequently and with the most varied associations of any of John's symbols."[33] Koester also adds,

---

30. R. E. Brown, *Gospel According to John (I–XII)*, 104–5.

31. Toussaint, "Significance of the First Sign," 45–51.

32. Lightfoot, *St. John's Gospel*, 121.

33. Culpepper, *Anatomy of the Fourth Gospel*, 192–95. Culpepper lists the varied uses of the water motif throughout John's Gospel: water, water pots, rivers, wells, springs, the sea, pools, basin, thirst, and drink.

"Images of water, like those of light and darkness, create another rich and variegated motif in the Fourth Gospel."[34]

Although the Evangelist uses the symbol of water in various ways throughout his gospel, it seems that in this miracle his use of water stands in contrast to the wine that Jesus provides. Dodd suggests that water, "standing for the lower life, is contrasted with wine, standing for the higher."[35] In other words, water in this miracle stands to represent physical human life without Christ devoid of any true hope and joy. In that case, wine stands to represent the newness of life, the kind of life that is found in Christ.

However, it would also be appropriate to compare the symbol of water in the context of the Jewish religious institutions. In describing the stone water jars that Jesus used for the miracle, the Evangelist adds "the kind used by the Jews for ceremonial washing" (John 2:6). Thus, Culpepper concludes, "This scene fits the recurring theme of the fulfillment of Jewish expectations and the replacement of Jewish festivals and institutions."[36] Beasley-Murray concurs with this when he says, "There is an implicit contrast between water used for Jewish purificatory rites and wine given by Jesus; the former is characteristic of the old order, the latter of the new."[37] Jones, on the other hand, while agreeing with this, takes the symbolism a step further and suggests that water itself also represents something new: "What Jesus brings to the wedding feast increases the joy of the celebration and offers far more than ritual purification. In addition to that, at Cana water has a more complete symbolic function. It not only bears witness to another reality but also embodies something about that reality. As water served to purify the celebrants under the Jewish dispensation and to enable them to partake in the wedding feast, so the water from the vessels used in purification rites, when turned to wine by Jesus, enables the disciples to grasp more fully his identity. The one who will baptize with the Holy Spirit (1:33) begins his ministry by using water to bring his disciples to faith."[38] In short, water

---

34. Koester, *Symbolism in the Fourth Gospel*, 155. For a detailed examination of the different uses of the water as a symbol in the Fourth Gospel, see the chapter entitled "Water" in his book, 155–84.

35. Dodd, *Interpretation of the Fourth Gospel*, 138.

36. Culpepper, *Anatomy of the Fourth Gospel*, 193.

37. Beasley-Murray, *John*, 36.

38. Jones, *Symbol of Water*, 62–65.

is not only linked with the issue of purification, but it also demonstrates the change to which it points. As Jones clarifies further, "Water both represents the new beginning Jesus brings and manifests that beginning in and of itself."[39] This truth brings to mind the Evangelist's declaration in the Prologue of the Gospel: "For the law was given through Moses; grace and truth came through Jesus Christ." (1:17).

Third, the wine that Jesus provides at the wedding stands to symbolize the messianic kingdom. Throughout the Old Testament the messianic kingdom is often described in terms of wine (Isa 25:6; 27:2–6).[40] For instance, in Isaiah 25:6 the prophet joins the figures of a banquet and wine together to illustrate the joys of the messianic kingdom: "On this mountain the LORD Almighty will prepare a feast of rich food for all peoples, a banquet of aged wine–the best of meats and finest of wines." In Isaiah 27:2–6 the prophet also describes Israel as God's fruitful vineyard in the eschatological kingdom. Furthermore, an abundance of wine is often used in the Hebrew Scriptures to symbolize the blessings in the promised kingdom (Gen 49:11–12; Jer 31:12; Hos 2:22; 14:7; Joel 2:19, 24; 3:18; Amos 9:13–14; Zech 9:15–17; 10:7).[41] For instance, the prophet Joel declares expectantly, "In that day the mountains will drip new wine, and the hills will flow with milk; all the ravines of Judah will run with water" (3:18). The "new wine" that flows from the Lord's mountain symbolizes the abundance of messianic blessings in the eschatological kingdom. The prophet Amos's description of the "new wine" in the promised kingdom anticipates the fulfillment of the Davidic covenant (2 Sam 7; cf. 1 Chron 17; Ps 89) and the restoration of God's people in the promise land (Amos 9:13–14).

Given the rich symbol of wine that stands to represents the blessings and the abundance of joy in the messianic kingdom, then, it is not difficult to see the significance of Mary's statement to Jesus, "They have no more wine" (John 2:3). As Toussaint notes, "The lapse of wine was a picture of the obsolescence of Judaism. The old wine had run out and Christ the Messiah was here to bring the new. . . . The miracle shows the old order had run its course; now was the time for a new one."[42] What Judaism could not provide Jesus supplies in exceeding abundance!

39. Ibid., 220.
40. Toussaint, "Significance of the First Sign," 50.
41. Schnackenburg, *Gospel According to St. John*, 1:338.
42. Toussaint, "Significance of the First Sign," 50.

He demonstrates this by creating between 120 and 180 gallons of wine, which was far more than necessary for a Jewish wedding in Galilee. In short, by providing the exceeding abundance of wine, Jesus was demonstrating that as the promised Messiah He was now replacing the obsolescence of Judaism with the joy of His kingdom.

To summarize, the first miracle of Jesus turning water into wine at the wedding in Cana authenticated His Person as the promised Messiah of the Old Testament Scriptures and the divine Son of God. By providing an abundance of wine at a Jewish wedding feast, Jesus was demonstrating that as the Messiah, He is capable of ushering in the promised eschatological kingdom. The miracle gave the disciples a "preview" of the abundant blessings that would be theirs in the messianic kingdom. As Laney concludes correctly, "The turning of water to wine was an indication that the Messiah was present and the kingdom was imminent. The miracle gave the wedding guests a brief foretaste of the abundance of joy that would be theirs in Messiah's kingdom."[43] This miracle is an initial fulfillment of Jesus' promise to the disciples in the closing verses of chapter 1 (vv. 50–51), namely, that they would witness great revelation concerning the messianic identity of Jesus. The messianic titles heralded by John the Baptist and the disciples in the Johannine Testimonium (1:19–51) are being demonstrated through the miracle in 2:1–11. Not only this miracle, however, but also all seven miracles are designed to demonstrate Jesus as the promised Messiah and the divine Son of God (cf. 20:30–31). Thus, in many ways this miracle of Jesus is not only the first one recorded by the Evangelist, but it also stands as the representative sign for the rest of them. As Raymond Collins explains, "The account of the water-become-wine is the key to the Johannine signs just as much as it is the first of Jesus' miracles."[44]

It is important to keep in mind, however, that this miracle of Jesus turning water into wine has far broader significance than just the future fulfillment of the Messiah in His kingdom. In fact, the focus of Jesus' sign-miracles (σημεῖα) in the Fourth Gospel is primarily the Person of Jesus as the Christ, the divine Son of God (20:30–31). Although the

---

43. Laney, *John*, 68.

44. R. F. Collins, "Cana," 79–95. If the Evangelist intended to denote only the order of the first miracle, he probably would have used the word πρῶτον. By using the word ἀρχή, however, John probably intended to emphasize its significance as a representative sign.

Evangelist presents Jesus as the promised Messiah of the Old Testament Scriptures who will one day fulfill the messianic promises in the eschatological kingdom, his practical aim in demonstrating Jesus' Person is that his readers may believe (or continue to believe) in Him, and thereby partake of the eternal life, here and now. As Polhill describes correctly, "Eternal life is not merely future. It begins now in receiving in this life the life that is in Christ."[45] Thus, on a practical level, the miracle of Jesus turning water into wine demonstrates that as the Messiah He offers a new life filled with abundant joy, that is, eternal life.

The passage immediately following the first sign-miracle (σημεῖον), the cleansing of the Jerusalem temple by Jesus (2:11–22), may serve an important literary and theological function of confirming the claims of the first miracle (2:1–11). Although the two pericopes occur in two different geographical settings, the wine miracle in Galilee and the temple cleansing in Jerusalem, nevertheless, they seem to be linked literarily through their common theme. Polhill explains, "At first glance, the cleansing of the temple seems wholly unrelated to the miracle which precedes it. In actuality, there is a close relationship. The cleansing provides a context for understanding the miracle at Cana."[46] Thus Koester is correct to observe, "The account of Jesus' actions in the Jerusalem temple forms the companion piece to the miracle at Cana."[47] R. E. Brown also perceives this literary and thematic connection: "The cleansing of the temple by Jesus fits in with motifs already seen at Cana: replacement Jewish institutions, and an abundance of wine heralding the messianic times."[48]

Cleansing the temple in Jerusalem at the beginning of His ministry was Jesus' first public presentation to the nation Israel. Whereas the wine miracle in Cana was a "semi-private" demonstration of Jesus' messianic identity to His disciples, the cleansing of the Jerusalem temple was a public declaration to the nation Israel and its religious leaders. In so doing, Jesus presented Himself to the nation as the Messiah. At the coming of the Messiah in His eschatological kingdom, He is expected to begin His ministry in the temple to purify the nation and its priesthood (Mal

---

45. Polhill, "John 1–4," 453.

46. Ibid., 451.

47. Koester, *Symbolism in the Fourth Gospel*, 82.

48. R. E. Brown, *Gospel According to John (I–XII)*, 121.

3:1–3).[49] And, upon cleansing the temple, His expression, "My Father's house," was a self-claim to Jesus' messiahship (Ps 69:9). When Jesus cleansed the temple and said to the merchants, "Get these out of here! How dare you turn My Father's house into a market place!" (John 2:16), Jesus was probably alluding to the eschatological vision of the prophet Zechariah that describes that there will be no merchants in the house of the Lord (Zech 14:20–21).[50] In short, in cleansing the Jerusalem temple Jesus was demonstrating His messianic authority over His Father's house. Thus, these two pericopes of the wine miracle and the temple cleansing that are juxtaposed closely literarily, both confirm the messianic identity of Jesus that was heralded by John the Baptist and the disciples in the Testimonium in 1:19–51.

In recording this significant deed of Jesus' cleansing of the Jerusalem temple, coupled with the first sign-miracle of His turning water into wine, the Evangelist may have also had in mind the highlight of the universal emphasis of Jesus' messiahship. Not only is Jesus the promised Messiah of the Hebrew Scriptures who will establish the eschatological age, His promised kingdom will also include the Gentiles who will embrace and worship the King.[51] The prophet Zechariah wrote concerning the future messianic kingdom, "Then survivors from all the nations that have attacked Jerusalem will go up year after year to worship the King, the LORD Almighty, and to celebrate the Feast of Tabernacles" (14:6). The prophet Isaiah also predicted such a glorious day when the Gentiles will join Israel in worshipping the King: "And foreigners who bind themselves to the LORD to serve him, and to love the name of the LORD, and to worship him, all who keep the Sabbath without desecrating it and who hold fast to my covenant—these I will bring to my holy mountain and give them joy in my house of prayer. Their burnt offerings and sacrifices will be accepted on my altar; for my house will be called a house of prayer for all nations. The Sovereign LORD declares—he who gathers the exiles of Israel: 'I will gather still others to them besides those already gathered' (56:6–8)." After all, the original dwelling place that was filled with the glory of God in the Old Testament, the tabernacle in the

---

49. Koester, *Symbolism in the Fourth Gospel*, 82. For a more detailed discussion concerning the import of this scene, see R. E. Brown's commentary, *Gospel According to John (I–XII)*, 121–23.

50. Beasley-Murray, *John*, 39.

51. Köstenberger, *Encountering John*, 75–76.

wilderness and the Solomonic temple, were testimonies to the nations regarding the glory of the one true God, and invitation to the foreigners to come and join Israel in the worship of Yahweh (Exod 40; 1 Kgs 8). This universal emphasis of the Messiah's blessings is also relevant in the present age through all believers being placed into the Body of Christ, both Jews and Gentiles (cf. Eph 2:11–22). Jesus seems to allude to this concept as He spoke of the temple of His body (John 2:19–22). The universal emphasis of the Messiah is also certainly highlighted by the Evangelist throughout his gospel in such statements like, "For God so loved the world" (3:16), and "He is the Savior of the world" (4:42).

CONCLUSION

The Evangelist's purpose statement of the Fourth Gospel explicitly states that his selected sign-miracles (σημεῖα) are intended to reveal Jesus as the promised Messiah and the unique Son of God, and those who believe in Him are promised eternal life (cf. 20:30–31). Thus, all the sign-miracles in the Gospel of John reveal Jesus' Person as the divine Messiah who grants life to those who would believe. But, this theme of Jesus as the life-giving Messiah is particularly central in the first four chapters of the Gospel, particularly in the two sign-miracles recorded in the section commonly referred to as the Cana Cycle (2:1—4:54). The first sign-miracle (2:1–11), as the "beginning of signs" (ἀρχὴν τῶν σημείων), stands as the representative sign for the rest of the miracles to follow. The first miracle of Jesus turning water into wine at the wedding in Cana authenticated His Person as the promised Messiah and the divine Son of God. And, as a representative sign the Evangelist states that Jesus revealed His glory (δόξα) through this miracle, which will be true of all the miracles.

6

The Second Sign: Healing the Official's Son (4:43–54)

INTRODUCTION

THE FIRST TWO MIRACLES in the Gospel of John form a literary inclusio around the beginning chapters of the Gospel, commonly known as the Cana Cycle (2:1—4:54),[1] because of their common geographical and thematic settings. Geographically, both miracles take place in Cana of Galilee and thus form a literary bracket around these three chapters.[2] Thematically, both miracles develop the theme of the new life that is available in Christ to all who would believe on His Person. Whereas Jesus demonstrates His authority as the divine Messiah to grant new life by changing water into wine in the first miracle, He illustrates the same truth through restoring the official's son from the brink of death in the second miracle.[3] Before discussing the second sign-miracle of Jesus, however, it is imperative that its attendant contexts (3:1—4:42) be developed. These include Jesus' personal interview with Nicodemus in chapter 3 and His personal encounter with the Samaritan woman in chapter 4.

---

1. For an analysis of Jesus' first miracle in John 2, see the present writer's article, "Significance of Jesus' First Sign-Miracle." And, for a more comprehensive analysis of Jesus' seven sign-miracles in the Gospel of John, see the present writer's doctoral dissertation, "Relationship of the Seven Sign-Miracles."

2. Although the pericopes that fall in between the two miracles take place outside of Cana (i.e., Jerusalem, Judea, and Samaria), these three chapters begin and end with the miracles taking place in Cana, thus causing Brown, among others, to entitle these chapters, "From Cana to Cana," R. E. Brown, *Gospel According to John (I–XII)*, 95.

3. When the Evangelist describes Jesus' miracle of healing the official's son as the second sign-miracle (δεύτερον σημεῖον), he is probably referring to the second miracle Jesus performed in Cana of Galilee, and not necessarily the second miracle among the seven. This is probably so because the other miracles are not numbered by the Evangelist.

THE SETTING

Having declared Jesus as the promised Messiah by the testimonies of John the Baptist and the disciples in chapter 1,[4] the Fourth Evangelist demonstrates that, as the Messiah, He is capable of replacing the old system of Judaism with the new wine of His kingdom (2:1–11). And, as the divine Messiah, He offers eternal life to all who would believe on His Person. Jesus then demonstrated the significance of the first sign-miracle by cleansing the temple in Jerusalem, an authoritative act reserved for the Messiah at His Second Advent (2:12–22). He performed these signs at the beginning days of His ministry in order to reveal His messianic identity, as the one who will one day establish His promised kingdom. However, as the Messiah He offers new life to all who would believe on Him.

Then in chapter 3, the Evangelist reveals *how* one can partake of the new life that is in Christ through Jesus' personal interview with Nicodemus. Nicodemus is introduced as "a man of the Pharisees." He seems to represent the many Jews in Jerusalem who believed in Jesus because they saw the signs he was doing (2:23–25; cf. 3:2).[5] Nicodemus is also described as a member of the "Jewish ruling council," the Sanhedrin, a ruling body of elders among the Jews.[6] Culpepper suggests correctly that the figure of Nicodemus also stands to represent the Pharisees, for whom the law and oral traditions marked the way of entrance into God's kingdom.[7] In short, he was a perfect candidate for entering God's kingdom,[8] if the conditions for entrance were measured by "human

---

4. For an analysis of the christological and eschatological significance of John 1:19–51, a section commonly referred to as the "Testimonium," see the present writer's previous article, "Relationship of John 1:19–51," 323–37.

5. Culpepper, *Anatomy of the Fourth Gospel*, 134–36. There is a literary connection between Jesus' statement in the closing verses of chapter 2 and the opening verse of chapter 3 by the word ἄνθρωπος (2:25, 3:1). The Evangelist is probably suggesting by this that Nicodemus was a man who was moved by Jesus' signs to learn more about Him.

6. R. E. Brown suggests that Nicodemus almost certainly belonged to the highest governing body of the Jewish people, composed of the priests (Sadducees), scribes (Pharisees), and lay elders of the aristocracy, and that its seventy members were presided over by the high priest. *Gospel According to John (I–XII)*, 130.

7. Culpepper, *Gospel and Letters of John*, 134–35.

8. The "kingdom of God" (βασιλείαν τοῦ θεοῦ) is an expression rarely used in the Fourth Gospel, being used only twice (3:3, 5). The term βασιλεία, however, is used three times in 18:36. It is an expression used far more frequently in the Synoptic Gospels,

righteousness." However, Jesus makes it clear that he stood outside the kingdom.[9]

The condition for entering the Messiah's kingdom or eternal life according to Jesus is spiritual rebirth or a birth from above.[10] Laney combines the two ideas and insightfully suggests the phrase, "born again from above."[11] It is clear from Nicodemus's response, however, that he could not comprehend Jesus' statement beyond the natural realm. Thus, Jesus rebukingly explains to Nicodemus that the concept of spiritual rebirth is derived from the Hebrew Scriptures and that he should have been familiar with it. Jesus explains that to be "born again/from above" is to be born of water and the Spirit.[12] Laney correctly observes that he

---

being used more than fifty times (Matthew uses the parallel expression "kingdom of heaven"). The kingdom of God mentioned here is not to be confused with the universal kingdom of God which has always been operative (Ps 103:19). Rather, Jesus is referring to His messianic kingdom that was promised by the OT prophets. The context of these chapters indicates this. As Kent correctly explains, "Although the ultimate establishment of this kingdom will be on earth, at present believers are participating in a limited sense in certain aspects of that kingdom (Col 1:13)." *Light in the Darkness*, 58. Laney concurs by saying, "The kingdom is a present reality (Col 1:13) that will ultimately be realized in physical form (Matt 25:34, 26:29; Luke 22:30; 1 Cor 15:50; 2 Tim 4:18; Rev 20:1–6). *John*, 77. The term that the Evangelist uses to communicate this truth throughout his Gospel is "eternal life."

9. This is indicated possibly by the phrase that Nicodemus came to Jesus "at night" (νυκτὸς). Although the Evangelist is indicating the literal time of day when he approached Jesus, but like so many other instances in the Fourth Gospel the Evangelist seems to also clue a symbolic meaning (cf. 9:4; 11:10; 13:30). Besides, the light and darkness motifs have already been developed by the Evangelist in the Prologue (1:1–18) to represent spiritual light and darkness, respectively. Thus, Nicodemus who came to Jesus at "night" lived in spiritual darkness in spite of all his religious credentials.

10. The phrase "born again" (γεννηθῇ ἄνωθεν) can be translated to mean either spiritual rebirth or spiritual birth from above. See BAGD 77. s.v. "ἄνωθεν." This is probably one of John's many double meanings. For an excellent study of the Johannine double meanings in the Fourth Gospel, see Hamidkhani, "Johannine Expressions of Double Meaning."

11. Laney, *John*, 77.

12. Jesus' enigmatic statement "born of water and spirit" is a concept derived from the OT. Hodges suggests that "water and the Spirit" should be translated "water and wind," a double metaphor for the work of the Holy Spirit (cf. Isa 44:3–5; Ezek 37:9–10). "Water and Spirit," 206–20. Both the Isa and the Ezek passages describe the future restoration of Israel as a nation prior to the establishment of the messianic kingdom. Kent points out the similarity between the concept of being "born of water and Spirit" with the New Covenant truths expressed by the prophet Ezekiel (36:25–26), where the water symbolizes the cleansing aspect and the Spirit illustrates the impartation of a new life (heart). *Light in the Darkness*, 58.

is probably referring to the New Covenant promises of regeneration and the forgiveness of sins through faith in Christ and His sacrificial death for sins (3:16–17; cf. 1 Cor 11:25; Heb 7:22; 8:6–13; 10:15–22).[13] In short, then, the requirement for entering the Messiah's kingdom is spiritual rebirth from above by means of one's faith in Jesus' sacrificial provision. As Koester perceptively concludes, "Being born from above means coming to faith in Jesus, who came from above."[14] Thus, even Nicodemus, a man who possessed impeccable and impressive religious credentials, could enter the Messiah's kingdom and partake of the eternal life only if he placed his trust in the divine provision of Christ's sacrificial death for the forgiveness of sins.

If the Evangelist reveals *how* one can partake of the new life that Christ offers through Jesus' personal interview with Nicodemus in chapter 3, then he reveals *who* can enter into that life through His personal encounter with the Samaritan woman in chapter 4. The literary connection between these two chapters is made obvious through the sharp contrast between the two characters, Nicodemus and the Samaritan woman.[15] If Nicodemus was a "prime" candidate for entrance into the Messiah's kingdom, humanly speaking, then the Samaritan woman was the "least likely" of candidates for His kingdom. Culpepper correctly observes that she lacked all of Nicodemus's advantages.[16] Thus, the great barrier that Jesus crossed in reaching out to the Samaritan woman is highlighted by the Evangelist's parenthetical statement in verse 9: "For Jews do not associate with Samaritans."[17]

---

13. Laney, *John*, 79.

14. Koester, *Symbolism in the Fourth Gospel*, 164.

15. Culpepper points out the polarization of characters between the Samaritan woman and Nicodemus: "He was a Jew; she was a Samaritan. He was a respectful leader; she was a village peasant with five husbands in her past." He observes that there were four levels of barriers that Jesus had to cross in conversing with the woman: gender, nationality, race, and religion. He then concludes that "all four barriers are crossed and community is created." *Gospel and Letters of John*, 139. For a more detailed comparison between the two characters, see also Dockery's article, "Reading John 4:1–45," 127–40. He compares the two characters in a chart by laying them side-by-side on various aspects.

16. Culpepper, *Anatomy of the Fourth Gospel*, 136. He compares the two characters this way: "He is a male teacher of Israel; she is a woman of Samaria. He has a noble heritage; she has a shameful past. He has seen signs and knows Jesus is 'from God'; she meets Jesus as a complete stranger."

17. R. E. Brown succinctly describes the barriers between Jews and Samaritans: "The Samaritans are the descendants of two groups: (a) the remnant of the native Israelites

The setting of the story that takes place at Jacob's well and the subject of water provide much insight into the significance of Jesus' conversation with the Samaritan woman and the gift He was offering her. While Jesus was offering her "living water"[18] as the gift of eternal life, the woman, like Nicodemus, could not comprehend His offer beyond the natural realm.[19] It is obvious that Jesus was building on the scriptural metaphor of water (cf. Ps 36:9; Isa 55:1) to refer to the new life that He offers: "Everyone who drinks of this water will be thirsty again, but whoever drinks the water I give him will never thirst. Indeed, the water I give him will become in him a spring of water welling up to eternal life" (John 4:13–14).[20] Jesus' encounter with the Samaritan woman at Jacob's well is probably intended to be a reminder of the patriarchal blessings that took place by a well.[21] As such, Jesus was revealing His own Person as the promised Messiah of the Hebrew Scriptures who fulfills the patriarchal promises made to Abraham, Isaac, and Jacob long ago. When the woman

---

who were not deported at the fall of the Northern Kingdom in 722 BC; (b) foreign colonists brought in from Babylonia and Media by the Assyrian conquerors of Samaria (2 Kings xvii 24ff. gives an anti-Samaritan account of this). There was theological opposition between these northerners and the Jews of the South because of the Samaritan refusal to worship at Jerusalem. This was aggravated by the fact that after the Babylonian exile the Samaritans had put obstacles in the way of the Jewish restoration of Jerusalem, and that in the second century BC the Samaritans had helped the Syrian monarchs in their wars against the Jews. In 128 BC the Jewish high priest burned the Samaritan temple on Gerizim." *Gospel According to John (I–XII)*, 170.

18. "Living water" (ὕδωρ ζῶν) was commonly a designation for water that flowed from a spring, in contrast to the stagnant water taken from a cistern (cf. Jer 2:13). Koester points out that "living water" was used for purification purposes in Scripture (i.e., skin disease) (Lev 14:5–6, 50–52), bodily discharge (15:13), and corpse defilement (Num 19:17). *Symbolism in the Fourth Gospel*, 168. It is clear that the Johannine term "living water" has a double meaning, a characteristic that is common in the Fourth Gospel.

19. Polhill, "John 1–4," 454.

20. By "living water," Jesus was also speaking figuratively for the Holy Spirit (John 7:38–39). Jesus says later on in the Gospel, "If anyone is thirsty, let him come to me and drink. Whoever believes in me, as the Scripture has said, streams of living water will flow from within him" (v. 38). The Evangelist adds parenthetically following this verse, "By this he meant the Spirit, whom those who believed in him were later to receive. Up to that time the Spirit had not been given, since Jesus had not yet been glorified" (v. 39).

21. Both Isaac (Gen 24) and Jacob (Gen 29) met their wives (Rebekah and Rachel) by a well that confirmed God's promise made to Abraham (Gen 12:1–3; 15:1–21). Moses also met his wife, Zipporah, by a well (Exod 2:15–22). Bonneau makes an extensive comparison between John 4 and Gen 24, although he goes perhaps too far in his analogies. "Woman at the Well," 1252–59.

expresses her expectation for the coming Messiah, Jesus responds with the revelatory words, "I who speak to you am he" (v. 26). By using the expression "I am," Jesus was intentionally identifying Himself as the God of Abraham, Isaac, and Jacob.

The motifs of the water and the well in this story also anticipate the eschatological hope expressed by the Hebrew prophets. For instance, the prophet Isaiah, in envisioning the eschatological days, declares: "With joy you will draw water from the wells of salvation" (12:3). He then continues his prophetic exultation with these significant words: "In that day you will say: 'Give thanks to the LORD, call on his name; make known among the nations what he has done, and proclaim that his name is exalted . . .'" (Isa 12:4). The prophets certainly envisioned the last days as a time when the Messiah will not only fulfill His promises to the nation Israel but also as a time when the Gentile nations will be blessed by Him (cf. Gen 12:1–3). And, the conclusion of the Samaritan woman pericope certainly foreshadows in the present age the truth that will be fulfilled in the eschatological age (John 4:39–42). The story concludes with the Samaritans believing in the Messiah by faith in recognizing Jesus as "the Savior of the world" (v. 42). In short, the Messiah is not only the King of Israel, He is also the Savior of the world.

To conclude, the story of the Samaritan woman reveals that although she was outside of the Jewish community, not to mention her sinful lifestyle, by placing her faith in Jesus as the promised Messiah, her sins were washed away and she gained entrance into the kingdom. This obviously stands in contrast to Nicodemus who, in spite of being within the Jewish community, apparently did not walk away from his encounter with Jesus with a newly found life like the Samaritan woman.[22] These two pericopes reveal, then, that one can only receive eternal life and enter into the Messiah's kingdom by believing in Jesus, regardless of one's religious or ethnic background.

---

22. It is possible that Nicodemus did come to faith on the night of his encounter with Jesus in chapter 3, although it nowhere mentions it in the context. He more likely placed his trust in Jesus later on, for the Evangelist makes it clear that Nicodemus demonstrated his faith in burying the body of Jesus along with Joseph of Arimathea in 19:38–42.

THE SIGN

The miracle narrative begins with transitional verses that shift the scene from Samaria to Galilee (4:43–45).[23] Having ministered in Samaria for two days (v. 43; cf. 4:40), Jesus now returned to the place where He performed His first miracle. These verses also introduce the conclusion of the Cana Cycle (2:1—4:54) by bringing Jesus back to the same place where the theme of signs was introduced (2:11).[24] By designating the miracle as a "second sign" (δεύτερον σημεῖον), the Evangelist is probably indicating the literary inclusio that brackets these three chapters with the two Cana stories. The second miracle indicates a literary unit not only by its common geographical setting with the first miracle, it also advances the theme that has been highlighted throughout this section, namely, that Jesus is the one who gives life.[25] Both miracles develop the theme of the new life that is available in Christ to all who would believe on His Person. Whereas Jesus demonstrates His authority as the divine Messiah to grant new life by changing water into wine in the first miracle, He illustrates the same truth through restoring the official's son from the brink of death in the second miracle.

The miracle story begins with a description of a certain royal official whose son lay sick at Capernaum (v. 46).[26] Capernaum was a city

23. Although most commentators treat these verses (vv. 43–45) as introductory verses to the miracle narrative, R. E. Brown treats these verses separately as a "transitional passage." *Gospel According to John (I–XII)*, 186–89.

24. Borchert, *John 1–11*, 216.

25. Culpepper, *Gospel and Letters of John*, 144. Culpepper demonstrates that the theme of Jesus as the giver of life is developed in all the pericopes of the Cana Cycle: the Prologue (1:1–18); the wedding at Cana (2:1–12); the cleansing of the Jerusalem temple (2:13–25); the conversation with Nicodemus (3:1–21); John the Baptist's testimony and Jesus' following discourse (3:22–36); the Samaritan woman (4:1–42); and the official's son (4:43–54).

26. Although this story is somewhat similar to the Synoptic Gospels' account of the Centurion and his servant (Matt 8:5–13; Luke 7:1–10), the details of the stories are too different for them to be the same occasion. For instance, whereas the person requesting the healing to Jesus in the Fourth Gospel is described as a "royal official" (βασιλικός), the synoptic accounts describe the man as a "centurion" (ἑκατόνταρχος). Furthermore, whereas John describes a "son" (υἱός) who is sick, Luke describes a "servant" (δοῦλος), although Matthew uses the term παῖς which, according to Carson, could refer to either a son or a servant. *Gospel According to John*, 233–34. However, as Morris says correctly, "About the only things in common are some interesting verbal parallels and the healing at a distance." *Gospel According to John*, 288. For a more detailed contrast between this Johannine account with the synoptic story, see Köstenberger, *John*, 168–69.

located approximately eighteen miles northeast of Cana on the shore of Kenneret (the Sea of Galilee), and according to Laney, it was an important tax collection station on the international highway (the Via Maris).[27] Apparently, there was stationed a certain royal official, who was probably in the service of Herod Antipas, who ruled Galilee from Herod's capital at Tiberias, possibly in the service of Rome.[28] Borchert explains the possible background of the official: "Most scholarly opinion leans in favor of the man's having been in the service of Herod Antipas, a subordinate ruler (for the Romans) or tetrarch in charge of Galilee and Perea, the man who divorced his Nabatean wife and married Herodias (the divorced wife of Philip, Herod's half-brother; cf. Matt 14:1–12). This official may have been a military officer, but since he was from Capernaum (a town on the Sea of Galilee near the border of another tetrarchy), the official could have been involved in other duties such as revenue collection."[29]

Although the ethnic identity of the royal official is subject to debate without an explicit statement, A. H. Mead insists he is a Gentile officer in the service of Herod Antipas.[30] The contextual evidence seems to support this conclusion.[31] The verse immediately preceding the account of this miracle may provide a clue to his Gentile identity. At the closing of the Samaritan woman account in chapter 4, the Samaritans who came to faith as a result of the woman's testimony about Jesus declared: "We no longer believe just because of what you said; now we have heard for

27. Laney, *John*, 101. Köstenberger guesses that the travel involved a day's journey of about fourteen miles and adds that it was mostly uphill, since Cana lay in the Galilean hill country and Capernaum was located several hundred feet below sea level. *John*, 170.

28. Mead, "Basiliko/j in John 4:46–53," 69–72.

29. Borchert, *John 1–11*, 219.

30. Mead, "Βασιλικός in John 4:46–53," 70–71. He insists that based on Herod's close relationship with Tiberus, a Gentile would not have been out of place at his court. He further explains that the synoptic centurion, though certainly a Gentile, was in Herodian service also. Keener refers to him as "A Galilean Aristocrat." *Gospel of John*, 1:630.

31. Moloney proposes that the description of the Βασιλικός in the present Johannine context suggests a Gentile identity of the man. He explains, "He is the last in a series of characters who appear across 4:1–54. He is not from Cana, but from the border town of Capernaum, well known for the presence of Gentile soldiers. All the other characters in 4:1–54 are Samaritans, people from the world outside Judaism. It is most likely that this particular Βασιλικός is understood and presented to the reader by the author as a final example of the reception of the word of Jesus from the non-Jewish world." *Gospel of John*, 153.

ourselves, and we know that this man really is the Savior of the *world*" (v. 42, emphasis added). This verse seems to be a literary hinge to what follows, namely, the salvation of the Gentile household of the royal official (vv. 43–54).

The official's son lay sick in Capernaum, and was close to death (ἤμελλεν ἀποθνῄσκειν). Culpepper accurately observes, "Death is the problem, not a particular illness."[32] This is evident by the fact that the narrative repeatedly emphasizes that the son "lives" (vv. 50, 51, 53) as a result of the miracle. When this man heard that Jesus had come to Galilee, he went to Jesus and "begged" (ἠρώτα) him to come and heal his son (v. 47).[33] His faith becomes evident, because when Jesus granted his request, "he took Jesus at his word" (ἐπίστευσεν ὁ ἄνθρωπος τῷ λόγῳ ὃν εἶπεν αὐτῷ ὁ Ἰησοῦς) and departed (v. 50). And, his faith in Jesus' word was confirmed when his servants met him on the road of his return and informed him of the exact hour his son was healed (vv. 51–52). When the man realized that his son was healed the exact time Jesus spoke the words of healing, he and his whole household believed (ἐπίστευσεν) (v. 53).

THE SIGNIFICANCE

On the most obvious level, the miracle reveals that Jesus has the power to save from death even at a great distance. Jesus' word has the power to work miracles even though He Himself is far removed from the actual place.[34] Robert Sloan explains the significance of Jesus' healing the official's son at a distance.

While Jesus does not believe His presence is required—that is, that the miracle must be "seen"—the nobleman pleads with Him to "come down before my child dies." The nobleman assumes that healing can occur only with Jesus' presence. Thus, while we hear in John 4:50 that the man "believed" the word that Jesus spoke to him—healing at a distance evidently requires more faith than healing associated with

---

32. Culpepper, *Gospel and Letters of John*, 146.

33. Laney suggests that the desperation of the father's request is evident by the imperfect tense of the verb, and possibly indicates a persistent and repeated request. In other words, the man "kept on asking." *John*, 101. The man's desperation is also seen by the fact that he again asks Jesus to come down in verse 49.

34. For a helpful discussion on Jesus' absence in healing the official's son, see Sloan, "Absence of Jesus in John," 207–27.

presence—and therefore started off toward his own home, we are told again in verse 53 that it is also upon later hearing that the hour of his son's healing corresponded to the hour of Jesus' statement ("your son lives") that he "believed." The demand for physical presence, overcome by faith, has nonetheless its (sublimated) counterpart in the synchronizing of word and deed. As is customary in the Gospel of John, belief has different meanings, and in this case it seems clear that "belief" of 4:53 is corroborated and/or intensified by the nobleman's subsequent experience of learning of the temporal correspondence between the words of healing, spoken at a distance, and the act of healing. The believing of 4:53 is thus related not only to the amazing fact of healing, but the even more astounding fact of healing "from a distance." That is, the healing was unseen—it was done by Jesus, but in the *absence* of Jesus.[35]

The emphasis of this miracle, then, is the authority of the Messiah's word, and it is similar to the first miracle in that regard. Even in the first miracle of Jesus turning water into wine, it was the Messiah's spoken word that caused the miracle to occur. Thus, both miracles confirm the claims of the Prologue (1:1–18) that Jesus is the λόγος of God. In short, Jesus, as the divine Messiah, has the power and authority to command life to be.

The miracle also reveals deeper christological significance. There are aspects of this sign that reveal His Person as the promised Messiah. In healing the royal official's son from the brink of death, Jesus demonstrates yet another important aspect of the Messiah's role as predicted by the Old Testament Prophets, namely, His authority to bring healing and deliverance from the cruel fate of death (cf. Isa 25:8; 35:5–6; 53:4; 61:1). As Carson explains, "The one who transformed water into wine, eclipsing the old rites of purification and announcing the dawning joy of the messianic banquet, is the one who continues his messianic work, whether he is rightly trusted or not, by bringing healing and snatching life back from the brink of death."[36] It is significant that both sickness and death will be absent in the future messianic kingdom. The apostle John also envisioned such a blissful time in his Apocalypse: "He will wipe every tear from their eyes. There will be no more death or mourning or crying or pain, for the old order of things has passed away" (Rev 21:4). Therefore, as Laney concludes correctly, "In Jesus' healing of the

---

35. Ibid., 209–10.

36. Carson, *Gospel According to John*, 238.

official's son He was giving a foretaste of kingdom glory."[37] In short, then, by revealing His Person as the Messiah who will overcome death, Jesus was illustrating that He has the authority to grant eternal life even now to those who would believe.

The significant relationship between the theme of life and believing is therefore also one of the emphases of this miracle. Borchert correctly observes, "The Johannine theme of life and death is encapsulated in these two brief but powerful statements ('Go! Your son will live'). As indicated earlier, the man obeyed the word of Jesus without seeing the sign."[38] As Blum concludes, "Jesus' word has power to work, and people are simply to believe His word."[39] In short, the Evangelist demonstrates in this miracle a theme that he has developed throughout the beginning chapters of the Gospel, that is, Jesus, as the divine Messiah has the authority to give life. And, believing in Jesus and His Word results in the eternal life that only He can give.

This miracle also reveals yet another aspect of the Messiah's kingdom. If the ethnic identity of the royal official and his son is Gentile, as argued above, this sign emphasizes the universality of the eschatological kingdom of the Messiah (Isa 2:2–3; 42:6; Zech 8:23). The prophets of old have envisioned the days of the Messiah when the Gentile nations will join Israel in the worship of the King. And, this miracle shows that the blessings of the Messiah's redemptive work extends not only to the Jews, but to the Samaritans and Gentile nations as well (cf. Gen 12:3). Thus, Jesus is not only the promised Messiah of the Hebrew Scriptures He is also the Savior of the world.

The literary pattern of highlighting Jesus' encounter with a Jew (Nicodemus), a Samaritan (the Samaritan woman), and a Gentile (the royal official), brings to remembrance Jesus' command to His disciples to be His witnesses in Jerusalem, Judea, and Samaria, and to the ends of the earth (Acts 1:8).[40] It is conceivable that the apostle John had his Lord's command in mind in designing his gospel this way.[41] It is ironic, how-

---

37. Laney, *John*, 103.

38. Borchert, *John 1–11*, 220.

39. Blum, "John," 288.

40. Culpepper, *Gospel and Letters of John*, 129. Culpepper provides a helpful chart in demonstrating the similar geographical patterns in both the Gospel of John and the book of Acts.

41. Mead, "Βασιλικός in John 4:46–53," 71. R. E. Brown, however, fails to see what he calls a "linear progression of faith" in these chapters. He says, "We have already ex-

ever, in comparing the responses of the three individuals whom Jesus encountered in these chapters, that the only one who walked away from his encounter with Jesus without receiving eternal life was the Jewish teacher of the law. Whereas the other two who were initially outside the covenant community put their faith in the Messiah and thus received life eternal, Nicodemus could not abandon his works-based system of religious Judaism.

CONCLUSION

The Evangelist's purpose statement of the Fourth Gospel explicitly states that his selected sign-miracles are intended to reveal Jesus as the promised Messiah and the unique Son of God, and those who believe in Him are promised life eternal (cf. 20:30–31). Thus, all of the sign-miracles in the Gospel of John reveal Jesus' Person as the divine Messiah who grants life to those who will believe. But, this theme of Jesus as the life-giving Messiah is particularly central in the first four chapters of the Gospel. The first chapter of the Fourth Gospel, consisting of the Prologue (1:1–18) and the Testimonium (1:19–51), plays a significant role within the book by introducing the key concepts and themes that will be developed later in the Gospel. The Prologue and the Testimonium introduce Jesus as the divine Messiah who grants eternal life to those who would believe in Him, which He will provide by His redemptive and sacrificial death on the cross as the Passover Lamb. By introducing Jesus as the divine Messiah who grants life to all who would believe, the Evangelist provides a foretaste of the kind of revelations to come in the seven sign-miracles and their attendant contexts in the form of narratives and discourses.

The first two sign-miracles are recorded in the section of the Gospel commonly referred to as the Cana Cycle (2:1—4:54). The two Cana sign-miracles frame these three chapters as a literary unit with their common geographical and thematic settings. They both take place in Cana of Galilee, and they both develop the theme of newness of life that Jesus provides as the divine Messiah. The first sign-miracle (2:1–11), as the "beginning of signs" (ἀρχὴν τῶν σημείων), stands as a representative sign for the rest of the miracles to follow. The first miracle of Jesus turn-

---

pressed doubts that John intended a progression in faith from the Jews of ii–iii through the Samaritans (half-Jews) to the Gentiles at Cana." *Gospel According to John (I–XII)*, 197. The literary clues within these chapters show, however, an underlying geographical pattern.

ing water into wine at the wedding in Cana authenticated His Person as the promised Messiah and the divine Son of God. And, as a representative sign the Evangelist states that Jesus revealed His glory (δόξα) through this miracle (2:11), which will be true of all of the miracles. The second miracle of Jesus healing the royal official's son (4:43–54) brings the Cana Cycle to a close with Jesus performing his second miracle in Cana of Galilee. Whereas Jesus demonstrates His authority as the divine Messiah to grant new life by changing water into wine in the first miracle, this sign-miracle demonstrates the importance of believing in Jesus and obeying His word. It is believing in Jesus as the promised Messiah and the divine Son of God that results in deliverance from the realm of death into the life from above, or eternal life.

7

The Third Sign: Healing the Lame Man (5:1–16)

INTRODUCTION

THE LITERARY STRUCTURE OF the Fourth Gospel reveals that it is one of the most carefully crafted pieces of literature in the Bible. The Evangelist explicitly states in his purpose statement (20:30–31) that the aim of his gospel is to present Jesus as the promised Messiah of the Old Testament Scriptures and the unique Son of God. And, his primary means of revealing Jesus' Person as the divine Messiah is the seven sign-miracles (σημεῖα) and their attendant contexts of teaching, which are all recorded in the first twelve chapters of the Gospel, commonly referred to as the Book of Signs (2:1—12:50).[1] The first two sign-miracles of Jesus are strategically placed in the beginning chapters of the Gospel, often characterized as the Cana Cycle (2:1—4:54),[2] because they are both performed in Cana of Galilee, thus forming a literary bracket around these chapters.[3] The remaining sign-miracles of Jesus are also purposefully allocated throughout the following chapters of this section, frequently

1. Although the term "Book of Signs" in referring to the first twelve chapters of the Fourth Gospel is now widely accepted and used by most Johannine scholars to outline the book, it is mostly associated with Dodd (*Interpretation of the Fourth Gospel*, x), and R. E. Brown (*Gospel According to John [I–XII]*, cxxxviii). The first twelve chapters of the Gospel records the public ministry of Jesus, while the second section records the private Farewell Discourse of Jesus with His disciples (chaps. 13–17) and the Passion Narrative (chaps. 18–20). Dodd calls this latter section, the "Book of Passion," while Brown calls it, the "Book of Glory."

2. Borchert, *John 1–11*, 151–222.

3. These three chapters (chaps. 2–4) form a literary unit because they are not only bounded geographically by the Cana miracles but also thematically by presenting Jesus as the life-giving Messiah who grants eternal life to those who would believe. For a more detailed description of the significance of this section, see chapter 3 of the book. See also Moloney's important work, "From Cana to Cana," 185–213.

designated as the Festival Cycle (5:1—12:50).[4] These chapters are designated as such because the sign-miracles and their attendant narratives and discourses are set in the context of Jewish festivals.[5] This cycle begins with an "unnamed feast" (5:1–47; cf. 5:1) and then runs through a year of festivals from Passover (6:1–72; cf. 6:4) through Tabernacles (7:1—10:21; cf. 7:2), Dedication or Hanukkah (10:22–42; cf. 10:22), and then back to Passover (12:1).[6]

The literary structure of the Fourth Gospel is skillfully woven together with its profound theology. Whereas the Cana Cycle chapters reveal Jesus as the divine Messiah who grants life and emphasize the importance of believing in His Person to receive that life, the Festival Cycle chapters develop the theme of increasing opposition by the Jewish leadership to the one who grants life.[7] As Harold Songer explains cor-

4. See Moloney, *Signs and Shadows*.

5. Culpepper, *Gospel and Letters of John*, 148–49. Guilding has attempted to interpret the whole Gospel on the basis of the feasts, proposing that the Fourth Gospel had been developed as a set of festival lectionary readings in ancient Palestine synagogues. *Fourth Gospel and Jewish Worship*. Although her main thesis found little general acceptance in the field of Johannine studies, her emphasis nevertheless has alerted the students of the Fourth Gospel concerning the importance of the Jewish feasts to the background of the Gospel. As Moloney thus concludes in his critique of Guilding's work, "It is better to allow the context to determine the use of the feasts rather than vice-versa." *Gospel of John*, 165.

6. Borchert, "Passover and the Narrative Cycles," 308–9. It is important to note, however, that even among the commentators who designate this section as the Festival Cycle outline the chapters differently. While some scholars outline the section to include all of 5:1—12:50, some scholars prefer to include only 5:1—10:42. Those who include only chapters 5–10 see chapters 11–12 as developing the theme of Jesus moving toward His death and glory. Those who see chapters 11–12 as a separate unit from chapters 5–10 view the chapters 11–12 as setting the stage for the Passover of Jesus' sacrifice as the Passover Lamb. R. E. Brown thus designates chapters 11–12 as "Jesus Moves Toward the Hour of Death and Glory." *Gospel According to John (I–XII)*, 419–98. Burge similarly calls John 11–12 "Foreshadowings of Jesus' Death and Resurrection." *Interpreting the Gospel of John*, 76–77. I also prefer to separate John 11–12 from John 5–10, although the separation of these chapters is technically minor.

7. The Festival Cycle (5:1—12:50) begins with Jesus' healing of the lame man at the Pool of Bethesda on the Sabbath. The opposition and increasing hostility of the Jewish religious leaders toward Jesus is introduced by the statement in 5:16: "So, because Jesus was doing these things on the Sabbath, the Jews persecuted him." The statement in 5:18 also states: "For this reason the Jews tried all the harder to kill him; not only was he breaking the Sabbath, but he was even calling God his own Father, making himself equal to God." These two verses introduce and foreshadow the role of the Jewish leadership in the rest of the Gospel. Following the raising of Lazarus from the dead by Jesus in chapter 11, this section closes with the Jewish authorities plotting to kill Jesus in chapter 12.

rectly, "Two related motifs are woven carefully together in John 5–12—
the steady insistence that Jesus is God's Son come to grant life and the
steadily increasing hostility of the Jews toward Jesus."[8] Tenney is thus
perceptive in characterizing these chapters as periods of controversy
(chaps. 5–6), conflict (chaps. 7–11), and crisis (chap. 12).[9] As Jesus performs His miracles and delivers His accompanying discourses in the
context of the Jewish feasts, He was demonstrating in no uncertain terms
to be the one who fulfills the hopes and joys of the festivals. The religious
establishment vehemently opposed the messianic claims of Jesus in these
chapters, thus fulfilling the Evangelist's words in the Prologue: "He came
to that which was his own, but his own did not receive him" (John 1:11).
In short, Borchert's summary of these chapters seems appropriate: "In
the Cana Cycle the theme of believing seems to be center stage. In the
Festival Cycle the themes of conflict and rejection seem to occupy that
position."[10]

　　Although there are five sign-miracles (σημεῖα) that are recorded
within the Festival Cycle (5:1—12:50) section of the Fourth Gospel, this
book will analyze the third sign-miracle of Jesus' healing of the lame
man at the Pool of Bethesda (5:1–15) and its attendant narrative and
discourse.

JESUS' MIRACLE OF HEALING THE LAME MAN
AT THE POOL (5:1-15)

The opening words of the chapter, "Some time later" or more literally,
"After these things" (μετὰ ταῦτα), indicate a shift in the setting of the
Gospel narrative as well as the obvious temporal change (v. 1). The
Evangelist uses this phrase often to inform the reader that a change is
taking place in the story (cf. 2:12; 3:22; 4:43; 6:1). As Moloney insightfully points out, "The reader has been taken from the Galilean setting of
a miracle in 4:46–54, where a Gentile displayed his belief in the word of

---

Thus, these chapters are distinctly marked with vehement opposition and hostility by
the Jewish leadership to the one who claims to be the promised Messiah.

　　8. Songer, "John 5–12," 459–71.

　　9. Tenney, *John*, 103. Tenney correctly conveys the idea of increasing hostility of
the Jewish religious leaders towards Jesus, finally climaxing with their decision to kill
Jesus.

　　10. Borchert, *John 1–11*, 227.

Jesus, to another context: a Jewish feast in Jerusalem."[11] Moloney explains further this thematic shift: "The issue of belief has been the *leitmotif* of 2:1—4:54; now, as Jesus goes up to Jerusalem, the story turns to the feast of 'the Jews.' There has been a growing hostility between Jesus and 'the Jews' (cf. 1:19; 2:13–22). In 5:1 a negative tone is already struck as the narrator mentions a feast celebrated by 'the Jews.'"[12] Therefore, a change in the Gospel story is taking place not only temporally and geographically, but also thematically.

THE SETTING

The sign-miracle (σημεῖον) of Jesus healing the lame man at the Pool of Bethesda takes place when Jesus went up to Jerusalem for "a feast of the Jews." The lack of a specific description of the feast in 5:1 has caused many scholars to propose different feasts for the setting of the story.[13] Since Jews were obligated to go to Jerusalem at the three major feasts of Passover, Pentecost, and Tabernacles, it is probably safe to assume at least that it was one of these pilgrim feasts.[14] Although all three of these pilgrim feasts have been proposed with credible arguments, as Morris argues, it is not possible to identify the feast with any certainty.[15] Thus, as Alfred Edersheim correctly concludes, "We must be content to call it the unknown feast."[16] Besides, perhaps the Evangelist intentionally mentions the feast without its name because the focus of the miracle and its attendant context is a Sabbath controversy, and the unnamed feast is not thematically related to the miracle.[17] Carson explains: "If the other feasts are named, it is because the context in each case finds Jesus doing or saying something that picks up a theme related to it. By implication, if the feast in John 5 is not named, it is probably because the material in John 5

---

11. Moloney, *Signs and Shadows*, 4.

12. Moloney, *Gospel of John*, 167.

13. A textual variant reading ἡ ἑορτή (the feast) would probably indicate the feast as the Passover, but the external support for the reading without the definite article is strong. Therefore, the anarthrous ἑορτή (a feast) is the preferred reading. See Metzger, *Textual Commentary*, 207.

14. R. E. Brown, *Gospel According to John (I–XII)*, 206. Hoehner suggests that it probably refers to the Tabernacles and proposes a specific date of October 21–28, AD 31. *Chronological Aspects*, 59.

15. Morris, *Gospel According to John*, 299.

16. Edersheim, *Life and Times of Jesus*, 1:460.

17. Borchert, *John 1–11*, 228.

is not to be thematically related to it. The mention of *a feast of the Jews* in that case becomes little more than an historical marker to explain Jesus' presence in Jerusalem."[18] In short, although the feast remains unnamed, it quickly becomes evident that the focus of this pericope is that the miracle took place on the Sabbath (cf. 5:9). God designed the Sabbath as a time of physical and spiritual refreshment (cf. Exod 20:8–11; 23:12; Deut 5:12–15).[19] It was also a holy day and a time to remember Israel's covenantal relationship to Yahweh (cf. Exod 31:12–18). According to Leviticus 23:1–3, the holiness of the Sabbath places the day among the other appointed feasts of God, such as Passover, Unleavened Bread, and Tabernacles, although unlike the yearly feasts, the celebration of the Sabbath is weekly.[20] By the time of the first century, however, the Sabbath had been perverted. Through the excessive and restrictive legislation of the rabbis on how to observe this holy day, the Sabbath became a burden rather than a holy observance.[21] For instance, thirty-nine classes of labor are forbidden on the Sabbath (*Shabbath* 7.2). Thus, the Sabbath became associated with burden for the people, rather than a sign of deliverance as it was originally meant. It is little wonder then that Jesus chose to free the crippled man on the Sabbath. Jesus wanted to demonstrate that the Son of Man is Lord even of the Sabbath (cf. Mark 2:17–18).[22]

18. Carson, *Gospel According to John*, 241.

19. For a detailed discussion of the Sabbath, see R. J. Griffith, "Eschatological Significance of the Sabbath." See also McCann, "Sabbath," 4:247–52.

20. Yee, *Jewish Feasts and the Gospel of John*, 33.

21. A major section of the Mishna is devoted to the Sabbath rules. For the rules concerning Shabbat or Sabbath, see Neusner, *The Mishnah*.

22. Borchert forcefully argues (I believe for valid reasons) for a strategic literary and theological role of the Sabbath in this chapter, *John 1–11*, 230.

"The answer to the relationship of chap. 5 to the remaining six chapters of what is here called the Festival Cycle in John is not to be found in seeking to establish the unnamed feast of 5:1 as one of the other Jewish Festivals that would fall between the Passover of 2:13, 23 and the Passover of 6:4 as though John were trying to squeeze in another festival between two Passovers in a mere pedantic chronological report. This Gospel is far too organized and theologically sophisticated for such a haphazard approach.

"The entire discussion of chap. 5 is built upon the implications arising from a Sabbath controversy. Yet for years, I, like many others, struggled to discover the Johannine rationale behind the so-called unnamed feast.... The answer I am now convinced is offered by festival text of Leviticus 23. According to the text, festivals are holy convocations. The first day of Passover accordingly is a holy convocation in which no labor is to be done (Lev 23:7). It is in fact a Sabbath, according to the perspective of Leviticus. Thus,

THE SIGN

The scene of the miracle is described by the Evangelist as taking place in Jerusalem at the pool near the "Sheep Gate." The Sheep Gate (Neh 3:1, 32; 12:39) was located in the north wall of Jerusalem, and was a gathering place for the sick.[23] The Aramaic name for Sheep Gate is *Bethesda*, which means "house of mercy."[24] And, the Evangelist records that around the pool lay a great number of disabled people—the blind, the lame, and the paralyzed.[25] In the midst of all the disabled bodies lay a man who is an invalid and who had been in that condition for thirty-eight years. Obviously, the Evangelist specifies the length of time the man was in that condition in order to emphasize that a healing of such a condition

a Sabbath understanding of the festivals is absolutely crucial for sensing the Levitical and Johannine perspective on the festivals. Obviously this evangelist knew what he was doing. The festivals are thus to be perceived as holy convocations established by God in the Torah (Purim and Hanukkah being added later to the calendar), and they are in Leviticus by statement and implication linked to Sabbath and to the many restrictions on labor pertaining to Sabbath observations.

"With this understanding of festival in mind, the reason for the continual undercurrent of Sabbath in the Johannine Festival Cycle becomes, I believe, much clearer and more relevant to the Johannine portrayal of Jesus as the Lord, even in the festivals. It also renders any Bultmannian discussion of displacement of chap. 5 as a complete misunderstanding of the Gospel."

23. Culpepper, *Gospel and Letters of John*, 150.

24. Laney, *John*, 106.

25. Some manuscripts add verses 3b-4: "And they waited for the moving of the waters. From time to time an angel of the Lord would come down and stir up the waters. The first one into the pool after each such disturbance would be cured of whatever disease he had." The absence of the earliest and best witnesses for the verses, however, has led many scholars to omit them from the original. See Metzger, *Textual Commentary*, 209. See also Fee's article, "Authenticity of John 5:3b–4," 207–18. He also prefers to omit them from the original. There are some, however, who argue for the authenticity of these verses. See Hodges, "Angel at Bethesda–John 5:4," 39. Hodges proposes some strong arguments in favor of the text: (1) All known Greek manuscripts of John's Gospel, with the exception of less than a dozen, include the verse; (2) The antiquity of the passage is vouched for from Tertullian in the third century; (3) The reading was widely diffused in both the east and west as evidenced in the versions and church Fathers; (4) In view of its unique content and probable connection with the traditions of Bethesda itself, the material is unobjectionable on stylistic grounds; (5) The deliberate omission can be explained as motivated by a falsely perceived "pagan tinge"; (6) The statement about the assembled sick in v. 3 and the response of the invalid in v. 7 demand the presence of v. 4 in order to make John's text genuinely comprehensible. Although the external attestation for the reading that omits the verses are strong and therefore are difficult to argue against, internally, however, the verses in question do provide an explanation for the lame man's statement in v. 7.

was humanly impossible. Jesus chooses such a man to display His mercy and perform His miracle. It is interesting, however, that in contrast to the royal official who found Jesus and begged Him to heal his son (John 4:47), the invalid man does not even seek healing from Jesus. It is Jesus who takes the initiative to heal him: "Do you want to get well (ὑγιής)?" (5:6).[26] The man's response again stands in contrast to the royal official who approached Jesus with faith. While the royal official's faith was genuinely placed in Jesus (4:50, 53), the invalid man still clung to some "magical" connection between the stirring water and health (v. 7).[27] He apparently thought that a well-timed entry into the pool would guarantee healing. It is interesting, however, that Jesus heals him without the water at all. Jesus commanded the man to simply get up, pick up his mat, and walk (v. 8). Koester thus concludes, "At Bethzatha, Jesus' life-giving word did not work through the water but was an alternative to it."[28]

This joyous occasion for celebration was not met with anticipated exuberance, however. The liberation of the invalid man from his disease was met with frowns from the Jewish religious establishment. The Evangelist adds following the miracle, that the day on which the miracle took place was the Sabbath (v. 9). The Jews[29] reproved the invalid man who has just been healed by saying, "It is the Sabbath; the law forbids you to carry your mat" (v. 10).[30] Following the interrogation by the Jewish

26. The Evangelist uses the term ὑγιής often (5:6, 9, 11, 14, 15) and it seems to be an important term in the story. On a literal level, the term describes physical healing. See BAGD 832, s.v. "ὑγιής." Figuratively, healing the whole man can symbolize God's healing power of the whole man, including his spiritual life (cf. Acts 4:10). See Luck, "ὑγιής," 8:312. Thus, when Jesus asks the invalid man if he wanted to get well, perhaps He was referring to more than just the physical healing.

27. Koester, *Symbolism in the Fourth Gospel*, 172.

28. Ibid.

29. The Greek term for "the Jews" (οἱ Ἰουδαῖοι) in the New Testament may have four different meanings: (1) the entire Jewish people (2:6, 13; 3:1, 25; 4:9, 22; 5:1; 6:4; 7:2; 8:31; 11:55; 18:12, 35; 19:21, 40, 42); (2) the residents of Jerusalem and surrounding territory (11:8, 19, 31, 33, 36, 45, 54; 12:9, 11; 19:20); (3) the people hostile to Jesus (6:41, 52; 8:48, 52, 57; 10:19, 24, 31, 33; 18:20, 38; 19:7, 12, 14); (4) the religious authorities in Jerusalem (1:19; 2:18, 20; 5:10, 15, 16, 18; 7:1, 11, 13, 15; 8:22; 9:18, 22; 13:33; 18:14, 31, 36; 19:31, 38; 20:19). See Bratcher, "'Jews' in the Gospel of John," 401–9. In this case, the "Jews" refers to the religious leaders in Jerusalem.

30. Although no specific law prohibited the carrying of a mat on the Sabbath, the Jews may have had such passages as Jer 17:21–27 and Neh 13:15 in mind. These passages mention general restrictions on the activity of carrying a load. Furthermore, the Mishnah (*Shabbath* 7.2; 10:5) also prohibits someone from transporting an object from one domain to another.

religious leaders (vv. 11–13), once again Jesus took the initiative and found the man." Jesus said to the newly healed man, "See, you are well again. Stop sinning or something worse may happen to you" (v. 14). It is doubtful that Jesus was making a cause-and-effect statement related to the man's sickness. Such a direct correlation between personal sin and sickness was rejected by Jesus elsewhere (cf. 9:3; Luke 13:1–5).[31] It is more likely that Jesus was addressing the eschatological correlation between sin and judgment by the statement "something worse" in His warning to the paralytic.[32] W. H. Harris explains this connection: "To those held in the bondage of death and sin the Son offers life, and the only danger is that an individual will ignore that offer. To do so would be not to trust in the Son. And something worse, condemnation at the Last Judgment (John 5:29) would surely befall such a person."[33] In other words, Jesus was in essence warning the man who has just been healed from his physical sickness that he faces a more urgent issue, namely, his spiritual destiny. Thus, Jesus was demonstrating through this miracle that He has the divine authority to forgive sins.[34]

THE SIGNIFICANCE

This sign-miracle (σημεῖον) clearly reveals Jesus as the divine Son of God (cf. 20:31). On its most obvious level, this miracle demonstrates that Jesus has the divine power to heal a man who had been in his paralytic state for thirty-eight years! To heal someone who had been in such a state for so long would have been humanly impossible. Tenney thus correctly suggests this miracle demonstrates Jesus' power over the ravages of time: "Despite the long period of helplessness, during which his muscles would have become atrophied, he was so completely healed that he put his bedroll on his shoulders and walked away."[35] Whereas Jesus demonstrates His divine authority to heal from a distance in healing the official's son (4:43–54), in this miracle Jesus demonstrates His divine authority to overturn years of physical paralysis.

31. R. E. Brown, *The Gospel According to John (I–XII)*, 208.
32. Borchert, *John 1–11*, 235.
33. W. H. Harris, "Theology of John's Writings," 177.
34. Yee, *Jewish Feasts and the Gospel of John*, 40.
35. Tenney, "Topics from the Gospel of John—Part II," 148.

It becomes quickly apparent, however, that this miracle is intended to communicate a far deeper significance than just Jesus' ability to heal a physical illness. Because, if Jesus' ability to heal physically were His main focus, then He could have (and, should have) healed all the physically disabled bodies lying by the pool.[36] As mentioned previously, in healing the invalid man physically, Jesus was addressing a more significant and urgent spiritual issue. As is confirmed in His discourse immediately following the miracle (5:16–47), Jesus demonstrates His divine prerogative to forgive sin and grant eternal life to those who genuinely believe in His Person: "I tell you the truth, whoever hears my word and believes him who sent me has eternal life and will not be condemned; he has crossed over from death to life" (v. 24). The present tense of the verb describing the possession of eternal life "has" (ἔχει) indicates that it is not merely a future hope but a present reality of the quality of life that Jesus grants to those who believe in Him.[37] Robert Cook explains eternal life this way: "Eternal life is rightly viewed as 'life of the age to come' while being something to be experienced here and now (5:24). This eternal life is based upon a birth 'from above' which enables one to 'see the kingdom of God' already in this life (3:3)."[38] Furthermore, eternal life also has future consequences in that it precludes condemnatory divine judgment.[39] As Morris comments, "To have eternal life now is to be secure throughout eternity."[40] In short, it is a present experience of that reality that will be fully realized in the age to come.

The authority to grant life, along with the authority to forgive sin, reveals Jesus' divine Sonship (John 5:17–18). In the Old Testament the raising of the dead was a divine prerogative and it demonstrates God's sovereignty over life: "Am I God? Can I kill and bring back to life?" (2 Kgs 5:7).[41] In Deuteronomy 32:39 God Himself declares: "See now that I myself am He! There is no god besides me. I put to death and I bring to life, I have wounded and I will heal, and no one can deliver out of my hand." And, elsewhere Hannah also confesses, "The Lord brings death and makes alive; he brings down to the grave and raises up" (1 Sam 2:6).

36. Lockyer, *Miracles of the Bible*, 302.

37. Laney, *John*, 112.

38. Cook, "Eschatology in John's Gospel," 87.

39. Laney, *John*, 112.

40. Morris, *Gospel According to John*, 316.

41. Carson, *Gospel According to John*, 252–53.

The Old Testament Scriptures are clear that only God can give life (Gen 2:7; Job 33:4; Pss. 16:11; 36:9). Thus when Jesus claims that prerogative of Himself, He undoubtedly is asserting Himself as the divine Son of God. As the Father has "life in Himself," indicating that His self-existent life is a source of life to others, Jesus also possesses that same life and thus exercises that divine prerogative Himself (John 5:26; cf. 1:3).

Another aspect of Jesus' deeds that reveals His divine Sonship is judgment. In the Old Testament it is also clear that God alone is called the Judge (Gen 18:25; Judg 11:27), and He alone exercises final judgment (Pss 94:2; 105:7; Isa 2:4; 26:9; Mic 4:3). Because of the relationship between the Father and the Son, the authority to judge has been delegated to the Son by the Father (John 5:22, 27). Jesus Himself says that the divine authority to judge has been given to the Son by the Father because He is the Son of Man (v. 27). This apocalyptic title "Son of Man" (Dan 7:13) points to the eschatological judgment at the resurrection of the dead (John 5:28). And, at this eschatological judgment both the righteous and the wicked will be raised: "Multitudes who sleep in the dust of the earth will awake; some to everlasting life, others to shame and everlasting contempt" (Dan 12:2). Jesus also speaks of two kinds of resurrections: a resurrection to life (cf. John 6:39) and a resurrection to condemnation (John 5:29). The basis of one's destiny in this judgment will be one's deeds, whether good or evil (v. 29). It is to be noted that the deeds of good or evil in the Fourth Gospel correlate with belief or unbelief concerning the Son (cf. 3:18, 36). Carson explains this correlation well: "In the context of the Fourth Gospel, 'those who have done good' are those who have come to the light so that it may be plainly seen that what they have done they have done through God (cf. 3:21). Conversely, 'those who have done evil (things)' 'loved darkness instead of light because their deeds were evil' (3:19). John is not juxtaposing salvation by works with salvation by faith: he will shortly insist, 'The work of God is this: to believe in the one he has sent' (6:29)."[42] In other words, one's deeds "validate or refute" the faith professed (cf. Matt 7:16–18).[43] Morris concurs: "This does not mean that salvation is on the basis of good works, for this very Gospel makes it plain over and over that men

42. Ibid., 258.
43. Laney, *John*, 114.

enter eternal life when they believe on Jesus Christ. But the lives they live form the test of faith they profess."[44]

Although the Son's divine prerogative to judge is ultimately in the future, it also includes present consequences. Believing in the one God has sent results in eternal life here and now: "I tell you the truth, whoever hears my word and believes him who sent me has eternal life and will not be condemned; he has crossed over from death to life" (John 5:24). Conversely, rejecting the Son has present implications as well as future consequences: "Whoever believes in him is not condemned, but whoever does not believe stands condemned already because he has not believed in the name of God's one and only Son" (3:18). The Evangelist also echoes Jesus' words later: "Whoever believes in the Son has eternal life, but whoever rejects the Son will not see life, for God's wrath remains on him" (3:36). In sum, then, as both the life-giver and the Judge, the Son has the right to grant life to those who believe in His Person or to dispense judgment to those who reject the offer of life available through Him.

Although the divine Sonship of Jesus is the primary focus of this miracle and its attendant discourse, to be sure, there are also significant messianic implications. For instance, the miracle of Jesus healing the lame man provides yet another aspect of the Messiah's work in His coming kingdom, namely, the healing of the blind, the dumb, the mute, and the lame (cf. Isa 35:5–6; 61:1). Laney perceptively observes, "This miracle serves as another illustration of Jesus' rolling back the effects of sin and His foreshadowing in a small but significant way the characteristics of the future messianic kingdom."[45] In contrast to the Jewish religious leaders, who because of their blindness and pride could not see their own spiritual deformity and thus rebuke Jesus for having compassion on the social outcasts, Jesus embraces those shunned by their society. The kingdom of God will not include the Jews merely on the basis of their physical lineage (i.e., Nicodemus), but only on the basis of faith in the Messiah, the same Messiah who will extend His mercies to the poor and the sick.

The fact that Jesus chose to heal the paralytic on the Sabbath has significant messianic implications as well. On numerous occasions that Jesus performs miracles of healing, the gospel writers note that the mira-

---

44. Morris, *Gospel According to John*, 321–22.

45. Laney, *John*, 105–6.

cles took place on the Sabbath (Mark 3:1–6; Luke 13:10–17; 14:1–6; John 5:1–18; 9:1–14). For example, Jesus healed on the Sabbath in the Lucan account of a Jewish woman who had been crippled by a demonic spirit for eighteen years (13:10–13). The religious leaders became indignant of the fact that Jesus healed her on the Sabbath (v. 14). Observing the hypocrisy of the religious leaders who themselves work on the Sabbath in order to feed their animals (v. 15), Jesus rebuked them by saying, "Then should not this woman, a daughter of Abraham, whom Satan has kept bound for eighteen long years, be set free on the Sabbath day from what bound her?" (v. 16). Jesus' statement of freeing the woman on the Sabbath seems to correlate deliverance with the Sabbath day.

The Sabbath is intricately related to the nation Israel. It was given only to the nation of Israel to observe and is therefore a Jewish institution. The Sabbath came to be associated as a sign of the Mosaic covenant (cf. Exod 31:12–18). Although the Sabbath is a weekly feast, its principles carried over into Israel's observance of the Sabbath year (Deut 15:2) and the year of Jubilee (Lev. 25:8–13). In Isaiah, the year of Jubilee became associated with the eternal rest of the future eschatological age (Isa 58; 61:1–3). Because the Sabbath observance was given to the nation Israel with the giving of the law, it was operative only as long as the law was in effect. Thus, at the death of Christ the Sabbath is no longer in effect, being part of the Mosaic law. The Sabbath will again be instituted in the future, however, in the Great Tribulation (Matt 24:20) and in the millennial age (Isa 66:23; Ezek 46:1). The reinstitution of the Sabbath in the future will fulfill the typological role of rest in the messianic kingdom (Ps 95; Heb 3:7—4:13; John 5:17; Lev 23).[46] Saucy is thus correct to conclude, "Jesus' miracles prefigure the eternal rest and release sought for in the new sabbatical age."[47]

By healing the paralytic on the Sabbath, then, Jesus was presenting Himself as the promised Messiah who will inaugurate His anticipated kingdom and finally provide rest for the nation. In healing the invalid man on the Sabbath, Jesus was probably demonstrating the obsolescence of Judaism. The crippled man therefore perhaps ironically symbolizes the Jewish nation which could not see its own spiritual deformity as a result of the crippling system of Judaism. It is perhaps conceivable, then, that the thirty-eight-year reference that indicated the length of time

46. Griffith, "Eschatological Significance of the Sabbath," 319.

47. Saucy, "Miracles and Jesus' Proclamation," 288.

the lame man had been in his state, could have a dual meaning. The thirty-eight-year time reference could also symbolically represent the time Israel spent in the wilderness for disobedience and thus failing to enter into the promised land (cf. Deut 2:14).[48] Although many scholars dismiss the symbolic meaning of the number,[49] considering the context of the miracle and being cognizant of the Evangelist's affinity with dual meanings throughout his Gospel, however, this suggestion does present a possibility. In short, Jesus was demonstrating to the nation of Israel that just as their forefathers failed to enter the promised land because of their lack of belief in Yahweh, the only way to enter that promised rest is through their faith in the Messiah. It is significant to keep in mind, however, that eschatological truth in John is primarily christological, that is, to present the Person of Jesus as the promised Messiah.

CONCLUSION

The miracle of Jesus healing the paralytic at the Pool of Bethesda and its attendant discourse reveal Jesus as the divine Son of God. As the Son of God Jesus has the divine power to heal a man who had been physically lame for thirty-eight miserable years. His authority to heal physical paralysis demonstrates a far deeper significance, however. Jesus has the divine authority to forgive sin and grant eternal life to those who would believe in Him. Furthermore, He also has the divine authority to judge in the eschatological judgment. Thus, as both the life-giver and Judge, the Son has the right to grant life to those who believe in Him or dispense judgment to those who reject the offer of life available through the Son. In addition, while this miracle primarily demonstrates Jesus' divine Sonship, it also reveals Jesus as the promised Messiah of the Hebrew Scriptures. His healing the paralytic man provides yet another aspect of the Messiah's work in His coming kingdom. And, by healing the paralytic on the Sabbath, Jesus was demonstrating to the nation Israel that He is the promised one who will inaugurate the kingdom and provide Sabbath rest for the nation. However, the promised eschatological rest can be experienced through belief in Him, here and now.

48. Jones, *Symbol of Water*, 127–28.
49. R. E. Brown, *Gospel According to John (I–XII)*, 207.

8

The Fourth Sign: Feeding the Five Thousand (6:1–15)

INTRODUCTION

THE OPENING WORDS OF the chapter, "After these things" (μετὰ ταῦτα), indicate a shift in the setting of the Gospel narrative as well as the obvious temporal change (6:1). The Evangelist uses this phrase often in his Gospel to inform the reader that a change is taking place in the story (cf. 2:12; 3:22; 4:43; 5:1). Moloney points out that the expression introduces a new place of setting (the Sea of Galilee), a new set of characters (a multitude and the disciples), and a change in time (the Passover).[1] This setting will remain the same throughout the entire chapter, including the immediately subsequent miracle of Jesus walking on the Sea of Galilee (John 6:16–21) and the accompanying discourse of Jesus on His miracle of feeding the five thousand (vv. 22–71). All three occasions occur on or around the Sea of Galilee, all three occasions involve both the multitude and the disciples, and all three occasions take place near the Passover.[2] In fact, it is really the Passover Feast that ties the three pericopes together in this chapter, both literarily and thematically. Literarily, the Festival Cycle (5:1—10:42) now moves into the second stage, following the third sign-miracle that took place on the Sabbath in John 5.[3] Thematically, all three pericopes in this chapter reveal the Person of Jesus as the divine Messiah from the background of

1. Moloney, *Signs and Shadows*, 30.

2. The only exception to this common setting is that the miracle of Jesus walking on the sea does not involve the multitude of people, but includes only the disciples. Bock notes that the Sea of Galilee was also called the Sea of Tiberias by John's time, named after a city created on its shores in AD 26. *Jesus According to Scripture: Restoring*, 446–47.

3. Borchert, *John 1–11*, 249.

the Passover and the exodus events.[4] Borchert explains this overarching
theme of the chapter this way:

> In this context reminiscent of Israel's first generation, the cross-
> ing of the sea (6:1) and the coming of the crowd out to a lonely
> arid mountain region (6:3) formed a picture-perfect setting for
> considering how Jesus could be related to the stories of the exo-
> dus. Therefore it should be no surprise that the stories of Jesus
> in this chapter deal with a miraculous feeding and the control of
> the sea. Moses had been mentioned as a witness in the conclud-
> ing arguments of the last chapter (5:45–46). Now the evangelist
> introduces the New Moses in the wilderness. . . . Passover epito-
> mizes God's claiming and releasing of his people as well as his
> preservation of the people by supplying them with food and res-
> cuing them from the threatening sea. Passover is a multifaceted
> identifying celebration, and the evangelist knew it well.[5]

Thus, Borchert is right to conclude that the Fourth Evangelist's
references to the Passover Feast are meant to be more than just time
indicators. In this chapter, that is especially the case.

THE SETTING

The setting of this miracle is described in the first four verses of the
chapter (6:1–4). These opening verses provide the following details for
the miracle: who, where, when, and why.[6] These verses describe Jesus'
actions as the disciples and a multitude of people gathered on the moun-
tainside by the Sea of Galilee when the Passover Feast was approaching.[7]
The Evangelist also described the reason the crowd of people was following Jesus: "because they saw the miraculous signs he had performed on
the sick" (v. 2). As Culpepper correctly points out, however, the emphasis
is that the Passover Feast was approaching (v. 4).[8] The Passover Feast in
view here is probably referring to the year AD 32, just one full year be-

---

4. Borchert, "Passover and the Narrative Cycles," 309.

5. Borchert, *John 1–11*, 249.

6. Moloney, *Gospel of John*, 195.

7. Ibid. Moloney also suggests that the use of the definite article "the mountain"
(εἰς τὸ ὄρος) may be a first hint that Jesus is adopting a position parallel to Moses who
received the law on a mountain (cf. Exod 19).

8. Culpepper, *Gospel and Letters of John*, 154–55.

fore Christ's crucifixion.[9] This would put this miracle near the beginning of Jesus' third year of ministry. Dwight Pentecost explains the change in the nature of Jesus' earthly ministry during His third and final year: "The accusation by the leaders that Jesus was demon-possessed (Matt 12:24) and the death of John the Baptist (Matt 14) brought about a turning point in the life of Christ. He no longer pursued a public ministry but rather devoted Himself to teaching the Twelve how to continue the ministry that the Father entrusted to Him."[10] The ministry of Jesus and the miracles He performed were no longer for the nation primarily but more so for the benefit of His disciples, in order to prepare them for ministry even in His absence. Although Jesus certainly did continue to perform miracles during His final year, they were done so in the midst of much opposition and unbelief. This miracle of Jesus feeding the five thousand is a case in point.

THE SIGN

While the miracle was performed to satisfy the physical hunger of the crowd, Jesus was primarily instructing the Twelve concerning the nature of ministry they would eventually face.[11] This is evident by the exchanges that take place between Jesus and His disciples before He performs the miracle (John 6:5–9). Jesus first asked Philip, "Where shall we buy bread for these people to eat?" (v. 5)[12] The Evangelist informed the reader, however, that Jesus asked the question to test Philip's faith (v. 6). Jesus already knew what He was going to do. Philip's answer, along with Andrew's response, revealed however that the disciples could not see the situation beyond the natural possibilities (vv. 7–9). Jesus, in His omniscience created the perfect scenario in which to demonstrate His omnipotence.

The miracle is described in verses 10–13. Having instructed the disciples to seat the multitude, Jesus provided the bread, and the people ate as much as they wanted. The Evangelist recorded that there were about five thousand "men" (οἱ ἄνδρες), which probably means that there were

9. Hoehner, *Chronological Aspects*, 143. I am following Hoehner's chronology of dating Christ's crucifixion on AD 33, after a three and one-half year earthly ministry.

10. Pentecost, *Words and Works of Jesus Christ*, 231.

11. Köstenberger, *Encountering John*, 99.

12. Moloney suggests that Jesus' question is meant to parallel the question that Moses asked Yahweh in the desert: "Where am I to get the meat to give all these people?" (Num 11:13). *Gospel of John*, 197.

considerably more people who benefited from Jesus' provision. The Matthean account of the miracle adds that this number did not include the women and children (14:21). W. H. Harris describes the enormity of this miracle this way: "The fourth sign-miracle, the multiplication of the bread (John 6:1–15), brings the reader face-to-face with the supernatural again, but this time on a far 'grander' scale than the changing of water into wine at Cana, the healing of the nobleman's son at Cana, or the cure of the paralytic at Bethesda in Jerusalem."[13] The people ate until they were "completely satisfied" (ἐνεπλήσθησαν). Laney humorously yet correctly points out, "No one was left thinking, *Another piece of bread would be nice.*"[14]

Moloney suggests that the promise of Psalm 23:1 is fulfilled: "The LORD is my shepherd, I shall not want."[15] The point of the miracle is that Jesus provided abundantly. This is attested by the fact that twelve full baskets were left over (John 6:12–13).

The fact that there were twelve full baskets left over seems to be significant, in that all four of the gospel writers explicitly mentioned it (cf. Matt 14:20; Mark 6:43; Luke 9:17). Carson suggests, for instance, that the twelve baskets signify that "the Lord has enough to supply the needs of the twelve tribes of Israel."[16] While this is certainly possible, it is more likely that Jesus was demonstrating to His disciples that as the divine Messiah, He is able to provide for their needs abundantly.[17] What's more, the ministry of "feeding" the people will characterize the disciples' ministry when Jesus is glorified. Pentecost explains the principle this way:

> Jesus was primarily instructing the Twelve concerning the nature of the ministry for which they were being prepared. They would face multitudes who were shepherdless sheep and starved spiritually. It would be their responsibility to "give them something to eat." The followers of Christ do not have the ability of them-

13. W. H. Harris, "Theology of John's Writings," 177.

14. Laney, *John*, 106.

15. Moloney, *Gospel of John*, 198. Moloney also interestingly points out that the Evangelist's mention of the grass recalls Ps 23:2: "He makes me lie down in green pastures."

16. Carson, *Gospel According to John*, 271.

17. As Keener notes in his commentary, the number twelve simply underlines afresh the abundance of the miracle and that there is no need to allegorize the baskets. He further emphasizes that twelve is the maximum number of baskets that these disciples could have reasonably carried. *Gospel of John*, 1:669.

selves to meet the spiritual need of the people, but when they make available what they have to the Lord, the Lord can take it and multiply it and use them to minister to the multitudes. The ministry belongs to the Lord, but it is carried on through His disciples as His agents. It is not what the disciples have that makes them good shepherds. Rather, it is what they give of themselves to the Lord that He can use to meet people's needs. To discharge the ministry entrusted to them, disciples must depend on Him and make themselves available to Him. Only in this way can they be shepherds to the hungry sheep.[18]

Tenney concurs in saying, "Quietly but effectively Jesus enlisted the aid of the disciples in the enterprise so that they might realize the full extent of His powers."[19]

Although Jesus may have been successful in teaching His disciples an invaluable lesson through this "field-trip" miracle, the response of the multitude was a different matter altogether (John 6:14–15). The witness of the miracle led the people to a profession of faith, albeit a superficial one: "Surely this is the Prophet who is to come into the world" (v. 14). Their reference to "the Prophet who is to come into the world" is probably to the eschatological figure of a Moses-like prophet (Deut 18:15–19), although Jewish messianic expectations in the first century were diverse.[20] Surely Jesus' provision of bread in the wilderness area prompted the Jewish crowd to think of Moses's role in providing manna.[21] The people must have reasoned that since Moses had fed the people in the wilderness and also delivered them out of Egyptian bondage, Jesus could also lead the nation out of their Roman bondage since He also fed the people.[22] Besides, there was a first-century Jewish expectation that the Messiah would renew the miracle of manna to mark the opening of the messianic era: "And it will happen at that time the treasury of manna will come down again from on high, and they will eat of it in those years because these are they who will have arrived at the consummation of time" (2 Bar 29:8).[23] The Jewish crowd may even have had in

18. Pentecost, *Words and Works of Jesus Christ*, 233.

19. Tenney, "Topics from the Gospel of John—Part II," 149.

20. Beasley-Murray, *John*, 88–89. For diversity of opinion concerning the Jewish messianic expectations, see also Meeks, *Prophet-King*, 91–98.

21. Carson, *Gospel According to John*, 271.

22. Meeks, *Prophet-King*, 1–2.

23. Klijn, "2 Baruch," 630–31.

mind passages like Psalm 132:15: "I will abundantly bless her provision; I will satisfy her needy with bread."[24] This miracle, which was clearly perceived to be a messianic miracle by the Jews, ignited in the crowd the hopes of deliverance from their oppressive plight. Laney explains the scenario this way:

> The Roman domination of Palestine in the first century kindled strong nationalistic hopes among the Jews. Although there was no consistent concept of "the anointed one" at the time of Jesus, the Jews of His day longed for a dynamic and powerful figure who could lead them in their political struggle against Rome. Suffering so long under Roman rule, the Jewish people must have been eager for an anointed king from their own ranks. Jesus had the qualities and credentials that commended Him to leadership, and the people decided to "make Him king by force." By popular demand they intended to force kingship upon Him.[25]

However, Jesus rejects this superficial offer of kingship (John 6:15). Moloney correctly concludes, "Jesus' gift of bread has led to the arousal of a messianic expectation that he is not prepared to accept."[26] Moloney also says elsewhere, "Jesus is not prepared to accept their acclamation or their desire to impose their messianic criteria on him."[27] Besides, it was clear to Jesus that the crowd was only interested in crowning Him for physical benefit (cf. 6:26). It became quickly apparent that the multitude's faith has not progressed much from verse 2: "A great crowd of people followed Jesus because they saw the miraculous signs he had performed on the sick."

THE SIGNIFICANCE

The significance of this miracle is attested by the fact that it was included by all four of the gospel writers and that it was the only miracle recorded by all four evangelists other than the resurrection of Jesus. On its most obvious level, this miracle demonstrates that Jesus is the Creator who is capable of commanding into existence whatever He wills through His authoritative word. This miracle validates the Evangelist's earlier asser-

---

24. This messianic psalm anticipates the eschatological kingdom of the Messiah in fulfillment of the Davidic covenant (2 Sam 7:12–16).

25. Laney, *John*, 123.

26. Moloney, *Signs and Shadows*, 37.

27. Moloney, *Gospel of John*, 199.

tion made in the Prologue that Jesus is the Creator: "Through him all things were made, without him nothing was made that has been made" (1:3; cf. Col 1:16). As Jesus was able to command into existence the best quality wine from water to satisfy all the guests at a wedding in Cana (cf. John 2:1–11), here Jesus was able to abundantly satisfy, with bread, the hunger of five thousand men, possibly even up to ten to fifteen thousand people. The miracle in essence demonstrated His deity (cf. 20:31). And, as the divine Creator, Jesus is able to provide for the needs of people.

The accompanying "Bread of Life" discourse (6:22–71) illustrated, however, that Jesus' miracle of feeding the five thousand had far deeper christological significance. Like the other sign-miracles in the Fourth Gospel, this miracle was intended to primarily reveal the Person of Jesus. It is evident that the multitude that witnessed Jesus' miracle did not comprehend its meaning beyond the natural and physical realm. When the multitude came looking for Jesus on the other side of the Sea of Galilee some time after the miracle, Jesus rebuked them saying, "Truly, truly, I say to you, you seek Me, not because you saw signs, but because you ate of the loaves, and were filled" (v. 26). As Borchert correctly points out, "They failed to recognize the sign in the miracle. The meaning of 'sign' in this Gospel is that it points beyond the physical, concrete reality to the reality of revelation."[28] The familiar phrase "Truly, truly I say to you" (Ἀμὴν ἀμὴν λέγω ὑμῖν) is a formula frequently used by Jesus to announce a crucial idea in light of the misunderstanding of truth on the part of His audience (cf. 1:1; 3:3; 5:19). Instead of following Jesus because He provided physical food, the multitude should have followed Him because He offers food that endures, namely, eternal life (6:27).[29]

The theme of "eternal life" (ζωὴν αἰώνιον) once again takes center stage in Jesus' discourse evidenced by the fact that the words "life" (ζωὴν), "living" (ζῶν), or "will live" (ζήσει), occur at least eighteen times just in this pericope alone (vv. 22–71). As the "Bread of God" (ὁ ἄρτος τοῦ θεοῦ) who comes down from heaven, Jesus gives eternal life to the

---

28. Borchert, *John 1–11*, 262.

29. Barrett thinks the whole discourse is summarized in these two verses (vv. 26–27): "The main theme is simply given out. Men are foolishly concerned not with the truth, but with food for their bodies. They must learn that there is bread which conveys not earthly but eternal life, and earn it; yet they will not earn it, for it is the gift of the Son of man, whom God has avouched. The whole discourse is summarized here. Jesus is the Son of man, and it is in communion with him that men have eternal life." *Gospel According to St. John*, 282.

world (vv. 33). This phrase "comes down" (καταβαίνων) is also a common phrase in this discourse, and is used in reference to the incarnation of Jesus (cf. 1:14).[30] The "Bread of God" who comes down from heaven gives life to the world. This is reminiscent of the title bestowed on Jesus by the Samaritans, whom they referred to as "the Savior of the world" (4:42). As the "Bread of Life" (ὁ ἄρτος τῆς ζωῆς), Jesus is the life-giving Son of God who grants eternal life to those who believe in Him.[31] Or, as W. H. Harris observes, Jesus is the giver *and* sustainer of eternal life, similar to the "living water" imagery in John 4.[32]

As it has been the emphasis throughout the Fourth Gospel, while eternal life is a present existence given to those who believe in Jesus here and now, it is also a foretaste of the future reality that will ultimately be realized in glory. The future aspect of eternal life is also certainly emphasized here in this passage, as Jesus promises to raise up on the last day (ἀναστήσω αὐτὸ ἐν τῇ ἐσχάτῃ ἡμέρᾳ) those who have believed in Him and thus possess eternal life (6:39). The promise to "raise up on the last day" is reiterated three other times in Jesus' discourse (cf. vv. 40, 44, 54). As a result of Jesus' "coming down" from heaven and becoming the sacrificial lamb for the sin of the world, He is able to grant eternal life to those who believe in Him, and He will also raise them up at the last day.[33]

The backdrop behind this particular miracle clearly reveals the messianic motif that is woven into the fabric of all seven of the sign-miracles in the Fourth Gospel. Just as this miracle revealed the divine Sonship of Jesus, it also demonstrated His messiahship (cf. 20:30–31). The Passover background behind Jesus' miracle and His subsequent discourse is unmistakably tied to Israel's deliverance from the Egyptian

30. The phrase is used seven times in Jesus' discourse (6:33, 38, 41, 42, 50, 51, 58) and is probably one of John's many double meanings in his Gospel, referring to both the bread that came down during the wilderness experience and Jesus' incarnation.

31. Jesus' self-declaration "I Am the Bread of life" (Ἐγώ εἰμι ὁ ἄρτος τῆς ζωῆς) in verse 35 is the first of seven "I Am" statements with a predicate. The other six are (with slight variations, depending on the translation): I Am the Light of the World (8:12); I Am the Gate or the Door (10:7, 9); I Am the Good Shepherd (10:11, 14); I Am the Resurrection and the Life (11:25); I Am the Way, the Truth, and the Life (14:6); I Am the True Vine (15:1, 5). These will be discussed more in detail in the fifth sign-miracle.

32. W. H. Harris, "Theology of John's Writings," 177.

33. Note the irony in this passage of Jesus' "coming down" (καταβαίνων) to grant eternal life and His "raising up" (ἀναστήσω) in the eschatological resurrection those who believe in Him.

bondage under Moses's leadership.[34] Koester's description of Moses's miracles in the Exodus account in comparison to Jesus' miracle in John 6 is strikingly similar:

> Moses was the most important miracle-working prophet in Israel's history. There had been no one like him "for all the signs and the wonders which the Lord sent him to do in the land of Egypt" (Deut 34:11). Moses' "signs" included miraculous demonstrations of divine authority (Exod 4:8–9, 28–31) and the plagues inflicted on the Egyptians (7:3; 8:23; 10:1–2). The last and greatest of these "signs" (11:9–10 LXX) was the slaying of the firstborn of every household in Egypt, which was commemorated each year at Passover, when unleavened bread was eaten (12:17). Moses also worked wonders in the wilderness. When the people murmured because they had nothing to eat, God told Moses, "Behold, I will rain bread from heaven for you" (16:4). In the morning the people discovered something on the ground that was white and tasted like wafers made with honey; they called it manna (16:14, 31). This "bread from heaven" continued to appear throughout the forty years Israel wandered in the desert. After entering the promised land, they celebrated the Passover on the plains of Jericho. The next day the manna ceased, "and the people of Israel had manna no more, but ate the fruit of the land of Canaan that year (Josh 5:12).[35]

By performing His miracle of feeding the five thousand, Jesus clearly intended to reveal His messianic identity, for there are indications in the Scriptures that signs like those of the Mosaic period would accompany those of the messianic age.[36] As the Hebrew prophets declared long ago, signs and wonders, like in the days of Moses, will characterize God's deliverance for Israel at the Messiah's advent (Mic 7:15; Isa 48:20–21). For instance, the prophet Micah records God's promise of future deliverance to His people in the eschatological kingdom: "As in the days when

---

34. For a good discussion on the significance of the Passover Feast behind this miracle, see Borchert, *John 1–11*, 249–50; idem, "Passover and the Narrative Cycles," 303–16.

35. Koester, *Symbolism in the Fourth Gospel*, 90–91. Köstenberger asserts correctly that in keeping with Jewish expectation, that "Jesus is presented as the antitype to Moses: he is not merely used by God to provide bread for his people, but is himself sent by God as the life-giving 'bread' who gives life for the world." *John*, 196.

36. Koester, *Symbolism in the Fourth Gospel*, 91.

you came out from the land of Egypt, I will show you miracles" (7:15).[37] And, judging from the fact that the multitude designated Jesus as the eschatological figure of a Moses-like prophet (Deut 18:15–19) and tried to make Him king by force, they apparently did make this connection (John 6:14–15).

Jesus' revelation of His own messianic identity went far beyond what the multitude could understand, however. While the people could not see beyond a political Messiah who could bring them physical relief and provide for their physical needs, Jesus was addressing their spiritual need for the eternal life that He offers. Tenney describes how people just could not relate to Jesus' miracle and His message: "The discourse on the Bread of Life spoke of spiritual not material sustenance, and His emphasis on the resurrection at the last day (John 6:54) must have seemed totally irrelevant to them. Furthermore, His declaration, 'Truly, truly, I say to you, unless you eat the flesh of the Son of Man and drink His blood, you have no life in yourselves' (6:53), mystified them. Even many of His disciples left Him because they could not understand the meaning of His words. The interpretation of the sign which had been given to demonstrate His sufficiency for human need proved to be an insurmountable obstacle to their faith."[38]

Although the multitude was expecting a political Messiah who would bring them temporal relief and provide for their materialistic needs, Jesus was presenting Himself as the divine Messiah who through His sacrificial death provides eternal life to those who believe in Him (v. 51). While the multitude expected Jesus to establish His kingdom by overthrowing the Romans and providing for their physical needs, Jesus was not proclaiming a kingdom that is materialistic in nature. As Homer Kent correctly says, "Although the Messianic Kingdom would be a literal kingdom, its basis was a spiritual revolution in which men's hearts would first be changed and in which perfect righteousness would prevail

---

37. As mentioned previously, the first-century Jewish noncanonical writings also described the Messiah's kingdom that will be characterized by signs and wonders similar to the Mosaic period: "And it will happen at that time the treasury of manna will come down again from on high, and they will eat of it in those years because these are they who will have arrived at the consummation of time" (2 Bar 29:8).

38. Tenney, "Topics from the Gospel of John—Part II," 149.

(cf. John 3:3)."[39] In sum, then, as the "Bread of Life" Jesus is the giver and sustainer of eternal life, both now and forever.[40]

CONCLUSION

The Passover Feast provided the backdrop for Jesus' two sign-miracles (σημεῖα) in John 6 and His "Bread of Life" discourse sandwiched in between them. The miracle of feeding the five thousand (6:1–15) during the Passover brought natural comparison of Jesus with another "sign" worker, Moses, who predicted that a prophet like him would arise (Deut 18:15). People reasoned that since Moses had fed the people in the wilderness and also delivered them out of Egyptian bondage, Jesus could also lead the nation out of their Roman bondage since He also fed the people. The Passover background of this miracle was unmistakably tied to Israel's deliverance from Egyptian bondage under Moses's leadership. Moses, as the prophet of God, also worked sign-miracles to demonstrate divine authority (Deut 34:11). Apart from the signs he performed in Egypt, he also performed great signs in the wilderness for the benefit of the nation. Throughout the wilderness dwelling, Israel received "bread from heaven" that fed the nation. Jesus' miracle of feeding the five thousand was a "sign" to reveal His messianic identity, for there are indications in the Scriptures that the messianic age would be accompanied by signs like those of the Mosaic period. As the Hebrew prophets declared long ago, God's deliverance for Israel at the Messiah's advent will be characterized by signs and wonders that was present when Moses led the nation out of Egypt (Mic 7:15; Isa 48:20–21). The feeding of the multitudes thus anticipated the day when God will abundantly provide for His people in the eschatological banquet.

---

39. Kent, *Light in the Darkness*, 102.
40. W. H. Harris, "Theology of John's Writings," 177.

9

The Fifth Sign: Walking on the Sea (6:16–21)

INTRODUCTION

THE SIGN OF JESUS walking on the Sea of Galilee shared the same setting with both His previous miracle of feeding the five thousand (6:1–15) and the accompanying Bread of Life discourse (6:22–71). As mentioned previously, this miracle was also closely related to the Passover background and the exodus motif. Borchert aptly describes the common setting behind these two miracles of Jesus and His following discourse: "The Passover is again moved to center stage (6:4) and linked with two signs (6:5–21) which point back to the two great events from the Exodus: God's control of the sea and God's provision of manna. The dialogue on bread which follows, however, moves the reader's attention away from manna per se to the question of Jesus' origin and his purpose in giving himself as bread for the life of the world (6:38 and 41–42 and 51)—namely the imminent self-sacrifice of Jesus (his flesh and blood; 6:51–58). He is the bread from heaven and his death is that means which provides life for the world."[1] Borchert also correctly points out elsewhere that God's provision of food and water is indelibly attached to Israel's history (cf. Ps 78:13–30), and that these two symbols are especially woven into the fabric of these two stories.[2] Therefore, although this miracle of Jesus walking on the sea may appear out of place initially, it fits rather neatly in the chapter both literarily and thematically.[3]

1. Borchert, "Passover and the Narrative Cycles," 309–10.
2. Borchert, *John 1–11*, 249.
3. R. E. Brown, *Gospel According to John (I–XII)*, 255. Brown also sees the Passover background and the exodus motif in these miracles: "Thus, there are OT passages, particularly among those dealing with the Exodus, that help to explain why the episode of

THE SETTING

The sign took place immediately following Jesus' previous sign of feeding the five thousand. Jesus had just escaped the people who intended to make Him into a political king by force for their self-serving interests, and thus He had withdrawn to a mountain by Himself (John 6:14-15). The synoptic gospel writers emphasized that Jesus went up on the mountain by Himself to pray (Matt 14:23; Mark 6:46). They also added that Jesus had specifically instructed the disciples to get into the boat and go on ahead of Him to the other side of the sea, while He dismissed the crowd (Matt 14:22; Mark 6:45). Mark alone noted, however, that as the disciples got onto the lake, the sun went down and the wind picked up, and Jesus was up in the hills praying and He saw them in their toil against the wind (Mark 6:45–48). Laney describes the dangerous situation in which the disciples found themselves: "The Sea of Galilee is usually a very calm body of water during the morning hours. In the afternoon, however, the lake is often stirred up by the Mediterranean winds that funnel through the valleys of Galilee and swoop down upon the placid water. Particularly stormy weather can make the Sea of Galilee look like a boiling cauldron. Such were the conditions as the disciples rowed against the wind toward Capernaum."[4]

It was not just the strong wind and the waves that terrified the disciples, however. It was also dark. While all three evangelists emphasized that it was "evening time" (ὀψία) (Matt 14:23; Mark 6:47; John 6:16), John alone added the fact that it was "dark" (σκοτία), and that Jesus had not yet come to them (v. 17). While darkness certainly does indicate the absence of light on a literal level, the Evangelist's affinity for double meanings in His Gospel leads us to believe that he intended to communicate a deeper symbolic meaning (cf. 3:2; 13:30). Carson correctly points out that there is a linkage between the darkness of night and the absence of Jesus.[5] Jesus created yet another perfect opportunity to reveal His Person to His disciples who will carry on His ministry in His absence, even in the midst of fierce opposition from the world (cf. John 14–17).

Jesus' walking on the sea may have fitted in with the general Passover motif of ch. vi of John and thus have stayed in close association with the multiplication."

4. Laney, *John*, 124–25.

5. Carson, *Gospel According to John*, 274.

THE SIGN

The sign of Jesus walking on the Sea of Galilee was the most "private" among the Johannine sign-miracles, in that only His disciples witnessed it. This miracle is sandwiched between the previous miracle of Jesus feeding the five thousand (6:1–15) and His Bread of Life discourse (6:22–71), so that it appears to be a two-part instruction for the disciples. The fearful situation that the disciples found themselves in was meant to symbolize not only the turmoil and disillusionment they must have been feeling in their hearts, but also the hostile reality that they would soon face. Laney perceptively describes what the disciples must have been experiencing in their hearts and why they needed to be reassured by their master: "The miracle of Jesus walking on the Sea of Galilee was intended as an encouragement to the disciples, who had just seen Jesus reject an offer of kingship. Recognition of His royal, messianic Person by the Jews was what they had been working for. But Jesus had refused the offer. The twelve may have been wondering, *Have we been mistaken? Have we put our faith in the wrong person?* Jesus answered such questions and strengthened their faith through the miraculous sign that followed."[6] The disciples also needed to be prepared for the turbulent times that lay ahead of them in the Lord's absence. Tenney insightfully describes why Jesus needed to teach His beloved disciples this invaluable object-lesson: "Ahead of them loomed greater dangers than the storm: the rising enmity of the Jewish hierarchy; the doubts and fears engendered by misunderstanding; the collapse of their expectations of an immediate kingdom; and the bewilderment that would accompany Jesus' departure from them. He wanted them to learn that He was Master of the forces of nature and that He could avert what seemed to be inevitable peril. His presence would be the permanent guarantee of their safety."[7]

Coming on the heels of Jesus' previous miracle of feeding the five thousand (6:1–15), it becomes evident what the Master's two-fold instruction intended to communicate. Opposition and hardship from the world of darkness will characterize the disciples' ministry of feeding the people by offering the words of life. Just as the miracle of feeding the five thousand revealed that Jesus is able to multiply whatever the disciples offer Him in obedience unto His glory, this miracle revealed that hard-

6. Laney, *John*, 124.
7. Tenney, "Topics from the Gospel of John—Part II," 150.

ship and opposition, even hatred from the world, will characterize this glorious ministry. But in the midst of their terrifying situations, Jesus' presence will strengthen and guide them. As Blum correctly concludes, "The two signs on the land and lake reveal Jesus as the Provider of 'bread' which gives life and as the Savior who intercedes for and protects his own. He intervenes in their times of trouble and brings them to safety."[8] Pentecost's summary of this miracle insightfully clarifies Jesus' intended object lesson for the disciples: "This incident was designed to reveal to these men that obedience to Christ does not remove all obstacles to the completion of His will. When the obstacles come, even though disciples may do their utmost, they cannot overcome the obstacles themselves. But Christ is cognizant of all difficulties. He is present with His own in their problems. Trials must be born in faith. The faith that first prompted a disciple to obedience must persist throughout the course of events involved in obedience to the will of God."[9] The strength and comfort that the disciples will have in the terrifying situations, however, will depend on their perspective of who Jesus is. And this sign is designed to reveal just who Jesus is.

THE SIGNIFICANCE

The sign of Jesus walking on the Sea of Galilee reveals first and foremost Jesus' Person as the divine Son of God and the promised Messiah. While many have characterized this sign as a nature-miracle because of the synoptic accounts' emphasis on Jesus calming the storm, it should be observed that the Fourth Evangelist does not even explicitly mention such an act of Jesus, though it is certainly implied.[10] The main focus of the miracle is the divine name by which Jesus identifies Himself to the disciples, namely as the "I Am" (Ἐγώ εἰμι). Although some interpret this expression as a mere statement of His self-identification, "It is I" (cf. 6:20), considering the use of the " I Am" (Ἐγώ εἰμι) expressions throughout this Gospel in revealing the Person of Jesus, it is possible that the expression reveals the deity of Jesus.[11] Furthermore, given the

---

8. Blum, "John," 294.

9. Pentecost, *Words and Works of Jesus Christ*, 235.

10. R. E. Brown, *Gospel According to John (I–XII)*, 254.

11. Barrett, for instance, believes that the expression "I Am" is just a statement of self-identification: "In this passage it is probable that ἐγώ εἰμι means simply "It is I." *Gospel According to St. John*, 281. See also Carson, *Gospel According John*, 275. He also believes it is probably just a self-identifying statement.

Passover background and the exodus motif throughout this whole chapter, it is entirely probable that Jesus is identifying Himself as the very God who revealed Himself to Moses (cf. Exod 3:14, LXX). W. H. Harris believes that the reason why this miracle interjects Jesus' miraculous feeding account (John 6:1–15) and His Bread of Life discourse (6:22–71) is to prepare the reader that Jesus is the one who bears the divine name, because Jesus soon thereafter identifies Himself as the "Bread of life" by using the expression "I Am" (6:35, 41, 48, 51).[12] In short, in identifying Himself with the expression "I Am," it is possible, even probable, that Jesus was revealing His deity to the disciples.[13]

The command "Don't be afraid" (μὴ φοβεῖσθε) that accompanied Jesus' expression of His divine name, must have alerted the disciples that they were witnessing a theophany. In the OT, the expression "Don't be afraid" often accompanies the appearance of God/the Angel of the Lord (cf. Gen 15:1; 26:24; 46:3; Isa 41:13–14; 43:1, 3). Besides, the disciples were fully aware of the fact that in the Hebrew Scriptures Yahweh Himself has unique authority over the terror of the sea (Exod 14–15; cf. Deut 7:2–7; Job 9:8; 38:16; Pss 29:3; 65:8; 77:20; 89:10; 93:3–4; Isa 43:1–5; 51:9–10).[14] Thus, R. E. Brown is right to conclude, "This was a miracle that gave expression to the majesty of Jesus, not unlike the Transfiguration."[15]

The expression of the divine name "I Am" (Ἐγώ εἰμι) also has significant messianic implications. The divine name "I Am" is also the covenant name by which Yahweh revealed Himself repeatedly to Abraham and his descendants. Throughout the OT God used this covenant name to reveal Himself to the descendants of Abraham, in order to remind them that God will fulfill the promise He had made to their ancestor. For instance, God appeared to Isaac in a nocturnal theophany to reassure him of the promise He made with Abraham: "I Am the God of your father Abraham; do not fear, for I Am with you. I will bless you, and multiply your descendants, for the sake of My servant Abraham"

12. W. H. Harris, "Theology of John's Writings," 177.

13. For a detailed discussion on the "I Am" statements in Scripture, see the appendix in R. E. Brown's commentary where he devotes an entire section on the "I Am" statements. *Gospel According to John (I–XII)*, 532–38.

14. Moloney, *Signs and Shadows*, 39. See also C. Brown's article, "Miracle," 3:371–81. Brown believes that Yahweh's subsequent provisions for His people in leading them through the Red Sea and providing food and drink also exhibits Yahweh's control over nature.

15. R. E. Brown, *Gospel According to John (I–XII)*, 254–55.

(Gen 26:24). God reiterates this reassurance of the same promise to Jacob in his dream at Bethel: "I Am the LORD, the God of your father Abraham and the God of Isaac; the land on which you lie, I will give it to you and your descendants. Your descendants shall also be like the dust of the earth, and you shall spread out to the west and to the east and to the north and to the south; and in you and in your descendants shall all the families of the earth be blessed. And behold, I Am with you, and will keep you wherever you go, and will bring you back to this land; for I will not leave you until I have done what I have promised you" (Gen 28:13–15). Thus, in using this phrase "I Am" to identify Himself Jesus is claiming to be the very God who revealed Himself to the patriarchs, and in whom all the patriarchal promises will ultimately be fulfilled in His eschatological kingdom.

To summarize, the main focus of this miracle of Jesus walking on the sea was to reveal His identity to His disciples. Jesus is the one who bears the divine name "I Am" (Ἐγώ εἰμι). The sign was personally designed by Jesus to prepare His disciples for the kind of ministry that lay ahead of them, which will be characterized by much hardship and intense opposition from the world. And, there will be times when the disciples would be terrified. And, this miracle demonstrated to the disciples that as the very God who wields authority over forces of nature, Jesus controls the very circumstances surrounding them. And, His divine presence will be with them even during His earthly absence because He is the great "I Am" (Ἐγώ εἰμι).

CONCLUSION

The Passover Feast provided the backdrop for Jesus' two sign-miracles (σημεῖα) in John 6 and His accompanying Bread of Life discourse sandwiched in between them. The miracle of feeding the five thousand (John 6:1–15) during the Passover brought natural comparison of Jesus with another "sign" worker, Moses, who predicted that a prophet like him would arise (Deut 18:15). Continuing the same theme of relating the days of Moses with the coming of the eschatological age by the similarity of their miracles, the subsequent sign of Jesus walking on the Sea of Galilee (John 6:16–21) revealed yet another aspect of His identity as the promised Messiah and the unique Son of God. Yahweh's provision for His people in leading them through the Red Sea and exhibiting His control over nature, finds similar parallel with Jesus' walking on the Sea of Galilee to protect His disciples. Jesus revealed Himself by using the divine name Yahweh used when He revealed Himself to Moses on Mount Sinai (John 6:20; cf. Exod 3:14). In using this divine name Himself Jesus was claiming to be the very God who revealed Himself to the patriarchs, and in whom all the patriarchal promises will be fulfilled in His eschatological kingdom.

10

The Sixth Sign: Healing the Man Born Blind (9:1–41)

INTRODUCTION

THIS SIGN-MIRACLE OF JESUS' healing of the blind man takes place in a different time and setting than the previous two. The miracle of Jesus healing the blind man takes place in Jerusalem, whereas the two Passover miracles in John 6 take place in Galilee. This miracle comes on the heels of Jesus' "I Am the Light of the World" discourse at the Jewish Feast of Tabernacles and His resumed conflict with the Jewish religious authorities in Jerusalem. During the feast in Jerusalem, He claimed to be the Light of the World who defeated darkness of sin and death. And, Jesus followed this claim with the astonishing promise, "Whoever follows me will never walk in darkness, but will have the light of life" (8:12). Jesus' healing of the blind man is an authentication of His claim to be the Light of the World. Therefore, it is imperative to examine this miracle in the context of the whole Feast of Tabernacles, which begins in John 7.

The opening words of the chapter, "After this" or more literally, "After these things" (μετὰ ταῦτα) once again indicate a shift in the setting of the Gospel narrative as well as the obvious temporal change (7:1). As indicated earlier, the Evangelist uses this phrase often in his Gospel to inform the reader that a change is taking place in the story (cf. 2:12; 3:22; 4:43; 5:1; 6:1). The Evangelist also informs the reader that "the Jewish Feast of Tabernacles" (ἡ ἑορτὴ τῶν Ἰουδαίων ἡ σκηνοπηγία) was near (7:2). And, there is no further mention of a feast until 10:22, where the Evangelist notes: "Then came the Feast of Dedication at Jerusalem." It seems fitting then that 7:1–10:21 forms a literary unit for John.[1] As

1. Moloney, *Gospel of John*, 232–33. Not all scholars see these chapters as a literary unit, however. For instance, Beasley-Murray and Carson recognize the connection between chaps. 7–8, but not 9–10. Beasley-Murray argues that chaps. 7–8 are a unit, but

Moloney correctly concludes, "John 7:1—10:21 is entirely dedicated to the presence of Jesus in Jerusalem for the celebration of Tabernacles."[2] Borchert says that these chapters form the third stage of the Festival Cycle, and that they continue the background of the exodus motif. The focus shifts in these chapters, however, from Passover to the Festival of Tabernacles and the wilderness experience.[3] Craig Keener also agrees that the miracle of Jesus' healing of the blind man in John 9 is connected with the Feast of Tabernacles of John 7–8: "This narrative demonstrates Jesus' claims in the previous context and chronologically follows directly on Jesus' departure from the temple on the last day of the festival (7:37; 8:59). It probably begins not far from the temple (cf. 9:7)."[4]

that chap. 9 is a sign introduction for chap. 10. *John*, 148–49). Carson also agrees that chaps. 7–8 are a unit, but he is not certain whether chaps. 9–10 are a unit because of the Feast of Dedication. *Gospel According to John*, 359. R. E. Brown stands somewhere in the middle of these two views, in that he designates chap. 9 as "Aftermath of Tabernacles." *Gospel According to John (I–XII)*, 359.

2. Ibid. Moloney lists a number of indications from 7:1—10:21 that point to a succession of events that take place during the feast:

1. The expression (μετὰ ταῦτα) appears in 7:1, but never again in 7:2—10:21.
2. The Jews' Feast of Tabernacles was at hand (v. 2).
3. The brothers and Jesus go up to Jerusalem for the feast (v. 10).
4. Encounters take place "about the middle of the feast" (v. 14).
5. Further encounters take place "on the last day of the feast" (v. 37).
6. In 8:12 Jesus speaks "again" (πάλιν), indicating that the feast is still being celebrated.
7. The same expression reappears in v. 21, maintaining the time line.
8. Although there is a continuation of time, a change of place occurs in v. 59.
9. Jesus' exit from the temple leads directly into 9:1. "Passing by," He sees the man born blind (9:1).
10. The temporal unity across 7:1—10:21 is not broken until the narrator announces the Feast of Dedication.

3. Borchert, *John 1–11*, 277.

4. Keener, *Gospel of John*, 1:775. He further demonstrates the connection of the chapters by observing, "This section opens with the healing of a blind man (9:1–7) and closes with the recognition that this miracle was not what one expected from a demon (10:21). The narrative between includes Pharisaic charges that Jesus' healing cannot be from God (9:16, 22, 24), a response from the formerly blind man that challenges the logic of their paradigm (9:25, 27, 31–33), and a response from Jesus, who reverses the charge and shows that it is his opponents who are not from God (9:40—10:18). Jesus' claim in this section to be the good shepherd (10:11) implicitly advances his previous claim to deity (8:58)."

The Feast of Tabernacles was a fall harvest festival and one of the three feasts Jews were required to attend in Jerusalem (Deut 16:16).[5] It occurred annually in the fall and commemorated the wilderness experience of Israel and God's supernatural provision for the nation during that time. The Tabernacles was regarded as the most popular of the three pilgrimage feasts, commonly referred to as "the feast of the LORD" (Lev 23:30; Judg 21:19), or simply as "the feast" (1 Kgs 8:2, 65; 2 Chron 7:8; Neh 8:14; Isa 30:29; Ezek 45:23, 25). Laney explains why the Tabernacles was the most popular and well-attended: "Most of the first-century Jews were farmers and their lives depended on their crops. Their work prevented many farmers from attending the spring festivals of Passover and Pentecost. But once the harvest was over and the crops were stored, they could stop laboring and enjoy themselves for a while. Thus Sukkoth became the most popular and well-attended feast."[6]

The feast consisted of a seven-day festival beginning on the fifteenth day of the seventh month, Tishri (September–October), followed by an eighth day observed as a Sabbath. The people constructed temporary huts (i.e., "tabernacles") of leafy branches on their rooftops or along the roads, and lived in them during the festival.[7] According to Gale Yee, "the eighth day was set apart from the seven days of festivities and functioned as a conclusion for the feast to help people make the transition back to normal life."[8]

Moloney explains the activities of the eighth day: "After the seven days of celebration in the booths, there was an additional day, an eighth day, recalling the protection of YHWH during the exodus period. On this eighth day those celebrating the feast no longer dwelt in their booths, there was no procession, and the water ritual ceased. The eighth day was dedicated to Israel's request for a superabundance of rain as a sign of YHWH's special and continuing care for the people."[9]

The Feast of Tabernacles involves both historical and prophetic aspects. The feast not only celebrated God's care for Israel in the past but also anticipated the day when God would establish Israel securely in the

5. The instructions for the Feast of Tabernacles are found in Lev 23:33–43 and Deut 16:13–15.

6. Laney, *John*, 138.

7. Kent, *Light in the Darkness*, 113.

8. Yee, *Jewish Feasts and the Gospel of John*, 72.

9. Moloney, *Signs and Shadows*, 67.

land under the leadership of the Messiah. Laney observes, "The celebration looks back to the wilderness wanderings when the people lived in temporary shelters (Lev 23:39, 42–43), and looks ahead prophetically to Israel's kingdom joy when the nation is regathered in the land (Zech 14:16)."[10] As the two themes of light and rain dominate the eschatological passage of Zechariah 14, the two images of water and light became the focus of the feast.[11] It makes sense, then, that Jesus claims that He is both the source of living water (John 7:37–39) and that He is the Light of the World (8:12) during this particular feast. He is presenting Himself as the promised Messiah in whom all the eschatological promises will be realized.

THE SETTING

As mentioned above, the words μετὰ ταῦτα (7:1) indicate that a new setting is taking place in the story. The entire section (7:1—10:21) that revolves around the theme of the Jewish Feast of Tabernacles takes place in Jerusalem. For the Evangelist, Jerusalem stands as the center of opposition and unbelief. The people's opposition and unbelief are represented and epitomized by the religious leaders in Jerusalem. The Evangelist begins this entire section by describing that "the Jews" (religious authorities) in Jerusalem were waiting there for Jesus so that they could take His life (7:1).[12] The Jewish religious leaders who vehemently opposed Jesus' healing of the paralytic on the Sabbath in John 5 resume their opposition to Jesus here. In these chapters, however, the opposition to Jesus increases from hostility to hatred, and even intent to murder. In fact, in chapters 7–8 alone, the Evangelist records that the Jewish officials sought

10. Laney, *John*, 138.

11. Yee, *Jewish Feasts and the Gospel of John*, 73–74. Moloney discusses the three major elements of ritual during the feast: (1) the water libation ceremony (Sukkah 4:9–10); (2) the ceremony of light (Sukkah 5:1–4); (3) the rite of facing the temple (Sukkah 5:4). *Signs and Shadows*, 66–70.

12. The Greek term for "the Jews" (οἱ Ἰουδαῖοι) in the New Testament may have four different meanings: (1) the entire Jewish people (2:6, 13; 3:1, 25; 4:9, 22; 5:1; 6:4; 7:2; 8:31; 11:55; 18:12, 35; 19:21, 40, 42); (2) the residents of Jerusalem and surrounding territory (11:8, 19, 31, 33, 36, 45, 54; 12:9, 11; 19:20); (3) the people hostile to Jesus (6:41, 52; 8:48, 52, 57; 10:19, 24, 31, 33; 18:20, 38; 19:7, 12, 14); (4) the religious authorities in Jerusalem (1:19; 2:18, 20; 5:10, 15, 16, 18; 7:1, 11, 13, 15; 8:22; 9:18, 22; 13:33; 18:14, 31, 36; 19:31, 38; 20:19). See Bratcher, "'Jews' in the Gospel of John," 401–9. In this case, the "Jews" refers to the religious leaders in Jerusalem.

to "seize" or arrest Jesus four times (7:30, 32, 44; 8:20). Four other times it is said that they even sought to kill Him (7:1, 19, 25; 8:37). It becomes evident, then, that the theme of growing conflict between Jesus and the religious leaders in chapters 7–8 provides the setting for Jesus' miracle of healing the blind man in John 9.

The Evangelist also informs the reader of the change in time by indicating that the Jewish Feast of Tabernacles was near (7:2). If the Passover events in chapter 6 took place in the spring of AD 32, then this particular Feast of Tabernacles occurred in the fall of AD 32, about six months before Christ's crucifixion.[13] As the Feast of Tabernacles drew near, Jesus' brothers (half-brothers) came to Him and "challenged" Him to go to the feast in Jerusalem to promote His messiahship (7:3–4). The Evangelist parenthetically notes that the brothers said this cynically out of their unbelief (v. 5). Jesus responds by saying, however, that His time had not yet come (vv. 6–8).[14] Jesus always lives in submission to the Father's divine timetable, and He is cognizant of "the hour" (ἡ ὥρα) of His approaching death, which will take place at the next Passover.[15] For the Evangelist, time indications are just as much theological as they are chronological.

The setting of the Feast of Tabernacles in chapters 7–8 emphasizes two significant claims of Jesus that will foreshadow His miracle of healing the blind man in chapter 9. On the last day of the feast Jesus proclaimed that He is the giver of living water (7:37) and that He is the Light of the World (8:12). As mentioned previously, two important elements connected with the Feast of Tabernacles were water and light. T. C. Smith explains succinctly the significance of Jesus' claims in the context of the festival:

> Water and light were used in two ceremonies observed at the feast. One of these was the rite of water libation. Each day during a festival the priests went to the Pool of Siloam and filled a golden jar with water. This jar, containing about a gallon of water, was brought to the Temple and poured into a silver bowl on the altar

13. See Hoehner, *Chronological Aspects*, 143.

14. By using the term ὁ καιρός Jesus was referring to the divine time that the Father has set for Him to go to Jerusalem. See Carson, *Gospel According to John*, 307–8.

15. When Jesus tells His brothers that He is not going up (ἀναβαίνω) to Jerusalem because His time (ὁ καιρός) has not yet come, the Evangelist is indicating a play on words to indicate that it was not yet the time to go up to the Father and be glorified. See R. E. Brown, *Gospel According to John (I–XII)*, 308.

as a symbol of the prayers for rain. At one time this rite of water libation had some historical association with the giving of water to the Israelites in the desert, but from the time of Zechariah it was in some way connected with the prayers of the people for rain in the next agricultural year. Another significant rite of the feast of Tabernacles was the lighting of the candelabra in the court of women. This rite was probably originally observed in connection with the coming of the radiance of God on the day of fall equinox as the Mishnah suggests (Sukkah 5:4). It is apparent that when Jesus said, "If any man thirst, he is to come to me and drink" (7:37) and "I am the light of the world" he meant to manifest himself in the context of the festival rituals. He directed attention to himself as the water of life and the light of the world.[16]

In short, the miracle of Jesus' healing of the man who was blind from birth created the perfect case study to demonstrate that, as the divine Messiah, He was the source of life and light (cf. 1:4). For the Evangelist, both the "living water" and "light" stand to symbolize eternal life (cf. 4:10–14; 1:4–9).

THE SIGN

The miracle of Jesus healing the blind man in chapter 9 begins without a noticeable literary break from the previous chapter, thereby indicating its connection with the previous setting. The opening words of the chapter, "As He went along" (Καὶ παράγων), seem to indicate that Jesus is not far removed from the events of the feast, either temporally or literarily. Borchert is thus correct to say, "The Tabernacles motif in John is brought to a conclusion in a powerful way through the story of the healing of the blind man."[17] Culpepper is also right to link this miracle with the previous chapter: "Having revealed himself as 'the light of the world,' Jesus now gives sight to a blind man."[18] In fact, the opening verse of this chapter reads, "As he went along, he saw a man blind from birth" (v. 1). Furthermore, immediately before His divine touch on the man born blind Jesus says to His disciples, "While I Am in the world, I Am the light of the world" (v. 5). He probably wanted to make sure that they made the connection between His claim and deed. Like the previous miracles, it

---

16. T. C. Smith, "Book of Signs," 454.

17. Borchert, *John 1–11*, 310.

18. Culpepper, *Gospel and Letters of John*, 174.

was of paramount importance to Jesus that His disciples comprehend the significance of His deeds, which reveal His Person.

The miracle account is narrated in the following two verses (vv. 6–7). Having applied some mud to the man's eyes, Jesus commands him to go and wash in the Pool of Siloam.[19] The Evangelist notes that the man went and washed, and came home seeing. The man did precisely what Jesus commanded him to do. In obeying Jesus' command, the man demonstrated the presence of his genuine faith. Being congenitally blind, the man overcame great obstacles to believe Jesus' word. The man's faith, however, stands in stark contrast to those who witness the miracle. His neighbors (vv. 8–12) and the Pharisees (vv. 13–34) express skepticism and unbelief. The closing verses of this chapter reveal that the man's initial faith that resulted in his physical sight now results in his spiritual sight as Jesus discloses His identity to the man (vv. 35–39). The man's expression of his faith indicates a proper belief: "'Lord, I believe,' and he worshiped him" (v. 37).[20]

THE SIGNIFICANCE

The closing verses of this chapter (vv. 35–41) reveal not only the genuine and saving faith of the blind man, but they also reveal the significance of Jesus' miracle. In healing the man born blind Jesus was illustrating the spiritual blindness of all men, who are born in sin and without hope (cf. Eph 2:1–3; Rom 3:9–20). And, just as the man who was born with congenital blindness could only be healed by Jesus' divine touch, only

---

19. Koester suggests that the name of the pool indicates a messianic interpretation of the sign: "The word *Siloam*, or *Shiloah* as it was sometimes written (Isa 8:6; cf. Neh 3:15), was similar to the word Shiloh, which many Jews understood to be a name for the Messiah. One of the most important messianic passages in the Old Testament literally said, 'The scepter shall not depart from Judah, nor the ruler's staff from between his feet, until Shiloh comes, and to him shall be the obedience of the peoples' (Gen 49:10). By the first century, Jewish interpretation took Shiloh as a reference to the Messiah, and this view is widely attested in later sources. By explaining that Siloam was the pool of the 'one who has been sent,' the fourth evangelist apparently alludes to this common Jewish tradition, suggesting that Siloam was in fact the pool of the Messiah whom God has sent." *Symbolism in the Fourth Gospel*, 103.

20. Keener rightly observes that the blind man himself becomes a paradigm of growing discipleship in John: "When he confesses Jesus openly, he moves from recognizing him as a 'man' (9:11) to a 'prophet' (9:17) and a man from God (9:33), and with Jesus' revelation recognizes him as 'Son of Man' (9:17) and 'Lord' (9:35–37)." *Gospel of John*, 1:775–76.

the divine Messiah who is the Light of the World can grant eternal life to those who believe in Him.[21] Pentecost's summary of the relationship between this miracle and Jesus' "I am the Light of the World" discourse is insightful:

> This incident of the healing of the blind man was an authentication of all that Christ claimed for Himself in the public teaching at the Feast of Tabernacles. There He claimed to be the Light of the World (John 8:12), and here He brought light to one born blind. There He claimed to liberate men from sin, Satan, and death (John 8:36), and here He liberated a man from darkness. There He claimed to be the sinless One (John 8:46), and here He defended His sinlessness and offered to forgive the sins of those who would trust in Him. There He claimed to be the preexistent God (John 8:58), and here He was worshiped as God.[22]

Therefore, this miracle demonstrates the spiritual blindness of all men desperately in need of life from one who is both the giver of eternal life and the Light of the World.

This miracle of Jesus' healing of the blind man also reveals much about the identity of the Healer. In the Old Testament God Himself is associated with the giving of sight to the blind (cf. Ps 146:8).[23] For instance, on the occasion when God disclosed His divine name to Moses as the "I Am" (Exod 3:14), He also revealed His divine attributes by saying, "Who gave man his mouth? Who makes him deaf or mute? Who gives him sight or makes him blind? Is it not I, the LORD?" (Exod 4:11). In healing the blind man, then, Jesus was revealing His deity. This miracle also has deep messianic implications. The Hebrew Scriptures are also clear that giving sight to the blind would be a sign of messianic activity. The prophet Isaiah predicted, for instance, that the Messiah would be "a light to the Gentiles" and "open eyes that are blind" (42:6–7). Furthermore, the healing of a man blind from birth illustrates one of the characteristics of the messianic kingdom when "the eyes of the blind will be opened" (Isa 35:5). In fulfillment of these messianic prophecies Jesus gives sight to the blind (cf. Matt 9:27–31; 12:22–23; 15:30; 20:29–34; 21:14). The miracle then provides a foretaste of the messianic blessings to be realized in the

---

21. For a detailed description of the many divergent views in the Jewish and Greco-Roman cultures, see Keener's commentary, *Gospel of John*, 1:777–78.

22. Pentecost, *Words and Works of Jesus Christ*, 292.

23. W. H. Harris, "Theology of John's Writings," 177–78.

promised kingdom when "the eyes of the blind will see" (Isa 29:18). As the promised Messiah of the Old Testament Jesus will give sight to the blind in His coming kingdom. But the future work of the Messiah reveals far greater implications in the present as the Messiah grants spiritual sight (eternal life) to those who believe in Him, here and now.

This miracle is also significant in that it demonstrates Jesus' authority not only to grant life to those who believe but also to judge those who reject the Son (cf. John 5:22).[24] Jesus Himself declares, "For judgment I have come into this world, so that the blind will see and those who see will become blind" (9:39). The Pharisees were a perfect case in point. When they ask Jesus if He is condemning them, He responds: "If you were blind, you would not be guilty of sin; but now that you claim you can see, your guilt remains" (vv. 40–41). The Pharisees who, being spiritually blind themselves were too proud to admit their blindness, whereas the blind man received his sight from the one who is the true Light who gives light to every man who puts his trust in Him by faith (cf. 1:9). R. E. Brown's summary of this miracle in its context is both perceptive and eloquent: "This is a story of how a man who sat in darkness was brought to see the light, not only physically but spiritually. On the other hand, it is also a tale of how those who thought they saw (the Pharisees) were blind themselves to the light and plunging into darkness. The story starts in vs. 1 with a blind man who will gain his sight; it ends in vs. 41 with the Pharisees who have become spiritually blind."[25]

The judgment of the Pharisees is the subject of the following chapter in Jesus' "I Am the Good Shepherd" discourse (10:1–21).[26] This discourse presents Jesus as the Good Shepherd who cares for His flock. In contrast to the Pharisees who, being compared to a thief and a robber, come in to steal, kill and destroy the sheep, Jesus is He who lays down His life for the sheep. As the Messiah Jesus is the Gate or Door for the sheep (v. 7). In contrast to the Pharisees who are illegitimate and false teachers, thereby having no divine authority (cf. Matt 7:29), Jesus is the promised Messiah of the Scriptures who has come to care for the sheep. In the

24. Keener, *Gospel of John*, 1:794.

25. R. E. Brown, *Gospel According to John (I–XII)*, 377.

26. The "I Am the Good Shepherd" discourse of Jesus in chapter 10 continues in the context of the Tabernacles story begun in 7:1. The stories in this section fit so neatly that R. E. Brown says, "The internal construction of the story shows consummate artistry; no other story in the Gospel is so closely knit. We have here Johannine dramatic skill at its best." *Gospel According to John (I–XII)*, 376. See also Keener, *Gospel of John*, 1:797–99.

Old Testament, God Himself is seen to be the faithful shepherd of His people (Gen 49:24; Ps 23:1; 80:1; Isa 40:10–11; Zech 10:3).[27] The imagery of the Good Shepherd also presents Jesus as the promised Messiah. The prophet Ezekiel, for instance, anticipated the day when the Messiah will care for His sheep as the Good Shepherd: "I will establish one shepherd over them, and he shall feed them, My servant David. He shall feed them and be their shepherd. And I, the LORD, will be their God, and My servant David a prince among them; I, the LORD, have spoken" (34:23–24; cf. Isa 55:3–4; Jer 23:5–6; Mic 7:14).

To summarize, then, the miracle of healing the man born blind reveals Jesus as the divine Messiah who, as the Light of the World, delivers men from darkness of sin and death by granting eternal life to those who believe in Him. And, as the Messiah Jesus is the Good Shepherd who lays down His life for the sheep.

CONCLUSION

The Fourth Evangelist skillfully weaves together the literary structure of the Fourth Gospel with its profound theology. Whereas the Cana Cycle (John 2–4) presents Jesus as the divine Messiah who grants life to those who believe in Him, the Festival Cycle (John 5–10) develops the theme of increasing opposition by the Jewish leadership to the one who grants that life. The sign-miracles that are recorded in these chapters reveal Jesus' Person in the context of Jewish festivals, demonstrating in no uncertain terms that as the Messiah, Jesus is the one who fulfills the joys and hopes of the festivals. These messianic claims of Jesus are vehemently opposed by the religious leaders in these chapters, thereby fulfilling the Evangelist's words at the outset of the Gospel: "He came to that which was his own, but his own did not receive him" (1:11). However, as the Bread of Life and the Light of the World, the Son offers life to those who would believe in Him, while at the same time rendering judgment to those who reject that offer. Furthermore, as the Good Shepherd and Door of the sheep, the Messiah will protect those who belong to Him, even laying down His life for them. As the Passover of "the hour" draws near, that prediction will soon become a reality.

---

27. Laney, *John*, 185. For a detailed discussion on the general background of the sheep and shepherd image, see Keener's commentary, *Gospel of John*, 1:799–801.

11

The Seventh Sign: Raising Lazarus from the Dead (11:1–44)

INTRODUCTION

THE MIRACLE OF RAISING Lazarus from the dead is the seventh and climactic sign of Jesus in the Fourth Gospel. It completes the selected Johannine signs that are designed to present Jesus as the promised Messiah and the Son of God (cf. 20:30–31). If the first miracle of Jesus turning water into wine in Cana is the first or representative one among the signs (ἀρχὴν τῶν σημείων), then this miracle of Jesus raising Lazarus from the dead is the seventh and climactic sign in revealing His Person.[1] The miraculous sign of raising Lazarus from the dead climactically confirms Jesus' authority to give life (5:21) and to resurrect the dead (5:28–29). It also demonstrates Jesus' own claim to be "the resurrection and the life" (11:25).[2]

THE SETTING

The miracle of Jesus raising Lazarus from the dead takes place in the context following the Jewish Feast of Dedication (10:22–42) and

1. For a more detailed discussion on the significance of the first and seventh sign-miracles of Jesus, see chapter 2, "Σημεῖα and the Fourth Gospel," in the book. The first and seventh miracles bracket the seven signs with the theme of revealing Jesus' glory (2:11, 11:4; cf. 12:41).

2. Keener perceptively observes the literary and theological connections between the first and last of Jesus' sign-miracles: "This climactic sign of Jesus' ministry joins the opening sign in framing Jesus' public ministry. The opening sign (2:1–11) recounts Jesus' benevolence at a wedding; the last involves it at a funeral. The joy of weddings and mourning of funerals could function as opposites in ancient literature." *Gospel of John*, 2:835.

preceding the Passover of Jesus' death (chaps. 12–20). The temporal indication "Then came" (Ἐγένετο τότε) in 10:22 seems to note that the events of 10:22–42 took place some time after the events of 7:1— 10:21. The events of 7:1—10:21 describe the occurrences during the Feast of Tabernacles, while the events of 10:22–42 describe the Feast of Dedication.[3] There must have been some three months of time that passed in between the two festivals.[4] While on the surface it may appear that the Feast of Dedication has little to do with Jesus' miracle of raising Lazarus from the dead, the messianic expectations that are involved in the festival may indicate Jesus' actions and the Evangelist's decision to place the narrative here.

The Feast of Dedication (also known as Hanukkah) was not a biblical festival. Judas Maccabeus instituted it to commemorate the cleansing and rededication of the temple in 164 BC after Antiochus Epiphanes IV had defiled it (cf. 1 Macc 1:10–67; 4:41–61; 2 Macc 6–7).[5] The festival was celebrated with the use of lamps in the temple, synagogue, and home, and so it also came to be known as the "Feast of Lights" (Josephus *Antiquities* 12.325). The celebration came to represent the deliverance and freedom of God's people. Borchert explains the background of the feast in the context of John 10.

> I believe chap. 10 represents a new theme that builds upon the inadequacy of the Jewish leadership and the rejection of Jesus' messianic calling evident throughout the Tabernacles section of John (chaps. 7–9). But the Festival of Dedication (which is the focus of chap. 10) also has a messianic aspect because that festival had been celebrated as a memorial to the rejection of false rulers, epitomized by Antiochus IV (Epiphanes), who among other things desecrated the temple by slaughtering a pig on the altar of sacrifice and also erected a statue of Zeus (Jupiter) in the most holy place, the inner sanctuary of the temple. The subsequent victory and expulsion of the Syrians from Israel in 164 B.C. under Judas Maccabeus and the accompanying reconsecration of the temple was thereafter established in the Jewish calendar as a

3. R. E. Brown, *Gospel According to John (I–XII)*, 401–12. See also Borchert, *John 1–11*, 327–45.

4. The Feast of Tabernacles takes place in the fall, while the Feast of Dedication takes place in the winter.

5. For a detailed discussion of the Maccabean events, see Hoehner's article, "Maccabees," 3:196–200. See also Hoehner's article on the whole intertestamental period, "Between the Testaments," 1:177–94.

national religious freedom festival, which at that time definitely implied messianic expectations.[6]

The background behind the Feast of Dedication reveals the Jews' skeptical question to Jesus in John 10:24: "How long will you keep us in suspense? If you are the Christ, tell us plainly." The Jews were rejecting Jesus because while He was claiming to be the Messiah, He was not measuring up to their great "Maccabean-style" deliverer expectations.[7] Jesus' talk of sheep and eternal life must have baffled the people's minds. Jesus must show the people that the true messianic deliverance is a spiritual one rather than a political one. As the divine Messiah, Jesus offers eternal life to those who believe in His name. And, He is able to offer them eternal life because He will soon go up to Jerusalem for the Passover, where He will vicariously offer up His life as the Passover Lamb for the forgiveness of sins. As the Good Shepherd, Jesus must lay down His life for the sheep (10:11, 15).

The Feast of Dedication (10:22–42) not only reveals the background behind the people's rejection of Jesus as the Messiah, it also provides the temporal context in the story that the time of Jesus' "hour" is drawing near. As Jesus' "hour" draws near, the polarization of people's opinion concerning Jesus grows further and further apart. On the one hand, the religious leaders in Jerusalem cement their hatred of Jesus in trying to stone Him because He claims to be the divine Son (vv. 30–39). On the other hand, many of the people on the other side of the Jordan place their faith in Jesus (vv. 40–42). This growing polarization of opinions provides the setting for Jesus' miracle of raising Lazarus from the dead in chapter 11. And, the climactic sign of Jesus' miracle of raising Lazarus will provide the ultimate evidence for faith and, at the same time, the ultimate cause for unbelief, and eventually murder.

THE SIGN

The miracle of Jesus' raising of Lazarus is recorded in the midst of a lengthy narrative (11:1–57). This chapter can be divided as follows: introduction (vv. 1–6); Jesus' dialogue with the disciples (vv. 7–16); Jesus' dialogue with Martha (vv. 17–27); Jesus' dialogue with Mary and the mourners (vv. 28–37); Jesus' miracle of raising Lazarus from the dead

6. Borchert, *John 1–11*, 328.

7. Laney, *John*, 200.

(vv. 38–44); the responses to Jesus' miracle (vv. 45–54); and Jesus' Passover pilgrimage (vv. 55–57). In typical form of a Johannine sign this miracle is also accompanied by Jesus' interpretation of its meaning, but with one exception. While the miracles in John 5, 6, and 9 are followed by Jesus' discourse in interpreting the sign, here the meaning is discussed before the miracle.[8]

The story begins by describing the grim situation in the home of Jesus' three loved ones. Lazarus was sick (v. 1). The opening verses also introduce the new characters who will play a significant part of the events in the chapters to come: Lazarus, Mary, and Martha. Mary is the one who will anoint Jesus and wipe His feet with her hair in the following pericope (12:1–11). Apparently, the siblings knew Jesus well (cf. Luke 10:38–42); thus, the sisters' request for Jesus to come and heal their brother: "Lord, the one you love is sick" (John 11:3). Jesus, however, does not go immediately to heal Lazarus. Rather, He assures them with this enigmatic statement: "This sickness will not end in death. No, it is for God's glory so that God's Son may be glorified through it" (v. 4). Like many other Johannine sayings, this statement has a dual meaning.[9] In one sense Jesus gives the assurance that Lazarus's sickness will not be the end of the story; he will be raised and the miracle will reveal Jesus' glory. In another sense these events will lead inevitably to Jesus' death at the Passover, and there the Father will glorify Him. The Evangelist notes that Jesus loved Lazarus (v. 5). Yet Jesus stayed two more days before going to Lazarus (v. 6). Laney is correct to say, "The delay indicates that Jesus was operating by a divine plan and according to a divine timetable."[10] Culpepper points out, "This enigmatic response continues the pattern of Jesus rebuffing requests and acting only in response to the Father's direction (cf. 2:4; 7:3–10)."[11]

Having waited two days until Lazarus died, Jesus leads the disciples to where he lay dead (v. 7). Songer perceptively characterizes Jesus' decision to go back to Judea as, "a journey to give life to Lazarus, but a march of death for Him."[12] The disciples try to deter Him from going because they knew the danger awaiting Him there: "But Rabbi, a short while ago

8. Culpepper, *Gospel and Letters of John*, 185.

9. Borchert, *John 1–11*, 350.

10. Laney, *John*, 204.

11. Culpepper, *Gospel and Letters of John*, 186.

12. Songer, "John 5–12," 467.

the Jews tried to stone you, and yet you are going back there?" (v. 8). Jesus answers His disciples with another enigmatic statement: "Are there not twelve hours of daylight? A man who walks by day will not stumble, for he sees by this world's light. It is when he walks by night that he stumbles, for he has no light" (vv. 9–10). Tenney is right in saying that "Jesus felt assured of safety while pursuing the course defined for Him by the will of God."[13] In other words, His death will be voluntary and it will happen according to the Father's set time. Jesus' conversation with His disciples also reveals that the purpose of Jesus' delay is twofold: first, to reveal His glory as the one who has authority over life and death; and second, to instruct and develop faith in the disciples, including Mary and Martha (vv. 11–16).

If the opening verses of the narrative and Jesus' discussion with the disciples present the occasion and purpose for the miracle (vv. 1–16), then His discussion with Martha reveals the nature and theology of the miracle (vv. 17–27). These verses begin with an explicit statement concerning Lazarus's death: he had been dead for four days (v. 17). Jesus wanted to make certain that there could not be a shadow of doubt concerning His miracle.[14] Knowing that Jesus could have come in time to save Lazarus because Bethany was less than two miles from Jerusalem, Martha perplexingly questions His delay (vv. 18–22). And, even when Jesus reassures Martha that her brother will rise again, those words mean little comfort to her because she thought Jesus was referring to the eschatological resurrection (vv. 23–24).[15] While it is true that there will be an eschatological resurrection, Jesus wants Martha to know that as the Messiah and the Son of God, He has the authority over life and death. Jesus said to her, "I Am the resurrection and the life. He who believes

13. Tenney, "Topics from the Gospel of John—Part II," 153.

14. The Evangelist's explicit statement concerning the length of time Lazarus had been dead probably reflects the Jewish tradition that the soul hovered near the body for three days after burial but left after that. Borchert explains this tradition: "The general belief was that the spirit of the deceased hovered around the body for three days in anticipation of some possible means of reentry into the body. But on the third day it was believed that the body lost its color and the spirit was locked out. Therefore the spirit was obliged to enter the chambers of Sheol (the place of the dead)," *John 1–11*, 354.

15. The belief in the resurrection of the dead in the last days is clearly taught in the Hebrew Scriptures (cf. Ps 16:8–11; Isa 26:14; Dan 12:1–4). While the Sadducees denied the resurrection in the first century, the Pharisees affirmed it. The common people usually shared the beliefs of the Pharisees. Thus, it is not surprising that Martha confessed her faith in that doctrine.

in me will live, even though he dies; and whoever lives and believes in me will never die. Do you believe this?" (vv. 25–26).[16] Songer correctly interprets this statement: "The dead who believe in Jesus will rise, and the living who believe will never die spiritually."[17] Dodd's interpretation is similar to Songer's, but more specific in separating the two claims. He paraphrases this way: "I am the resurrection: he who has faith in me, even if he dies, will live again. I am the life: he who is alive and has faith in me will never die."[18] Jesus is reiterating the truth He has been teaching all along, namely, that eternal life begins here and now, and those who believe in Him already have that life. Martha's response reflects her settled conviction: "Yes, Lord. I believe that you are the Christ, the Son of God, who was to come into the world" (v. 27).[19] She believed in Jesus even before seeing the miracle.

While Jesus' discussion with Martha reveals the nature of the miracle and His divine authority over life and death (vv. 17–27), His discussion with Mary reveals Jesus' humanity (vv. 28–37). Jesus is "deeply moved in spirit and troubled" (v. 33). Jesus even "wept," so that those around Him could say, "See how he loved Lazarus" (vv. 35–36).

These verses reveal the tenderness of Jesus' heart, and that must have ministered to Mary deeply to know that Jesus has not only the power and authority over life and death, but that as the Good Shepherd He also cares for her. Jesus' display of His love and compassion also sets the stage for His miracle of raising Lazarus from the dead.

The miracle account of Jesus raising Lazarus from the dead is recorded in only a few verses (vv. 38–44). Like the other miracles of Jesus, it only takes the simple command of His word to raise Lazarus who had been dead for four days. As the divine Messiah, there is power and authority in His word (cf. 2:7; 4:50; 5:8). When Jesus calls Lazarus by name (v. 43), He must have been fulfilling His role as the Good Shepherd

16. Jesus' "I Am the resurrection and the life" (Ἐγώ εἰμι ἡ ἀνάστασις καὶ ἡ ζωή) statement in 11:25 is the fifth of seven "I Am" (Ἐγώ εἰμι) statements with a predicate in the Fourth Gospel. It is a strong affirmation of His deity.

17. Songer, "John 5–12," 467.

18. Dodd, Interpretation of the Fourth Gospel, 365.

19. The titles confessed by Martha about Jesus (ὁ Χριστὸς ὁ υἱὸς τοῦ θεοῦ) are the same two titles mentioned in the Evangelist's purpose statement (20:30–31) as the aim of the sign-miracles. The perfect tense of the verb "I believe" (πεπίστευκα) reflects the presence of her faith in Jesus already.

who calls His sheep by name (cf. 10:3).[20] Jesus also said, "My sheep hear my voice . . . and I give them eternal life, and they will never perish" (10:27–28). This miracle demonstrates a central theme that has been developed throughout these chapters, namely, that Jesus is the life-giving Son of God.

The closing verses of this chapter describe the aftermath of Jesus' climactic miracle (vv. 45–57). The reaction of the people to the sign was twofold: some believed in Jesus, while others rejected Him with skepticism and unbelief. Some of the people even went to report Jesus' miracle to the religious authorities. The unbelief of the Jewish religious leaders reaches its climax at this point. Jesus' climactic sign of raising Lazarus from the dead was "the straw that broke the camel's back." The Sanhedrin convenes and decides to put an end to Jesus' life. Caiaphas's judgment to sacrifice Jesus' life for the good of the nation ironically predicts the kind of death Jesus would soon experience (vv. 49–53). The following verses describe Jesus' final Passover pilgrimage up to Jerusalem (vv. 54–57). The "hour" to be given as the "Passover Lamb" has finally come. He will give Himself voluntarily and vicariously. He gives His life, so that others may live through Him. As the "Lamb of God" He will take away the sin of the world (cf. 1:29). His sacrificial death will prove true to His claim: "I Am the good shepherd. The good shepherd lays down his life for the sheep" (10:11).

THE SIGNIFICANCE

The significance of this miracle is indicated by the fact that it is the seventh sign among the Johannine miracles. As the seventh sign, it is both completing and climactic. It is completing in that these seven miracles are specifically chosen by the Evangelist to present Jesus as the Christ and the Son of God. It is climactic in that this miracle of Jesus raising Lazarus from the dead brings to a climax a theme that has been building up throughout the miracles and their attendant contexts, namely, that as the promised Messiah and the divine Son of God Jesus has the authority to give eternal life to those who believe in Him (5:22; 14:6). The seventh sign is also climactic in that this miracle of Jesus raising Lazarus from the dead brings the people's opinions and responses to a climactic end. For those who seek to believe, this miracle provides the ultimate

---

20. Culpepper, *Gospel and Letters of John*, 189.

evidence for faith in Jesus as the promised Messiah and the divine Son of God (11:27; cf. 20:30–31). But for those who persist in unbelief, this miracle provides the ultimate grounds for rejecting Jesus. The degree of opposition to Jesus has grown deeper and deeper to the point where the religious leaders decide resolutely to take His life.

The significance of Jesus' miracle of raising Lazarus from the dead is also seen in the fact that this miracle provides hope beyond this life. In raising Lazarus from the dead, Jesus demonstrates His authority to reverse the effects of sin and death (cf. Gen 2:17; Rom 5:12).[21] And, by His own death and resurrection, Jesus provides forgiveness of sins and offers life. Tenney eloquently explains that this miracle of Jesus raising Lazarus from the dead, "declared Him to be the Master of man's last and most implacable enemy, death."[22]

This miracle therefore also has profound messianic and eschatological implications. The Hebrew Scriptures are clear that the Old Testament saints expressed their confidence of everlasting hope that will be realized in the Messiah's kingdom (Ps 16:9–11; cf. Isa 26:19–20; Dan 12:2).[23] Even Martha in this miracle narrative professes her belief in the eschatological resurrection: "I know he will rise again in the resurrection at the last day" (John 11:24). Her faith in the eschatological resurrection was probably based on the prophetic words of Daniel who stated that, "many of those who sleep in the dust of the earth shall awake, some to everlasting life, some to shame and everlasting contempt" (Dan 12:2). However, Jesus responds to Martha by saying, "I Am the resurrection and the life" (John 11:25). Jesus was refashioning Martha's belief concerning the resurrection, in that while there will certainly be the eschatological resurrection, those who believe in Him already have eternal life, here and now. In other words, faith in Jesus will result in eternal life both now and hereafter.[24]

21. Laney, *John*, 214.

22. Tenney, "Topics from the Gospel of John—Part II," 154.

23. Köstenberger, in his commentary points out Old Testament instances of raising of the dead that include Elijah's raising of the widow's son (1 Kgs 17:17–24); Elisha's raising of the son of the Shunammite woman (2 Kgs 4:32–37); Elisha's "posthumous" raising of the dead man (2 Kgs 13:21); and the witch of Endor's illicit summoning of Samuel from the dead at King Saul's request (1 Sam 28). He then observes correctly by saying, "Raising of the dead were generally viewed in light of the final resurrection and as an expression of God's power to bring it about." *John*, 321–22.

24. Moloney, *Signs and Shadows*, 161.

The climactic sign of Jesus' raising of Lazarus is also significant in that it serves as a sign of judgment on the unbelieving Israelite nation and its leaders. Jesus had previously stated that He would no longer perform public miracles to convince the nation that He was the Son of God, and that the only sign left to give the nation would be the sign of Jonah, which is the resurrection of Jesus (cf. Matt 12:38–40).[25] The persistence of unbelief and rejection on the part of the Jewish religious leaders sealed their fate in their resolutely deciding to take Jesus' life. Their determined will does not waver until they arrest Jesus and hand Him over to be crucified and die a criminal's death. The proximity of this seventh and climactic miracle to the Passover events, both literarily and chronologically, reveals the Evangelist's obvious intent to show that Jesus' imminent and inevitable fate is entirely according to the Father's will. Jesus will go up to Jerusalem for the Passover to die as the Passover Lamb. As the Lamb of God He will take away the sin of the world. With Jesus' sacrificial death, Jesus will forever change the Passover.

CONCLUSION

The seventh miracle of Jesus raising Lazarus from the dead is the completing and climactic sign. This miracle completes the Evangelist's selected sign-miracles (σημεῖα) to demonstrate Jesus' Person as the promised Messiah and the divine Son of God. Just as the first sign-miracle of Jesus turning water into wine is the representative sign, the seventh sign-miracle of Jesus raising Lazarus from the dead is the completing and climactic sign. It is climactic in that it is the greatest of Jesus' seven miracles recorded in this Gospel. The miracle of raising Lazarus from the dead climactically authenticates Jesus' authority to grant eternal life to those who believe in Him. In raising Lazarus from the dead, Jesus was also demonstrating the validity of His own claims that He will rise again, and that He has the power and authority to do so. This miracle also illustrates Jesus' claims that He will raise people at the eschatological resurrection. However, the eternal life that Jesus gives begins here and now for those who believe in Him.

---

25. Pentecost, *Words and Works of Jesus Christ*, 344.

PART THREE

Conclusion of Jesus' Miracles in the Fourth Gospel

12

The Significance of John 12 and John 13–20 in their Relationship to the "Book of Signs"

THE SIGNIFICANCE OF JOHN 12

CHAPTER 12 OF THE Fourth Gospel plays a significant role in the argument of the book for the Evangelist, both literarily and theologically. First, this chapter serves as a literary "hinge" between the Book of Signs (chaps. 2–11) and the Book of Glory (chaps. 13–20). It brings the public ministry of Jesus to a close and anticipates "the hour" of His death. Borchert is also correct to say that this chapter both "concludes the Festival Cycle and foreshadows the dawning of the Farewell Cycle."[1] Laney's description of this chapter is also accurate: "Chapter 12 is a key turning point in John's development of the life of Christ. It describes a point of crisis in Jerusalem and the transition in Jesus' career from public to private ministry."[2] Second, this chapter serves a theological purpose in validating the claims made about Jesus in the Book of Signs, as His sacrificial death and triumphant resurrection confirm His Person as the promised Messiah and the divine Son of God. This chapter demonstrates further that as the promised Messiah of the Scriptures, His vicarious death will purchase redemption not only for His people but also for the whole world (cf. 1:29; 3:16–17; 4:42). Chapter 12 includes three significant symbolic acts that demonstrate the implications of Jesus' Passover death: Mary's anointing of Jesus in Bethany (vv. 1–11); Jesus' triumphal entry into Jerusalem (vv. 12–19); and the coming of the Greeks to seek Jesus (vv. 20–36). As Moloney accurately states, "The theme of Jesus'

---

1. Borchert, "Passover and the Narrative Cycles," 311.
2. Laney, *John*, 219.

death, so prominent in 11:1–54, dominates all these events."[3] Then, the chapter concludes with the Evangelist's summary of Jesus' ministry and the people's responses to Him in terms of belief and unbelief (vv. 37–50).

The chapter begins with the Evangelist's chronological note that it was just six days before the Passover (v. 1). His temporal reference is theological in that he wants to emphasize that the events that are about to take place are closely related to the Passover. He first describes the account of Jesus' anointing in Bethany (v. 3). Mary's anointing of Jesus' feet with her hair was probably an expression of her love and devotion to her Lord. It may also have been an expression of her gratitude for raising her brother from the dead, as the setting indicates (vv. 1–2). But, Jesus reveals that such action symbolically prepared him for His burial (vv. 7–8). The anointing for burial probably represents preparations for a king's death. Beasley-Murray correctly suggests, "John wishes to show that Jesus enters Jerusalem as the king who has been anointed for burial, as one destined for exaltation via the suffering of death."[4] Culpepper's description of Jesus' burial is also insightful: "The anointing may also serve the kingship motif that will be prominent during the trial and death of Jesus. He is anointed, just as he will ride in procession into the city, but the anointing ironically is an anointing of his feet, not by the high priest but by a woman, and he rides in procession not on a stallion but on a donkey. He will be elevated and enthroned, in a sense, but his lifting up will be on a cross with the inscription over him, 'The King of the Jews.' The anointing for this king, fittingly, is an anointing of his body for burial."[5] Thus, the anointing of Jesus anticipated His predetermined and sacrificial death. It symbolizes Jesus' messianic identity as the Lamb of God who takes away the sin of the world (1:29; cf. Isa 53).

Jesus' triumphal entry into Jerusalem further confirmed the messianic identity of Him as King (vv. 12–19). By entering Jerusalem riding on a donkey, Jesus was presenting Himself to the nation as the promised Messiah of the Hebrew Scriptures (Ps 118:25–26; Zech 9:9). The Evangelist records that the great crowd that gathered for the Passover Feast greeted Jesus with a royal coronation as the messianic King. Having witnessed Jesus' miracle of raising Lazarus from the dead, they were ready

3. Moloney, *Gospel of John*, 348.

4. Beasley-Murray, *John*, 208.

5. Culpepper, *Gospel and Letters of John*, 193.

to crown Him King. What they did not know, however, was that the King was coming to die.[6] Borchert thus says, "The so-called Triumphal Entry in John is hardly to be viewed in terms of triumph."[7] Beasley-Murray describes the crowd's misunderstanding of Jesus' entry into Jerusalem, and how Jesus sought to correct their misconception:

> The enthusiasm of the crowd is uncomfortably reminiscent of the attempted messianic rising mentioned in 6:14–15. The Evangelist's stating at this point in the narrative that Jesus procured a donkey on which to ride into Jerusalem emphasizes the intention of Jesus to correct a false messianic expectation, for to enter the city on a donkey instead of on a horse, which was associated by Jews with war (cf. Isa 31:1–3; 1 Kgs 4:26), was itself a demonstration of the peaceable nature of the mission of Jesus, and the relation of the event of Zech 9:9 makes that move explicit; for Zech 9:9–10 describes the *joyous* coming of the King—Messiah—he is righteous, gentle, bringing salvation, riding on a donkey, proclaiming peace to the nations. Nothing further from a Zealotic view of the Messiah could be imagined.[8]

While Jesus was presenting Himself as the messianic King, He was not coming to institute the eschatological kingdom. Rather, He was coming to die for the sins of the world.

That Jesus was coming to die for the sins of the whole world is symbolically represented with the coming of the Greeks to seek the Lord (John 12:20–36). With the coming of the Greeks, Jesus reveals to His disciples that "the hour" of His death had come (vv. 23–24). Jesus' death will provide eternal life for all: "But I, when I am lifted up from the earth, will draw all men to myself" (v. 32). It has been the Fourth Evangelist's emphasis throughout his Gospel that Jesus, the promised Messiah of the Hebrew Scriptures, is also the Savior of the world (4:42; cf. 1:12; 3:16–17; 6:33; 8:12). Morris is thus correct to say, "Jesus was the Savior of the world and this group of Gentiles symbolically represents the world seeking its salvation from Jesus."[9]

---

6. Laney thus suggests that what is commonly referred to as the "Triumphal Entry" should be referred to as the "Royal Entry," since Jesus is coming to die. He suggests that the phrase "Triumphal Entry" should be reserved for Jesus' Second Advent. *John*, 222–24.

7. Borchert, "The Passover and the Narrative Cycles," 311.

8. Beasley-Murray, *John*, 210.

9. Morris, *Gospel According to John*, 592.

In contrast to the Gentiles who came looking for Jesus, however, many of the Jews will reject Him as the Messiah. The Evangelist brings this chapter, or the whole Book of Signs, to a close by summarizing the polarizing responses of the people in terms of belief and unbelief. The Evangelist has emphasized throughout his Gospel that as Jesus' ministry progressed, the public opinion about Him became increasingly polarized. Fewer and fewer people stayed neutral about Him. Jesus was seen as either being from God or He was thought to be an agent of Satan, as the Jewish religious leaders held. The Evangelist summarized the rejection of Jesus in these words: "Even after Jesus had done all these miraculous signs in their presence, they still would not believe in Him" (v. 37). But, as the Evangelist concludes, the prophets anticipated this kind of a response regarding the Messiah (Isa 53:1; 6:10).

THE SIGNIFICANCE THE "BOOK OF GLORY" (JOHN 13–20)

The latter part of the Fourth Gospel commonly known as the Book of Glory or Book of Passion plays a significant role in the book along with chapter 12. The sacrificial death and triumphal resurrection of Jesus validate the christological and messianic claims expressed in the first eleven chapters, particularly His sign-miracles. The Book of Glory can be generally divided into two portions: the Farewell Discourse (chaps. 13–17) and the Passion and Resurrection Narratives (chaps. 18–20). The Farewell Discourse, or more commonly known as the "Upper Room" discourse, relates Jesus' instructions to His disciples to prepare them for His impending death. This section describes the last week of Jesus' life spent with His disciples, highlighted by the night preceding the crucifixion. That night was spent celebrating the Passover with the disciples. In the Farewell Discourse Jesus prepares His disciples by revealing many truths concerning His departure, the coming of the Holy Spirit, the Church, and the disciples' relationship with Him and with one another (chaps. 13–16). Furthermore, He also prays to the Father for the disciples concerning their unity, sanctification, and protection in His absence (chap. 17).

The Passion Narrative of the Fourth Gospel fulfills the Evangelist's theme that Jesus is indeed the Messiah and the Son of God, who came from the Father's side to offer Himself sacrificially for the world as the Lamb. John leaves no doubt in these accounts that Jesus allows Himself to be arrested and crucified, thus demonstrating His voluntary and vicarious sacrifice. His whole life had been anticipatory of this "hour" and thus He was not a victim of circumstances. This section reveals the height of unbelief on the part of many such as Judas, the religious leaders, Pilate, and the nation. At the same time, John also reveals the height of belief on the part of many such as the beloved disciple, the women, Joseph of Arimathea, and even Nicodemus.

The resurrection of Jesus is John's ultimate proof in presenting Him as the Messiah and the Son of God, because only God Himself can resurrect life, as Jesus Himself predicted (cf. 2:19). Jesus' appearance to Mary Magdalene, Peter and John, the disciples, and Thomas was to authenticate His claims and thus strengthen them for service. The Evangelist's proof that Jesus is the promised Messiah and the divine Son of God climaxes with Thomas's exclamation: "My Lord and my God" (20:28). Interestingly, these two terms that are used to describe Jesus, "My Lord and my God" ('Ο κύριός μου καὶ ὁ θεός μου), are the exact words to describe the covenant name of God in the Septuagint (LXX).

CONCLUSION

Chapter 12 of the Fourth Gospel plays a significant role in the book, both literarily and theologically. Literarily, this chapter provides the bridge between the Book of Signs and the Book of Glory. Theologically, this chapter provides the perspective with which the Book of Signs should have been read and how the Book of Glory should be read. In other words, what significant claims have been made about Jesus in the Book of Signs, and how will they be confirmed and fulfilled in the Book of Glory? Chapter 12 includes three symbolic acts that explain the significance of Jesus' Passover death. First, Mary's anointing of Jesus symbolically anticipates the death and burial of the Messiah. Second, Jesus' triumphal entry into Jerusalem validates His messianic kingship. However, the messianic King has not come to establish His kingdom but to die sacrificially as the Passover Lamb. Third, the coming of the Greeks symbolically identifies Jesus as the messianic King who is also the Savior of the world.

The Book of Glory (chaps. 13–20) also plays a significant role in the book. These chapters validate the christological and messianic claims that are developed in the Book of Signs (chaps. 2–12). The sacrificial death and the triumphant resurrection of Jesus demonstrates His Person as the promised Messiah and the divine Son of God. And, as the divine

Messiah He has the power and authority to grant eternal life to those who believe in Him. These chapters convincingly validate Jesus' claim to be the resurrection and the life.

13

Conclusion and Summary

SOMEONE ANONYMOUS ONCE DESCRIBED the Fourth Gospel as a book in which a child can wade and an elephant can swim.[1] Kysar's summary of the Fourth Gospel eloquently confirms the accuracy of this perceptive description of this book:

> The beginning student may well find the thought of the gospel rather obvious and understand its symbolism in a straightforward manner. On the other hand, the lifetime scholar of the writing will still be wrestling with the nuances of the gospel in the fading years of his or her career. The gospel presents itself in a manner not unlike that of the mysterious cave that entices the mountain explorer. The entrance seems clear enough, but the deeper one moves into the opening the less illumination there seems to be and the more intense the darkness becomes. But, like the newly discovered mountain-side cave, the fourth evangelist and his gospel are irresistibly attractive to the historical explorer; the enigmas and mysteries of the gospel cry out for explication and beckon the student to undertake the probings of its inner recesses.[2]

Even a casual reader of this Gospel will agree that while its basic message and concepts are straightforward and simple to understand, one will also quickly realize that the background from which they are drawn is profoundly deep. The Fourth Gospel and its theology as a whole is immersed in the Old Testament Scriptures. The knowledge of the Hebrew Bible will therefore enhance one's appreciation of the Evangelist's deep theology.

---

1. Quoted in Kysar's *Fourth Evangelist and His Gospel*, 6.
2. Ibid.

The Fourth Evangelist reveals the aim of his Gospel towards the end of the book: "Jesus did many other miraculous signs in the presence of his disciples, which are not recorded in this book. But these are written that you may believe that Jesus is the Christ, the Son of God, and that by believing you may have life in his name" (20:30–31). The purpose of the Evangelist in writing his Gospel was to present the Person of Jesus as the promised Messiah of the Old Testament Scriptures and the divine Son of God. The means by which he has chosen to do so is the selected miracles and their attendant contexts. And, the seven sign-miracles of Jesus (σημεῖα) are strategically placed within the Gospel to demonstrate both His messiahship and His deity.

While the Evangelist reveals the purpose of his Gospel towards the end of the book, he prepares the stage for the christological revelations of his sign-miracles from the beginning. The opening chapter of the Gospel explicitly declares who Jesus is and thus prepares the reader for the kind of revelations to come in the rest of the book. The Prologue (1:1–18) announces the coming of the eternal Logos, who is now incarnate in Jesus. He has come from the Father's side, both to reveal the Father to the world and to grant eternal life to those who receive Him by faith. The Testimonium (1:19–51) explains that Jesus can grant life and the forgiveness of sins based on the sacrificial death He will die as the "Lamb of God" who takes away the sin of the world. As the Passover Lamb, Jesus will die a substitutionary and vicarious death for the sins of the whole world.

The seven sign-miracles in the Fourth Gospel are all recorded in the Book of Signs (2:1—12:50), which describes the public ministry of Jesus. They all demonstrate the claims made in the opening chapter of the Gospel in presenting Jesus as the promised Messiah and the divine Son of God (cf. 20:30–31). The first miracle of Jesus turning water into wine at a wedding in Galilee (2:1–11) first illustrates His deity by creating the finest of wine from jars of water. This miracle demonstrates the Evangelist's earlier claim that all things were made through the preincarnate Word (cf. 1:3). Second, this miracle also identifies Jesus as the promised Messiah of the Hebrew Scriptures. By providing an abundance of wine at a Jewish wedding feast, Jesus was demonstrating that as the Messiah He is capable of ushering in the promised eschatological kingdom and provide the joy associated with that kingdom.

However, this divine Messiah offers a new life filled with abundant joy, even here and now.

The second miracle of Jesus healing the royal official's son (4:43–54) also highlights the Person of Jesus as the Messiah and the Son of God. Whereas Jesus demonstrates His authority as the divine Messiah to grant new life by changing water into wine at a wedding in the first miracle, He illustrates the same truth through restoring the official's son from the brink of death in the second miracle. This miracle reveals that Jesus has the divine power to save one from death even at a great distance. As the incarnate Word, Jesus has the power and authority to command life to be. This miracle also identifies Jesus as the promised Messiah of the Old Testament Scriptures, as the power and authority to heal sickness and death are the characteristics of the Messiah in His promised kingdom. Furthermore, in healing the Gentile official's son from the brink of death, Jesus illustrates that the Messiah's kingdom will be universal and inclusive. This universal characteristic of the future messianic kingdom reveals Jesus to be the Savior of the world in the here and now, and He grants eternal life to all who believe in the Son.

The third miracle of Jesus healing the lame man at the Pool of Bethesda (5:1–15) also reveals Jesus as both the divine Son of God and the promised Messiah. This miracle clearly demonstrates that Jesus has the divine power to heal a man who has been in his paralytic state for thirty-eight years! However, this miracle demonstrates a far more significant issue, namely, Jesus' divine prerogative to forgive sin and grant eternal life to those who believe in His Person. To those who have been affected from the "crippling" damage of sin, the Son offers life. While the divine Sonship of Jesus is the primary focus of this miracle, it also has significant messianic implications. This miracle emphasizes an aspect of the Messiah's work in His coming kingdom, namely, the healing of the blind, the dumb, the mute, and the lame (cf. Isa 35:5–6; 61:1). It anticipates His glorious future kingdom where, literally, there will be no such diseases.

The fourth miracle of Jesus feeding the five thousand (John 6:1–15) also demonstrates His deity by demonstrating that Jesus is the Creator who is capable of commanding into existence whatever He wills through His word. As Jesus was able to command into existence the best quality of wine from water to satisfy all the guests at a wedding in Cana, here Jesus is able to abundantly satisfy the hunger of five thousand men with bread. As the divine Creator, Jesus is able to provide for the needs of people. The accompanying Bread of Life discourse reveals, however, that Jesus was illustrating that He is the provider of a deeper need of people, namely, spiritual life. As the Bread of Life, Jesus is able to grant eternal life to those who believe in Him. The Passover background of this miracle also reveals Jesus as the promised Messiah of the Hebrew Scriptures. By performing His miracle of feeding the five thousand Jesus clearly intended to reveal His messianic identity, for there are indications in the Hebrew Scriptures that the messianic age would be accompanied by signs like those of the Mosaic period (Mic 7:15; Isa 48:20–21). As the Messiah, He will die sacrificially as the Passover Lamb for the deliverance of the world, so that whoever would believe in Him can possess eternal life.

The fifth miracle of Jesus walking on the Sea of Galilee (John 6:16–21) also reveals His divine identity. This miracle identifies Jesus as the one with the divine name, "I Am" (Ἐγώ εἰμι), the name with which God Himself revealed to Moses (cf. Exod 3:14, LXX). As God, Jesus is able to protect His people from the dangers of the world. In fact, as He is able to control the wind and the waves of the sea, Jesus is the one who controls the circumstances of life. The divine name "I Am" also has deep messianic implications. It is the covenant name by which Yahweh repeatedly revealed Himself to Abraham and his descendants. The emphasis of the covenant name is given in order to remind them that God will fulfill the promises made to their ancestor. Therefore, in using this divine name Himself Jesus is claiming to be the very God who revealed Himself to the patriarchs, and in whom all the patriarchal promises will be fulfilled in His eschatological kingdom.

The sixth sign of Jesus healing the man born blind (John 9:1–41) is also revelatory, in that it reveals Jesus' Person as the divine Son of God and the promised Messiah of the Old Testament Scriptures. In healing a man with congenital blindness Jesus was demonstrating His deity, for only God can heal a man born blind. In healing the man born blind Jesus was also illustrating the spiritual blindness of all men, who are born in sin and without hope (cf. Eph 2:1–3; Rom 3:9–20). And, just as the man who was born with congenital blindness could only be healed by Jesus' divine touch, only the divine Messiah who is the Light of the World can grant life to those who believe in Him. Furthermore, the healing of the blind man from birth illustrates one of the characteristics of the messianic kingdom when "the eyes of the blind will be opened" (Isa 35:5). The miracle then provides a foretaste of the messianic blessings to be realized in the promised kingdom when "the eyes of the blind will see" (Isa 29:18). This same blessing is available spiritually through the divine Messiah, however, to those who believe in Him, here and now.

The seventh miracle of Jesus raising Lazarus from the dead (John 11:1–44) is the climactic sign in the Fourth Gospel. This miracle confirms one of the central themes of the whole Gospel, that as the divine Messiah Jesus has the authority to give eternal life to those who believe in Him (cf. 5:22; 14:6). By raising Lazarus from the dead Jesus was demonstrating that, as the "Resurrection and the Life," He possesses the authority to reverse the effects of sin and death (cf. Gen 2:17; Rom 5:12). Furthermore, by His death and resurrection, Jesus provides forgiveness of sin and offers life to those who believe in Him. This miracle also has profound messianic and eschatological implications, in that the Hebrew Scriptures are clear that the Old Testament saints expressed their confidence of everlasting life that will be realized in the Messiah's kingdom (Ps 16:9–11; cf. Isa 26:19–20; Dan 12:2). Jesus' claim "I am the Resurrection and the Life" indicates, however, that while there will certainly be the future eschatological resurrection, the resurrection life is already available to those who believe in Him.

The seven sign-miracles of Jesus demonstrate the Evangelist's claim that He is both the promised Messiah of the Old Testament Scriptures and the divine Son of God (cf. John 20:30–31). As the divine Messiah, Jesus has come to offer eternal life to those who would believe in His name. As the Lamb of God who takes the sin of the world, He offers the hope of forgiveness to those who are trapped in the death and darkness of sin. The Book of Glory (13:1—20:31) confirms and authenticates Jesus' own claims that He is indeed the promised Messiah and the divine Son of God. As the Messiah, Jesus will die a Passover Lamb's sacrificial and substitutionary death. However, His triumphant resurrection also validates His claim that He is indeed the Resurrection and the Life.

The seven sign-miracles of Jesus are intentionally designed by the Evangelist to be both revelatory and pragmatic in their aim. First, in revealing the Person of Jesus as the divine Messiah, they also reveal His glory (δόξα). The sign-miracles are bracketed with the theme of Jesus' glory (δόξα), as both the first and the seventh sign-miracles are specifically stated to have revealed His glory (2:11; 11:4, 40). Furthermore, the whole Book of Signs (chaps. 2–12) concludes with the Evangelist's own parenthetical statement of connection between the recorded signs-miracles with Jesus' glory (12:37–41). Just as God Himself revealed His glory through the wondrous works He performed on behalf of His people in Egypt (cf. Exod 15:11), here Jesus, as the divine Messiah, performs His sign-miracles (σημεῖα) in order to reveal His glory.

Second, the Johannine sign-miracles also have a pragmatic aim. They are designed to lead people to believe in Him (πιστεύω), or believe with a deeper understanding. In other words, the sign-miracles are designed by the Evangelist to produce or develop faith in his readers. However, while the sign-miracles are intended to produce a response of faith, they are also divisive. Although the Johannine signs are designed to lead people to a decision of faith, they also have an opposite effect that results in unbelief and rejection of the Person of whom the miracles testify. Thus, the Johannine sign-miracles have a double character of both revealing and veiling at the same time. To those who embrace the revelation of Jesus' Person by faith, the divine Messiah will grant forgiveness of sins and eternal life. And, to those who reject the revelation of Jesus' Person will remain in darkness and face judgment by the Son, not only in this life but also in the future eschatological judgment.

Bibliography

Abraham, Abram Kenneth. *Promises of the Messiah: New Testament Fulfillment of Old Testament Prophecies.* Westwood, NJ: Barbour and Company, 1987.

Adkisson, Randall Lynn. "An Examination of the Concept of Believing as a Dominant Motif in the Gospel of John." PhD diss., New Orleans Baptist Theological Seminary, 1990.

Alden, Robert L. "אוֹר." *TWOT* 1:18.

Alexander, Philip S. "The King Messiah in Rabbinic Judaism." In *King and Messiah in Israel and the Ancient Near East.* Proceedings from the Oxford Old Testament Seminar, ed. John Day. Sheffield: Sheffield Academic Press, 1998.

Alexander, Ralph H. "A New Covenant—An Eternal People (Jeremiah 31)." In *Israel: The Land and the People,* edited by H. Wayne House. Grand Rapids, MI: Kregel, 1998.

Allen, Ronald B. "Affirming Right-Of-Way on Ancient Paths." *Bibliotheca Sacra* 153 (January-March 1996): 3–11.

———. "By His Name, His Nature." *Moody Monthly* 89 (October 1989): 38–43.

———. "In His Law, the Surprise of His Grace." *Moody Monthly* 89 (December 1989): 42–46.

———. "In the Light of the Coming One." *Moody Monthly* 90 (February 1990): 30–33.

———. "The Land of Israel." In *Israel: The Land and the People,* edited by H. Wayne House. Grand Rapids, MI: Kregel, 1998.

———. "Our God: Consuming Fire and Warm Embrace." *Moody Monthly* 89 (September 1989): 34–39.

———. "Psalm 87, A Song Rarely Sung." *Bibliotheca Sacra* 153 (April–June 1996): 131–40.

———. "A Surprise of Wonder." *Moody Monthly* 90 (January 1990): 36–39.

———. "When God Reached Out to Abraham." *Moody Monthly* 89 (November 1989): 38–40.

———. "The Word as Divine Light: Its Unique Wisdom." In *Celebrating the Word,* edited by Earl Radmacher. Portland, OR: Multnomah, 1987.

Anderson, Paul N. *The Christology of the Fourth Gospel: Its Unity and Disunity in the Light of John 6.* Wissenschaftliche Untersuchungen zum Neuen Testament, ed. Martin Hengel and Otfried Hofius. Tübingen: J. C. B. Mohr (Paul Siebeck), 1996.

Anderson, Ward William. "Signs of Jesus' Messiahship: A Biblical-Theological Comparison of Old Testament Messianic Revelation with the Miracles in John 1–12." PhD diss., Bob Jones University, 1985.

Ashton, John. "Introduction: The Problem of John." In *The Interpretation of John,* edited by John Ashton. 2nd ed. Edinburgh: T. & T. Clark, 1997.

———. *Studying John: Approaches to the Fourth Gospel.* New York: Oxford University Press, 1994.

———. *Understanding the Fourth Gospel.* New York: Oxford University Press, 1991.

Bibliography

Bailey, Mark L. "Dispensational Definitions of the Kingdom." In *Integrity of Heart, Skillfulness of Hands: Biblical and Leadership Studies in Honor of Donald K. Campbell*, edited by Charles H. Dyer and Roy B. Zuck. Grand Rapids, MI: Baker, 1994.

Bailey, Mark L., and Thomas L. Constable. *New Testament Explorer: Discovering the Essence, Background, and Meaning of Every Book in the New Testament*. Swindoll Leadership Library, ed. Charles R. Swindoll. Nashville, TN: Word, 1999.

Ballard, Charles Warren. "The Relationship of the Prologue to the Argument of the Gospel of John as Evidenced by the Concepts 'Sight' and 'Truth.'" ThM thesis, Dallas Theological Seminary, 1982.

Barber, Cyril J. "Theology of the Resurrection in John's Gospel." ThM thesis, Dallas Theological Seminary, 1967.

Barbieri, Louis A., Jr. "The Future for Israel in God's Plan." In *Essays in Honor of J. Dwight Pentecost*, edited by Stanley D. Toussaint and Charles H. Dyer. Chicago: Moody, 1986.

Barrett, C. K. "Der Zweck des vierten Evangeliums." *Zeitschrift für systematische Theologie* 22 (1953): 257–73.

———. "The Dialectical Theology of St. John." In *New Testament Essays*. London: SPCK, 1972.

———. *Essays on John*. Philadelphia: Westminster, 1982.

———. *The Gospel According to St. John: An Introduction with Commentary and Notes on the Greek Text*. 2nd ed. Philadelphia: Westminster, 1978.

———. *The Gospel of John and Judaism*. Translated from the German by D. Moody Smith. Philadelphia: Fortress, 1975.

———. "The Lamb of God." *New Testament Studies* 1 (1954–55): 210–18.

———. "The Old Testament in the Fourth Gospel." *Journal of Theological Studies* 48 (1947): 155–69.

———. "The Parallels between Acts and John." In *Exploring the Gospel of John: In Honor of D. Moody Smith*, edited by R. Alan Culpepper and C. Clifton Black. Louisville, KY: Westminster John Knox, 1996.

———. "The Prologue of St. John's Gospel." In *New Testament Essays*. London: SPCK, 1972.

Barrosse, Thomas. "The Seven Days of the New Creation in St. John's Gospel." *Catholic Biblical Quarterly* 21 (1959): 507–16.

Barton, John. "The Messiah in Old Testament Theology." In *King and Messiah in Israel and the Ancient Near East*. Proceedings from the Oxford Old Testament Seminar, ed. John Day. Sheffield: Sheffield Academic Press, 1998.

Beale, G. K. "Revelation." In *It is Written: Scripture Citing Scripture: Essays in Honour of Barnabas Lindars*, edited by D. A. Carson and H. G. M. Williamson. Cambridge: Cambridge University Press, 1988.

Beasley-Murray, George R. *Gospel of Life: Theology in the Fourth Gospel*. Peabody, MA: Hendrickson, 1991.

———. *Jesus and the Kingdom of God*. Grand Rapids, MI: Eerdmans, 1986.

———. *John*. Word Biblical Commentary, ed. David A. Hubbard and Glenn W. Barker, vol. 36. Waco, TX: Word, 1987.

Becker, Jürgen. "Die Geschichte der johannieschen Gemeinden." *Theologische Rundschau* 47 (December 1982): 305–12.

————. "Wunder und Christologie: Zum Literarkritischen und Christologischen Problem der Wunder im Johannesevangelium." *New Testament Studies* 16 (January 1970): 130–48.

Bennett, Donald M. "The Revelation of Jesus Christ in the Miracles of John." ThM thesis, Dallas Theological Seminary, 1957.

Berger, Klaus. "Die Königlichen Messiastraditionen des Neuen Testaments." *New Testament Studies* 20 (October 1973): 1–44.

Bernard, J. H. *A Critical and Exegetical Commentary on the Gospel According to St. John.* International Critical Commentary, ed. A. H. McNeile. 2 vols. Edinburgh: T. & T. Clark, 1928.

Beutler, Johannes. "Der Alttestamentlich-Jüdische Hintergrund der Hirtenrede in Johannes 10." In *The Shepherd Discourse of John 10 and its Context: Studies by members of the Johannine Writings Seminar*, edited by Johannes Beutler and Robert T. Fortna. Cambridge: Cambridge University Press, 1991.

————. "Psalms 42/43 im Johannesevangelium." *New Testament Studies* 25 (October 1978): 33–57.

————. "The Use of 'Scripture' in the Gospel of John." In *Exploring the Gospel of John: In Honor of D. Moody Smith*, edited by R. Alan Culpepper and C. Clifton Black. Louisville, KY: Westminster John Knox, 1996.

Birch, B. C. "Number." *ISBE* 3:556–61.

Bittner, Wolfgang J. *Jesu Zeichen im Johannesevangelium.* Wissenschaftliche Untersuchungen zum Neuen Testament, ed. Martin Hengel and Otfried Hofius, vol. 26. Tübingen: J. C. B. Mohr (Paul Siebeck), 1987.

Blackburn, B. L. "Miracles and Miracle Stories." In *Dictionary of Jesus and the Gospels*, edited by Joel B. Green, Scot McKnight, and I. Howard Marshall. Downers Grove, IL: InterVarsity, 1992.

Blomberg, Craig L. *Jesus and the Gospels.* Nashville, TN: Broadman & Holman, 1997.

Blum, Edwin A. "John." In *The Bible Knowledge Commentary: New Testament*, edited by John F. Walvoord and Roy B. Zuck. Wheaton, IL: Victor, 1983.

Bock, Darrell L. *Jesus According to Scripture: Restoring the Portrait from the Gospels.* Grand Rapids, MI: Baker, 2002.

Boice, James Montgomery. *The Gospel of John: An Expositional Commentary.* 5 vols. Grand Rapids, MI: Zondervan, 1975.

————. *Witness and Revelation in the Gospel of John.* Grand Rapids, MI: Zondervan, 1970.

Bonneau, Norman R. "The Woman at the Well: John 4 and Genesis 24." *Bible Today* 67 (October 1973): 1252–59.

Booth, John Louis. "The Purpose of Miracles." ThD diss., Dallas Theological Seminary, 1965.

Borchert, Gerald L. *John 1–11.* New American Commentary, ed. E. Ray Clendenen, vol. 25a. Nashville, TN: Broadman & Holman, 1996.

————. "The Passover and Narrative Cycles in John." In *Perspectives on John: Method and Interpretation in the Fourth Gospel*, edited by Robert B. Sloan and Mikeal C. Parsons. Lewiston, NY: Edwin Mellen, 1993.

Borgen, Peder. "The Gospel of John and Hellenism: Some Observations." In *Exploring the Gospel of John: In Honor of D. Moody Smith*, edited by R. Alan Culpepper and C. Clifton Black. Louisville, KY: Westminster John Knox, 1996.

————. *Logos was the True Light: And Other Essays on the Gospel of John*. Trondheim, Norway: Tapir, 1983.

Bowker, J. W. "The Origin and Purpose of St. John's Gospel." *New Testament Studies* 11 (1965): 398–408.

Bratcher, Robert G. "'The Jews' in the Gospel of John." *Bible Translator* 26 (October 1975): 401–9.

Bromiley, G. W. "Stoics." *ISBE* 4:621–22.

Brooke, George J. "Kingship and Messianism in the Dead Sea Scrolls." In *King and Messiah in Israel and the Ancient Near East*. Proceedings from the Oxford Old Testament Seminar, ed. John Day. Sheffield: Sheffield Academic Press, 1998.

Brooks, Alan Duane. "Responses to the Light: Sight and Blindness in the Characters of John 9." PhD diss., Baylor University, 1991.

Brown, Colin. "Miracle." *ISBE* 3:371–81.

Brown, Raymond B. "The Prologue of the Gospel of John: John 1:1ñ18,î *Review and Expositor* 62 (fall 1965): 430ñ31.

Brown, Raymond E. *The Community of the Beloved Disciple*. New York: Paulist, 1979.

————. *The Gospel According to John (I–XII)*. Anchor Bible, ed. William Foxwell Albright and David Noel Freeman, vol. 29. New York: Doubleday, 1966.

————. *The Gospel According to John (XIII–XXI)*. Anchor Bible, ed. William Foxwell Albright and David Noel Freeman, vol. 29a. New York: Doubleday, 1970.

————. "The Gospel Miracles." In *The Bible in Current Catholic Thought*, edited by John L. McKenzie. New York: Herder & Herder, 1962.

————. *An Introduction to the New Testament*. Anchor Bible Reference Library, ed. David Noel Freedman. New York: Doubleday, 1997.

————. *New Testament Essays*. New York: Paulist, 1965.

————. "Other Sheep Not of This Fold: The Johannine Perspective on Christian Perspective on Christian Diversity in the Late First Century." *Journal of Biblical Literature* 97 (March 1978): 5–22.

Browning, Ruth H. "The Universality of John's Gospel." PhD diss., Boston University School of Theology, 1951.

Broyles, Craig C. "The Redeeming King: Psalm 72's Contribution to the Messianic Ideals." In *Eschatology, Messianism, and the Dead Sea Scrolls*, edited by Craig A. Evans and Peter W. Flint. Grand Rapids, MI: Eerdmans, 1997.

Bruce, F. F. *The Gospel of John*. Grand Rapids, MI: Eerdmans, 1983.

————. "The Time is Fulfilled: Five Aspects of the Fulfillment of the Old Testament in the New." The Moore College Lectures, 1977. Exeter: Paternoster, 1978.

Bühner, Jan. "The Exegesis of the Johannine 'I-Am' Sayings." In *The Interpretation of John*, edited by John Ashton. 2nd ed. Edinburgh: T. & T. Clark LTD, 1997.

Bultmann, Rudolf. *Das Evangelium des Johannes*. Gottingen: Dandenhoed & Ruprecht, 1941. Reprint, 1978.

————. *The Gospel of John: A Commentary*. Translated by G. R. Beasley-Murray, R. W. N. Hoard, and J. K. Riches. Philadelphia: Westminster, 1971.

————. "The History of Religions Background of the Prologue to the Gospel of John." In *The Interpretation of John*, edited by John Ashton. 2nd ed. Edinburgh: T. & T. Clark LTD, 1997.

Burge, Gary M. *Interpreting the Gospel of John*. Grand Rapids, MI: Baker, 1992.

Burkett, Delbert. *The Son of Man in the Gospel of John.* Journal for the Study of the New Testament Supplement Series, ed. David Hill, vol. 56. Sheffield: Sheffield Academic Press, 1991.

Burns, J. "Some Reflections on Coheleth and John." *Catholic Biblical Quarterly* 25 (1963): 414–16.

Burns, Rita J. "Jesus and the Bronze Serpent." *Bible Today* 28 (March 1990): 84–89.

Campbell, Donald K. "The Church in God's Prophetic Program." In *Essays in Honor of J. Dwight Pentecost,* edited by Stanley D. Toussaint and Charles H. Dyer. Chicago: Moody, 1986.

Campbell, J. Y. "The Origin and Meaning of the Term Son of Man." *Journal of Theological Studies* 48 (1947): 145–55.

Carroll, Kenneth L. "The Fourth Gospel and the Exclusion of Christians from the Synogogues." *Bulletin of the John Rylands Library* 40 (September 1957): 19–32.

Carson, D. A. *The Gospel According to John.* Grand Rapids, MI: Eerdmans, 1991.

———. "John and the Johannine Epistles." In *It is Written: Scripture Citing Scripture: Essays in Honour of Barnabas Lindars,* edited by D. A. Carson and H. G. M. Williamson. Cambridge: Cambridge University Press, 1988.

———. "The Purpose of the Fourth Gospel: John 20:31 Reconsidered." *Journal of Biblical Literature* 106 (December 1987): 639–51.

Carson, D. A., Douglas J. Moo, and Leon Morris. *An Introduction to the New Testament.* Grand Rapids, MI: Zondervan, 1992.

Carter, Gary L. "Christ as the True Light, the True Bread, and the True Vine in the Gospel of John." ThM thesis, Dallas Theological Seminary, 1980.

Charlesworth, James H. "The Dead Sea Scrolls and the Gospel according to John." In *Exploring the Gospel of John: In Honor of D. Moody Smith,* edited by R. Alan Culpepper and C. Clifton Black. Louisville, KY: Westminster John Knox, 1996.

———, ed. *The Old Testament Pseudepigrapha: Apocalyptic Literature and Testaments.* Vol. 1. Garden City, NY: Doubleday, 1983.

———, ed. *The Old Testament Pseudepigrapha: Expansions of the "Old Testament" and Legends, Wisdom and Philosophical Literature, Prayers, Psalms, and Odes, Fragments of Lost Judeo-Hellenistic Works.* Vol. 2. Garden City, NY: Doubleday, 1985.

Chumney, Edward. *The Seven Festivals of the Messiah.* Shippensburg, PA: Treasure, 1994.

Clark, D. K. "Signs in Wisdom and John." *Catholic Biblical Quarterly* 45 (April 1983): 201–9.

Cofield, James E. "Jesus in the 'New Moses' in the Gospel of John." ThM thesis, Dallas Theological Seminary, 1982.

Collins, John J. "The Expectation of the End in the Dead Sea Scrolls." In *Eschatology, Messianism, and the Dead Sea Scrolls,* edited by Craig A. Evans and Peter W. Flint. Grand Rapids, MI: Eerdmans, 1997.

Collins, Raymond F. "Cana (Jn. 2:1–12)—The first of his signs or the key to his signs?" *Irish Theological Journal* 47 (summer 1980): 79–95.

Comfort, Philip W., and Wendell C. Hawley. *Opening the Gospel of John: A Fresh Resource for Teaching and Preaching the Fourth Gospel.* Wheaton, IL: Tyndale, 1994.

Cook, W. Robert. "Eschatology in John's Gospel." *Criswell Theological Review* 3 (fall 1988): 79–99.

Cullmann, Oscar. *The Johannine Circle: Its Place in Judaism, among the Disciples of Jesus and in Early Christianity: A Study in the Origin of the Gospel of John.* Translated by John Bowden. Philadelphia: Westminster, 1976.

———. "A New Approach to the Interpretation of the Fourth Gospel." *Expository Times* 71 (1959): 8–12.

Culpepper, R. Alan. *Anatomy of the Fourth Gospel: A Study in Literary Design.* Philadelphia: Fortress, 1983.

———. *The Gospel and Letters of John.* Interpreting Biblical Texts, ed. Charles B. Cousar. Nashville, TN: Abingdon, 1998.

———. "The Pivot of John's Prologue." *New Testament Studies* 27 (October 1980): 1–31.

Currie, Charles C. "The Signs and Discourses in the Gospel of John." ThM thesis, Dallas Theological Seminary, 1955.

Curtis, A. Kenneth, J. Stephen Lang, and Randy Petersen. *The 100 Most Important Events in Christian History.* Grand Rapids, MI: Fleming H. Revell, 1991.

Dahood, M. "Ebla, Genesis and John." *Christian Century* 98 (April 1981): 418–21.

Dahms, J. V. "Isaiah 55:11 and the Gospel of John." *Evangelical Quarterly* 53 (April-June 1981): 78–88.

Daube, David. *The New Testament and Rabbinic Judaism.* London: Athlone, 1956.

Davis, John J. *Biblical Numerology: A Basic Study of the Use of Numbers in the Bible.* Grand Rapids, MI: Baker, 1968.

Davies, W. D. "Reflections on Aspects of the Jewish Background of the Gospel of John." In *Exploring the Gospel of John: In Honor of D. Moody Smith,* edited by R. Alan Culpepper and C. Clifton Black. Louisville, KY: Westminster John Knox, 1996.

Day, John. "The Canaanite Inheritance of the Israelite Monarchy." In *King and Messiah in Israel and the Ancient Near East.* Proceedings of the Oxford Old Testament Seminar, ed. John Day. Sheffield: Sheffield Academic Press, 1998.

De Jonge, M. "Jewish Expectations About the 'Messiah' According to the Fourth Gospel." *New Testament Studies* 19 (April 1973): 246–70.

———. "The Use of the Word CRISTOS in the Johannine Epistles." In *Studies in John.* Supplements to Novum Testamentum, ed. W. C. van Unnik, vol. 24. Leiden: E. J. Brill, 1970.

De Kruijf, Th. C. "The Glory of the Only Son (John 1:14)." In *Studies in John.* Supplements to Novum Testamentum, ed. W. C. van Unnik, vol. 24. Leiden: E. J. Brill, 1970.

Delling, Gerhard. "ἀρχή." *TDNT* 1:478–89.

Dembski, William A. *Intelligent Design: The Bridge Between Science & Theology.* Downers Grove, IL: InterVarsity, 1999.

Derickson, Gary W. "Viticulture and John 15:1–6." *Bibliotheca Sacra* 153 (January-March 1996): 34–62.

Derrett, J. Duncan M. "Fig trees in the New Testament." *Heythrop Journal* 14 (July 1973): 249–65.

———. "Water into Wine." *Biblesche Zeitschrift* 7 (January 1963): 80–97.

———. "Why and How Jesus Walked on the Sea." *Novum Testamentum* 23 (October 1981): 331–48.

Dockery, David S. "Reading John 4:1–45: Some Diverse Hermeneutical Perspectives." *Criswell Theological Review* 3 (fall 1988): 127–40.

Dodd, C. H. "The Background of the Fourth Gospel." *Bulletin of the John Rylands Library* 19 (July 1935): 329–43.

————. *The Interpretation of the Fourth Gospel.* Cambridge: Cambridge University Press, 1968.

————. *The Parables of the Kingdom.* Rev. ed. New York: Charles Scribner's Sons, 1961.

Dumbrell, William J. "Law and Grace: The Nature of the Contrast in John 1:17." *Evangelical Quarterly* 58 (January 1986): 25–37.

Dunn, James D. G. "John and the Synoptics as a Theological Question." In *Exploring the Gospel of John: In Honor of D. Moody Smith,* edited by R. Alan Culpepper and C. Clifton Black. Louisville, KY: Westminster John Knox, 1996.

Dyer, Charles H. "Biblical Meaning of Fulfillment." In *Issues in Dispensationalism,* edited by Wesley R. Willis and John R. Master. Chicago: Moody, 1994.

Earle, Ronald Leslie. "Concept of the Kingdom Program in the Gospel of John." ThM thesis, Dallas Theological Seminary, 1982.

Edersheim, Alfred. *The Life and Times of Jesus as Messiah.* Grand Rapids, MI: Eerdmans, 1971.

Elliott, Stephen D. "An Exposition of the Shepherd Figure in John 10:1–18." ThM thesis, Dallas Theological Seminary, 1971.

Ellis. E. Earle. *The World of St. John.* Grand Rapids, MI: Eerdmans, 1984.

Enz, J. J. "The Book of Exodus as a Literary Type for the Gospel of John." *Journal of Biblical Literature* 76 (1957): 208–15.

Evans, Craig A. "Jesus and the Dead Sea Scrolls from Qumran Cave 4." In *Eschatology, Messianism, and the Dead Sea Scrolls,* edited by Craig A. Evans and Peter W. Flint. Grand Rapids, MI: Eerdmans, 1997.

————. "On the Quotation Formulas in the Fourth Gospel." *Biblische Zeitschrift* 26 (1982): 79–83.

————. *Word and Glory: On the Exegetical and Theological Background of John's Prologue.* Journal for the Study of the New Testament Supplement Series, ed. Stanley E. Porter, vol. 89. Sheffield: Sheffield Academic Press, 1993.

Fee, Gordon D. "On the Authenticity of John 5:3b–4." *Evangelical Quarterly* 54 (October–December 1982) 207–18.

Feinberg, Paul D. "Dispensational Theology and the Rapture." In *Issues in Dispensationalism,* edited by Wesley R. Willis and John R. Master. Chicago: Moody, 1994.

Fish, John Huff, III. "Our Lord's Use of the Old Testament." ThD diss., Dallas Theological Seminary, 1965.

Flynn, Leslie B. *The Miracles of Jesus.* Wheaton, IL: Victor, 1990.

Forestell, J. Terence. *The Word of the Cross: Salvation as Revelation in the Fourth Gospel.* Rome: Biblical Institute Press, 1974.

Fortna, Robert Tomson. *The Fourth Gospel and Its Predecessor.* Philadelphia: Fortress Press, 1988.

————. *The Gospel of Signs.* Cambridge: Cambridge University Press, 1970.

Foubister, David Ronald. "The Nature and Purpose of Jesus' Miracles in the Gospels." PhD diss., Fuller Theological Seminary, 1981.

France, R. T. *Jesus & the Old Testament: His Application of Old Testament Passages to Himself and His Mission.* Downers Grove, IL: InterVarsity, 1971.

Freed, E. E. *Old Testament Quotations in the Gospel of John.* Leiden: Brill, 1965.

Freed, Edwin D. Ἐγώ εἰμι in John 1:20 and 4:25." *Catholic Biblical Quarterly* 41 (April 1979): 288–91.

Fruchtenbaum, Arnold G. *The Gospel and Letters of John.* Interpreting Biblical Texts, ed. Charles B. Cousar. Nashville, TN: Abingdon, 1998.

———. "Israel and the Church." In *Issues in Dispensationalism*, edited by Wesley R. Willis and John R. Master. Chicago: Moody, 1994.

———. *Israelogy: The Missing Link in Systematic Theology*. Tustin, CA: Ariel Ministries, 1989.

Fuller, Reginald H. *Interpreting the Miracles*. London: SCM Press, 1963.

Garland, David E. "The Fullfillment Quotations in John's Account of the Crucifixion." In *Perspectives on John: Method and Interpretation in the Fourth Gospel*, edited by Robert B. Sloan and Mikeal C. Parsons. Lewiston, NY: Edwin Mellen, 1993.

Gates, Sidney A. "The Conception of Eternal Life in John's Gospel and the Epistles." PhD diss., Southern Baptist Theological Seminary, 1937.

Geyser, A. "The Shmeivon at Cana of the Galilee." In *Studies in John*. Supplements to Novum Testamentum, ed. W. C. van Unnik, vol. 24. Leiden: E. J. Brill, 1970.

Gillingham, S. E. "The Messiah in the Psalms: A Question of Reception History and the Psalter." In *King and Messiah in Israel and the Ancient Near East*. Proceedings from the Oxford Old Testament Seminar, ed. John Day. Sheffield: Sheffield Academic Press, 1998.

Glasson, T. Francis. *Moses in the Fourth Gospel*. Naperville, IL: Alec R. Allenson, 1963.

Goldberg, Louis. "Historical and Political Factors in the Twentieth Century Affecting the Identity of Israel." In *Israel: The Land and the People*, edited by H. Wayne House. Grand Rapids, MI: Kregel, 1998.

González, Justo L. *The Story of Christianity: The Early Church to the Dawn of the Reformation*. Vol. 1. San Francisco: Harper & Row, 1984.

Gordon, Victor R. "Sign." *ISBE* 4:505–8.

Grant, Robert M. "The Origin of the Fourth Gospel." *Journal of Biblical Literature* 69 (December 1950): 305–22.

Grässer, Erich. "Die Antijüdische Polemik in Johannesevangelium." *New Testament Studies* 11 (1965): 74–90.

Grassi, Joseph A. *Loaves and Fishes: The Gospel Feeding Narratives*. Collegeville, MN: Liturgical, 1991.

Griffith, W. H. Thomas. "The Purpose of the Fourth Gospel." *Bibliotheca Sacra* 125 (July-September 1968): 254–62.

Griffith, Richard James. "The Eschatological Significance of the Sabbath." ThD diss., Dallas Theological Seminary, 1990.

Griffiths, D. R. "Deutero-Isaiah and the Fourth Gospel: Some Points of Comparison." *Expository Times* 65 (September 1954): 355–60.

Grigsby, Bruce Holeman. "The Source and Purpose of the Light Versus Dark Motif in the Fourth Gospel." ThM thesis, Dallas Theological Seminary, 1976.

Grisanti, Michael A. "Israel's Mission to the Nations in Isaiah 40–55: An Update." *The Master's Seminary Journal* 9 (Spring 1998): 39–61.

———. "The Relationship of Israel and the Nations in Isaiah 40–55." PhD diss., Dallas Theological Seminary, 1993.

Gromacki, Robert G. *New Testament Survey*. Grand Rapids, MI: Baker, 1974.

Gryglewicz, Feliks. "Das Lamm Gottes." *New Testament Studies* 13 (1967): 133–46.

Guilding, Aileen. *The Fourth Gospel and Jewish Worship: A Study of the Relation of St. John's Gospel to the Ancient Lectionary System*. Oxford: Oxford University Press, 1960.

Gundry, Robert H. *A Survey of the New Testament*. Rev. ed. Grand Rapids, MI: Zondervan, 1981.

Gunner, R. A. H. "Number." In *New Bible Dictionary*, edited by I. Howard Marshall, A. R. Millard, J. I. Packer, and D. J. Wiseman. 3rd ed. Downers Grove, IL: InterVarsity, 1996.

Guthrie, Donald. "The Importance of Signs in the Fourth Gospel." *Vox Evangelica* 5 (1967): 72–83.

———. *New Testament Introduction*. Downers Grove, IL: InterVarsity, 1970.

———. *New Testament Introduction*. 4th ed. Downers Grove, IL: InterVarsity, 1990.

Haenchen, Ernst. *A Commentary on the Gospel of John: Chapters 1–6*. Translated by Robert W. Funk. Vol. 1. Philadelphia: Fortress, 1984.

———. *A Commentary on the Gospel of John: Chapters 7–12*. Translated by Robert W. Funk. Vol. 2. Philadelphia: Fortress, 1984.

Hamidkhani, Saeed. "Johannine Expressions of Double Meaning: A Literary-Exegetical Analysis." ThM thesis, Dallas Theological Seminary, 1992.

Hanhart, K. "The Structure of John 1:35—4:54." In *Studies in John*. Supplements to Novum Testamentum, ed. W. C. van Unnik, vol. 24. Leiden: E. J. Brill, 1970.

Hanson, Anthony Tyrrell. "John 1:14–18 and Exodus 34." *New Testament Studies* 23 (October 1976): 90–101.

———. *The Prophetic Gospel: A Study of John and the Old Testament*. Edinburth: T. & T. Clark, 1991.

Harner, Philip B. *The "I Am" of the Fourth Gospel: A Study in Johannine Usage and Thought*. Philadelphia: Fortress, 1970.

Harris, Elizabeth. *Prologue and Gospel: The Theology of the Fourth Evangelist*. Journal for the Study of the New Testament Supplement Series, ed. Stanley E. Porter, vol. 107. Sheffield: Sheffield Academic Press, 1994.

Harris, Gregory H. "Satan's Deceptive Miracles in the Tribulation." *Bibliotheca Sacra* 156 (July-September 1999): 308–24.

Harris, W. Hall. "A Theology of John's Writings." In *A Biblical Theology of the New Testament*, edited by Roy B. Zuck and Darrell L. Bock. Chicago: Moody, 1994.

Harrison, Everett F. *Introduction to the New Testament*. Rev. ed. Grand Rapids, MI: Eerdmans, 1971.

———. *John: The Gospel of Faith*. Chicago: Moody, 1962.

———. "Judaism." *ISBE* 2:1150.

Heil, John Paul. *Jesus Walking on the Sea: Meaning and Gospel Functions of Matt 14:22–33, Mark 6:45–52 and John 6:15b–21*. Analecta Biblica: Investigationes Scientificae in res Biblicas, ed. Fritzleo Lentzen-Deis and Francis J. McCool, vol. 87. Rome: Biblical Institute Press, 1981.

Helfmeyer, F. J. "אות." *TDOT* 1:167–88.

Hengel, Martin. "The Interpretation of the Wine Miracle at Cana: John 2:1–11." In *The Glory of Christ in the New Testament: Studies in Christology*, edited by L. D. Hurst and N. T. Wright. New York: Oxford University Press, 1987.

Hendriksen, William. *The Gospel According to John*. New Testament Commentary. 2 vols. Grand Rapids, MI: Baker Book, 1953.

Hengel, Martin. "The Old Testament in the Fourth Gospel." *Horizons in Biblical Theology* 12 (June 1990): 19–41.

Hiebert, D. Edmond. *An Introduction to the New Testament*. Vol. 1. Winona Lakes, IN: BMH Books, 1975.

Hodges, Zane, C. "The Angel at Bethesda-John 5:4," *Bibliotheca Sacra* 136 (January-March 1979): 39.

———. "A Dispensational Understanding of Acts 2." In *Issues in Dispensationalism*, edited by Wesley R. Willis and John R. Master. Chicago: Moody, 1994.

———. "Water and Spirit—John 3:5." *Bibliotheca Sacra* 135 (July-September 1978): 206–20.

Hoehner, Harold W. "Between the Testaments." In *The Expositor's Bible Commentary*, edited by Frank E. Gaebelein, vol. 1. Grand Rapids, MI: Zondervan, 1979.

———. *Chronological Aspects of the Life of Christ*. Grand Rapids, MI: Zondervan, 1977.

———. "Israel in Romans 9–11." In *Israel: The Land and the People*, edited by H. Wayne House. Grand Rapids, MI: Kregel, 1998.

———. "Maccabees." ISBE 3:196–200.

Hofbeck, Sebald. *Semeion: Der Begriff des "Zeichen" im Johannesevangelium unter Berücksichtigung seiner Vorgeschichte*. Münsterschwarzacher Studien. Vol. 3. Münsterschwarzbach: Vier-Türme, 1966.

Hofius, Otfried. "Miracle." *NIDNTT* 2:626–33.

Hogan, Garry R., Jr. "The Manifestation of the Glory of God in the Gospel of John." ThM thesis, Dallas Theological Seminary, 1975.

Holloway, Richard. *Signs of Glory*. New York: The Seabury, 1982.

Holst, Robert Arthur. "The Relation of John, Chapter Twelve, to the So-Called Johannine Book of Glory." PhD diss., Princeton Theological Seminary, 1974.

Hook, H. Phillip. "The Doctrine of the Kingdom in Covenant Premillennialism." ThD diss., Dallas Theological Seminary, 1959.

Hooker, Morna D. "The Johannine Prologue and the Messianic Secret." *New Testament Studies* 21 (1974): 40–58.

Horbury, William. "Messianism in the Old Testament Apocrypha and Pseudepigrapha." In *King and Messiah in Israel and the Ancient Near East*. Proceedings from the Oxford Old Testament Seminar, ed. John Day. Sheffield: Sheffield Academic Press, 1998.

Hoskyns, Edwyn Clement. *The Fourth Gospel*. London: Faber and Faber, 1947.

House, H. Wayne. "The Church's Appropriation of Israel's Blessings." In *Israel: The Land and the People*, edited by H. Wayne House. Grand Rapids, MI: Kregel, 1998.

Houston, Walter. "'Today, in Your Very Hearing': Some Comments on the Christological Use of the Old Testament." In *The Glory of Christ in the New Testament: Studies in Christology*, edited by L. D. Hurst and N. T. Wright. New York: Oxford University Press, 1987.

Howard, Kevin, and Marvin Rosenthal. *The Feasts of the Lord*. Orlando, FL: Zion's Hope, 1997.

Howard, W. F. "The Common Authorship of the Johannine Gospel and Epistles." *Journal of Theological Studies* 48 (1947): 12–25.

Hudson, Donald James. "*Ego Eimi* in the Gospel of John." ThM thesis, Dallas Theological Seminary, 1963.

Hughes, Paul. "Moses' Birth Story: A Biblical Matrix for Prophetic Messianism." In *Eschatology, Messianism, and the Dead Sea Scrolls*, edited by Craig A. Evans and Peter W. Flint. Grand Rapids, MI: Eerdmans, 1997.

Hughes, R. Kent. *Behold the Lamb*. Wheaton, IL: Victor, 1984.

———. *John: That You May Believe*. Preaching the Word. Wheaton, IL: Crossway Books, 1999.

Hulbert, Terry C. "The Eschatological Significance of Israel's Annual Feasts." ThD diss., Dallas Theological Seminary, 1965.

Hunter, A. M. *The Gospel According to John.* Cambridge Bible Commentary, ed P. R. Ackroyd, A. R. C. Leaney, and J. W. Packer. Cambridge: Cambridge University Press, 1965.

———. "Recent Trends in Johannine Studies." *Expository Times* 71 (March, April 1960): 164–67, 219–22.

Jelinek, John A. "The Dispersion and Restoration of Israel to the Land." In *Israel: The Land and the People*, edited by H. Wayne House. Grand Rapids, MI: Kregel, 1998.

Johnson, Elliott E. "Prophetic Fulfillment: The Already and Not Yet." In *Issues in Dispensationalism*, edited by Wesley R. Willis and John R. Master. Chicago: Moody Press, 1994.

Johnson, S. Lewis, Jr. *The Old Testament in the New: an Argument for Biblical Inspiration.* Grand Rapids, MI: Zondervan, 1980.

———. "Paul and 'The Israel of God': An Exegetical and Eschatological Case-Study." In *Essays in Honor of J. Dwight Pentecost*, edited by Stanley D. Toussaint and Charles H. Dyer. Chicago: Moody, 1986.

Johnston, George. "*Ecce Homo!* Irony in the Christology of the Fourth Evangelist." In *The Glory of Christ in the New Testament: Studies in Christology*, edited by L. D. Hurst and N. T. Wright. New York: Oxford University Press, 1987.

Johnston, L. "The Making of the Fourth Gospel." *Scripture* 12 (January 1960): 1–13.

Jones, Larry Paul. "A Study of the Symbol of Water in the Gospel of John." PhD diss., Vanderbilt University, 1995.

———. *The Symbol of Water in the Gospel of John.* Journal for the Study of the New Testament Supplement Series, ed. Stanley E. Porter, vol. 145. Sheffield: Sheffield Academic Press, 1997.

Joyce, Paul M. "King and Messiah in Ezekiel." In *King and Messiah in Israel and the Ancient Near East.* Proceedings from the Oxford Old Testament Seminar, ed. John Day. Sheffield: Sheffield Academic Press, 1998.

Kaiser, Walter C., Jr. "The Land of Israel and the Future Return (Zechariah 10:6–12)." In *Israel: The Land and the People*, edited by H. Wayne House. Grand Rapids, MI: Kregel, 1998.

———. *The Messiah in the Old Testament.* Grand Rapids, MI: Zondervan, 1995.

Kallas, James. *The Significance of the Synoptic Miracles.* Greenwich, CT: The Seabury Press, 1961.

Kanhart, K. "The Structure of John 1:35—4:54." In *Studies in John.* Supplements to Novum Testamentum, ed. W. C. van Unnik, vol. 24. Leiden: E. J. Brill, 1970.

Keener, Craig S. *The Gospel of John: A Commentary.* 2 vols. Peabody, MA: Hendrickson, 2003.

———. *The IVP Bible Background Commentary: New Testament.* Downers Grove, IL: InterVarsity, 1993.

Kent, Homer A., Jr. *Light in the Darkness: Studies in the Gospel of John.* Grand Rapids, MI: Baker, 1974.

Kilpatrick, G. D. "The Religious Background of the Fourth Gospel." In *Studies in the Fourth Gospel*, edited by F. L. Cross. London: A. R. Mowbray & Co., 1957.

Kim, Seyoon. *"The 'Son of Man'" as the Son of God.* Wissenschaftliche Untersuchungen zum Neuen Testament, ed. Martin Hengel and Otfried Hofius, vol. 30. Tübingen: J. C. B. Mohr (Paul Siebeck), 1983.

Kim, Stephen S. "The Significance of Jesus' First Sign-Miracle in John." *Bibliotheca Sacra* 167 (January-March 2010): 201–15.

———. "The Relationship of the Seven Sign-Miracles of Jesus in the Fourth Gospel to the Old Testament." PhD diss., Dallas Theological Seminary, 2001.

———. "The Relationship of John 1:19–51 to the Book of Signs in John 2–12." *Bibliotheca Sacra* 165 (July-September 2008): 323–37.

Klijn, A. F. J. "2 Baruch." In *The Old Testament Pseudepigrapha: Apocalyptic Literature and Testaments*, edited by James H. Charlesworth, vol. 1. Garden City, NY: Doubleday & Company, 1983.

Knight, Harold. "The Old Testament Conception of Miracle." *Scottish Journal of Theology* 5 (1952): 355–61.

Knoppers, Gary N. "David's Relation to Moses: The Contexts, Content and Conditions of the Davidic Promises." In *King and Messiah in Israel and the Ancient Near East*. Proceedings of the Oxford Old Testament Seminar, ed. John Day. Sheffield: Sheffield Academic Press, 1998.

Koester, Craig R. *The Dwelling of God: The Tabernacle in the Old Testament, Inter-testamental Jewish Literature, and the New Testament.* The Catholic Biblical Quarterly Monograph Series, vol. 22. Washington, DC: The Catholic Biblical Association of America, 1989.

———. "Messianic Exegesis and the Call of Nathanael (John 1:45–51)." *Journal for the Study of the New Testament* 39 (June 1990): 23–34.

———. *Symbolism in the Fourth Gospel: Meaning, Mystery, Community.* Minneapolis, MN: Fortress, 1995.

Kossen, H. B. "Who were the Greeks of John xii 20?" In *Studies in John*. Supplements to Novum Testamentum, ed. W. C. van Unnik, vol. 24. Leiden: E. J. Brill, 1970.

Köstenberger, Andreas J. *Encountering John: The Gospel in Historical, Literary, and Theological Perspective.* Encountering Biblical Studies, ed. Walter A. Elwell. Grand Rapids, MI: Baker, 1999.

———. *John.* Baker Exegetical Commentary on the New Testament, ed. Robert Yarbrough and Robert H. Stein. Grand Rapids, MI: Baker, 2004.

———. *The Missions of Jesus and the Disciples according to the Fourth Gospel.* Grand Rapids, MI: Eerdmans, 1998.

Kruger, Paul A. "אוֹר." *NIDOTTE* 1:331–32.

Kysar, Robert. *The Fourth Evangelist and His Gospel: An Examination of Contemporary Scholarship.* Minneapolis, MI: Augsburg, 1975.

———. *John.* Augsburg Commentary on the New Testament, ed. Roy A. Harrisville, Jack Dean Kingsbury, and Gerhard A. Krodel. Minneapolis: Augsburg, 1986.

———. *The Maverick Gospel.* Rev. ed. Louisville, KY: Westminster/John Knox, 1993.

Lamarche, Paul. "The Prologue of John." In *The Interpretation of John*, edited by John Ashton. 2nd ed. Edinburgh: T. & T. Clark LTD, 1997.

Laney, J. Carl. "Abiding is Believing: The Analogy of the Vine in John 15:1–6." *Bibliotheca Sacra* 146 (January-March 1989): 55–66.

———. *John.* Moody Gospel Commentary, ed. Paul Enns. Chicago: Moody, 1992.

Larson, David L. "A Celebration of the Lord Our God's Role in the Future of Israel." In *Israel: The Land and the People*, edited by H. Wayne House. Grand Rapids, MI: Kregel, 1998.

LaSor, W. S. "Dead Sea Scrolls." *ISBE* 1:883–97.

Lee, Dorothy A. *The Symbolic Narratives of the Fourth Gospel: The Interplay of Form and Meaning.* Journal for the Study of the New Testament Supplement Series, ed. Stanley E. Porter, vol. 95. Sheffield: Sheffield Academic Press, 1994.

Leung, Donald Chung-Yiu. "The Development of Plot in John Chapters 2 through 4." ThM thesis, Dallas Theological Seminary, 1994.

Levey, Samson H. *The Messiah: An Aramaic Interpretation.* Los Angeles: Hebrew Union College Press, 1974.

Levy, David M. *The Tabernacle: Shadows of the Messiah.* Bellmawr, NJ: Friends of Israel Gospel Ministry, 1993.

Liddell, Henry George, and Robert Scott. *A Greek-English Lexicon.* 9th ed. Oxford: Clarendon, 1940.

Lightfoot, R. H. *The Gospel Message of St. Mark.* 2nd ed. Oxford: Oxford University Press, 1952.

———. *St. John's Gospel: A Commentary.* London: Oxford University Press, 1956.

Lindars, Barnabas. *The Gospel of John.* New Century Bible Commentary, ed. Matthew Black. Grand Rapids, MI: Eerdmans, 1982.

Lockyer, Herbert. *All the Miracles of the Bible.* Grand Rapids, MI: Zondervan, 1961.

Lohse, Eduard. "Miracles in the Fourth Gospel." In *What About the New Testament?: Essays in Honour of Christopher Evans,* edited by Morna Hooker and Colin Hickling. London: SCM Press, 1975.

Luck, Ulrich. "ὑγιής." *TDNT* 8:308–13.

Luter, A. Boyd. "Israel and the Nations in God's Redemptive Plan." In *Israel: The Land and the People,* edited by H. Wayne House. Grand Rapids, MI: Kregel, 1998.

Lutzer, Erwin W. *Seven Convincing Miracles: Understanding the Claims of Christ in Today's Culture.* Chicago: Moody, 1999.

MacDonald, George. *The Miracles of Our Lord.* Wheaton, IL: Harold Shaw, 1980.

MacGregor, G. H. C. *The Gospel of John.* Moffatt New Testament Commentary, ed. James Moffatt. London: Hodder and Stoughton, 1929.

Manson, T. W. *Studies in the Gospels and Epistles.* Philadelphia: Westminster, 1962.

Manson, W. "The Ἐγώ εἰμι of the Messianic Presence in the New Testament." *Journal of Theological Studies* 48 (1947): 137–45.

Marshall, I. Howard. "Johannine Theology." *ISBE* 2:1081–91.

———. "John, Epistles of." *ISBE* 2:1091–98.

Martyn, J. Louis. "A Gentile Mission That Replaced an Earlier Jewish Mission?" In *Exploring the Gospel of John: In Honor of D. Moody Smith,* edited by R. Alan Culpepper and C. Clifton Black. Louisville, KY: Westminster John Knox, 1996.

———. *The Gospel of John in Christian History: Essays for Interpreters.* New York: Paulist, 1979.

———. *History & Theology in the Fourth Gospel.* Rev. and enl. Nashville, TN: Abingdon, 1979.

Mason, Rex. "The Messiah in the Postexilic Old Testament Literature." In *King and Messiah in Israel and the Ancient Near East.* Proceedings from the Oxford Old Testament Seminar, ed. John Day. Sheffield: Sheffield Academic Press, 1998.

Master, John R. "The New Covenant." In *Issues in Dispensationalism,* edited by Wesley R. Willis and John R. Master. Chicago: Moody, 1994.

Mattill, A. J. "Johannine Communities behind the Fourth Gospel: Georg Richter's Analysis." *Theological Studies* 38 (June 1977): 294–315.

McCann, J. Clinton, Jr. "Sabbath." *ISBE* 4:247–52.

McCarthy, Ronald Wayne. "The Millennial Significance of the Miracles of Christ." ThM thesis, Dallas Theological Seminary, 1961.

McConville, J. G. "King and Messiah in Deuteronomy and the Deuteronomistic History." In *King and Messiah in Israel and the Ancient Near East*. Proceedings from the Oxford Old Testament Seminar, ed. John Day. Sheffield: Sheffield Academic Press, 1998.

McKnight, Scot. *A Light Among the Nations: Jewish Missionary Activity in the Second Temple Period*. Minneapolis, MN: Fortress, 1991.

McNamara, Martin. *Palestinian Judaism and the New Testament*. Good News Studies, ed. Robert J. Harris, vol. 4. Wilmington: Michael Glazier, 1983.

Mead, A. H. "The Βασιλικός in John 4:46–53." *Journal for the Study of the New Testament* 23 (February 1985): 69–72.

Meeks, Wayne A. *The Prophet-King: Moses Traditions and the Johannine Christology*. Supplements to Novum Testamentum, ed. W. C. van Unnik, vol. 14. Leiden: E. J. Brill, 1967.

Menken, M. J. J. "The Provenance and Meaning of the Old Testament Quotation in John 6:31." *Novum Testamentum* 30 (January 1988): 39–56.

Merrill, Eugene H. "Daniel as a Contribution to Kingdom Theology." In *Essays in Honor of J. Dwight Pentecost*, edited by Stanley D. Toussaint and Charles H. Dyer. Chicago: Moody, 1986.

Metzer, Bruce M. *A Textual Commentary on the Greek New Testament*. London: United Bible Societies, 1971.

Michaels, J. Ramsey. *John*. New International Biblical Commentary, ed. W. Ward Gasque. Peabody, MA: Hendrickson, 1984. Reprint, 1989.

———. "Nathanael Under the Fig Tree." *Expository Times* 78 (March 1967): 182–32.

Middleton, Thomas G. "The Christology of the Miraculous Signs in John 2–11 and John 21." ThD diss., New Orleans Baptist Theological Seminary, 1986.

Mills, Watson E. *Bibliographies for Biblical Research: The Gospel of John*. Vol. 4. Lewiston/Queenston/Lampeter: Mellen Biblical, 1995.

Miller, Gene. "The Nature and Purpose of the Signs in the Fourth Gospel." PhD diss., Duke University, 1968.

Minear, Paul S. "The Audience of the Fourth Evangelist." *Interpretation* 31 (October 1977): 339–54.

Mitchell, Daniel Roy. "The Person of Christ in John's Gospel and Epistles." ThD diss., Dallas Theological Seminary, 1982.

Mitchell, Kenneth R. "The Figure of the Vine in the Scriptures." ThM thesis, Dallas Theological Seminary, 1975.

Mitton, C. Leslie. "Modern Issues in Biblical Studies: The Provenance of the Fourth Gospel." *Expository Times* 71 (August 1960): 337–40.

Mlakuzhyil, George. *The Christocentric Literary Structure of the Fourth Gospel*. Analecta Biblica: Investigationes Scientificae in res Biblicas, ed. P. Albert VanHoye and P. Gerald O'Collines, vol. 117. Roma: Editrice Pontificio Istituto Biblico, 1987.

Moloney, Francis J. *Belief in the Word: Reading John 1–4*. Minneapolis, MN: Fortress, 1993.

———. "From Cana to Cana (John 2:1—4:54) and the Fourth Evangelist's Concept of Correct (and Incorrect) Faith." In *Studia Biblica 1978 II: Papers on the Gospels: Sixth International Congress on Biblical Studies, Oxford 3–7 April 1978*, edited by E. A. Livingstone. Journal for the Study of the New Testament Supplemental Series, ed. Ernst Bammel, Anthony Hanson, David Hill, and Max Wilcox, vol. 2. Sheffield: JSOT Press, 1980.

————. *Glory not Dishonor: Reading John 13–21*. Minneapolis, MN: Fortress, 1998.

————. *The Gospel of John*. Sacra Pagina Series, ed. Daniel J. Harrington, vol. 4. Collegeville, MN: Liturgical, 1989.

————. *The Johannine Son of Man*. Roma: LAS, 1976.

————. *Signs and Shadows: Reading John 5–12*. Minneapolis, MN: Fortress, 1996.

————. "Who is 'The Reader' in/of the Fourth Gospel?" In *The Interpretation of John*, edited by John Ashton. 2nd ed. Edinburgh: T. & T. Clark, 1997.

Moo, Douglas J. *The Old Testament in the Passion Narratives*. Sheffield: Almond, 1983.

Moore, Thomas S. "Luke's Use of Isaiah for the Gentile Mission and Jewish Rejection Theme in the Third Gospel." PhD diss., Dallas Theological Seminary, 1995.

Morgan, R. "Fulfillment in the Fourth Gospel: The Old Testament Foundations." *Interpretation* 11 (April 1957): 155–69.

Morris, Leon. *The Gospel According to John*. New International Commentary on the New Testament, ed. F. F. Bruce. Grand Rapids, MI: Eerdmans, 1971.

————. "Hellenism." ISBE 2:679–81.

————. *Jesus is the Christ: Studies in the Theology of John*. Grand Rapids, MI: Eerdmans, 1989.

————. "John, Gospel According to." ISBE 2:1098–107.

————. "John the Apostle." *ISBE* 2:1107–8.

————. *Reflections on the Gospel of John*. 4 Vols. Grand Rapids, MI: Baker, 1988.

Munn, R. James. "The Bread of Life Discourse." ThM thesis, Dallas Theological Seminary, 1983.

Neufeld, Dietmar. "'And When That One Comes': Aspects of Johannine Messianism." In *Eschatology, Messianism, and the Dead Sea Scrolls*, edited by Craig A. Evans and Peter W. Flint. Grand Rapids, MI: Eerdmans, 1997.

Neusner, Jacob. *Invitation to the Talmud*. Rev. and exp. ed. San Francisco: HarperCollins Publishers, 1984.

————. "Talmud." *ISBE* 4:717–27.

————. trans. *The Mishnah*. New Haven, CT: Yale University Press, 1988.

Nicol, W. *The Semeia in the Fourth Gospel*. Supplements to Novum Testamentum, ed. W. C. van Unnik, vol. 32. Leiden: E. J. Brill, 1972.

O'Brien, James Randall. "The Progression of the Mosaic Motif to the Johannine Concept of Messiah." ThD diss., New Orleans Baptist Theological Seminary, 1983.

O'Connor, Jerome Murphy. "Qumran and the New Testament." In *The New Testament and Its Modern Interpreters*, edited by Eldon Jay Epp and George W. MacRae. Atlanta: Scholars Press, 1989.

Oehler, W. *Das Johannesevangelium, eine Missionsschrift fur die Welt, der Gemeinde ausgelegt*. Gutersloh: Bertelsmann, 1936.

Okure, Teresa. *The Johannine Approach to Missions: A Contextual Study of John 4:1–42*. Wissenschaftliche Untersuchungen zum Neuen Testament, ed. Martin Hengel and Otfried Hofius, vol. 31. Tübingen: J. C. B. Mohr (Paul Siebeck), 1988.

Oluwafemi, Titus Oluwafidipe. "Jesus' Resurrection as the Ultimate 'Sign' of His Messianic Authority." PhD diss., Baylor University, 1979.

Owings, Timothy L. "John 2:1–11," *Review and Expositor* 85 (summer 1988): 533–37.

Patterson, Leon Bell. "A Comparative Study of the Johannine Concept of Eternal Life and the Synoptic Concept of the Kingdom." PhD diss., Southwestern Baptist Theological Seminary, 1959.

Pentecost, J. Dwight. *The Words and Works of Jesus Christ.* Grand Rapids, MI: Zondervan, 1981.

Peters, George W. *A Biblical Theology of Missions.* Chicago: Moody Press, 1972. Reprint, 1984.

Plummer, Alfred. *The Gospel According to St. John: with Maps, Notes and Introduction.* Cambridge: Cambridge University Press, 1880. Reprint, 1923.

Polhill, John B. "John 1–4: The Revelation of True Life," *Review and Expositor* 85 (summer 1988): 445–57.

Pollard, T. E. *Johannine Christology and the Early Church.* Society for New Testament Studies Monograph Series, ed. Matthew Black, vol. 13. Cambridge: Cambridge University Press, 1970.

Price, J. Randall. "Prophetic Postponement in Daniel 9 and Other Texts." In *Issues in Dispensationalism,* edited by Wesley R. Willis and John R. Master. Chicago: Moody Press, 1994.

Pritz, Ray A. "The Remnant of Israel and the Messiah." In *Israel: The Land and the People,* edited by H. Wayne House. Grand Rapids, MI: Kregel, 1998.

Proyen, Dirk Van. "The Attestation of the Miracles of John's Gospel to the Deity of Jesus Christ." ThM thesis, Dallas Theological Seminary, 1971.

Pryor, John W. *John: Evangelist of the Covenant People: The Narrative & Themes of the Fourth Gospel.* Downers Grove, IL: InterVarsity, 1992.

Radmacher, Earl D. "The Imminent Return of the Lord." In *Issues in Dispensationalism,* edited by Wesley R. Willis and John R. Master. Chicago: Moody, 1994.

Rainey, Frankie Earl, Jr. "'Σημεῖον' in the Fourth Gospel: A Clue to the Interpretation of the Gospel." PhD diss., Southwestern Baptist Theological Seminary, 1968.

Redding, David A. *The Miracles of Christ.* Westwood, NJ: Fleming H. Revell, 1964.

Reim, Günter. "Jesus as God in the Fourth Gospel: The Old Testament Background." *New Testament Studies* 30 (January 1984): 158–60.

———. *Studien zum alttestamentlichen Hintergrund des Johannesevangeliums.* Society for New Testament Studies Monograph Series, ed. Matthew Black, vol. 22. Cambridge: Cambridge University Press, 1974.

Reimer, David J. "Old Testament Christology." In *King and Messiah in Israel and the Ancient Near East.* Proceedings from the Oxford Old Testament Seminar, ed. John Day. Sheffield: Sheffield Academic Press, 1998.

Remus, Harold. *Jesus as Healer.* Understanding Jesus Today, ed. Howard Clark Kee. Cambridge: Cambridge University Press, 1997.

Reinhartz, Adele. "John 20:30–31 and the Purpose of the Fourth Gospel." PhD diss., McMaster University, 1983.

Rengstorf, Karl Heinrich. "Σημεῖον." *TDNT* 7:200–2691.

Renwick, A. M. "Gnosticism." *ISBE* 2:484–90.

Richards, H. J. *The Miracles of Jesus.* Mystic, CT: Twenty-Third Publications, 1975.

Richardson, Alan. *An Introduction to the Theology of the New Testament.* London: SCM Press, 1958.

———. *The Miracle-Stories of the Gospels.* New York: Harper & Brothers, 1942.

Riga, Peter. "Signs of Glory: The Use of Shmeivon in St. John's Gospel." *Interpretation* 17 (1963): 402–24.

Rigg, William H. *The Fourth Gospel and Its Shmeivon Message for Today.* London: Lutterworth Press, 1952.

Robertson, A. T. *The Divinity of Christ in the Gospel of John*. New York: Fleming H. Revell, 1916.

Robinson, H. W. "The Nature-Miracles of the Old Testament." *Journal of Theological Studies* (1943): 1–12.

Robinson, J. A. T. "The Destination and Purpose of St. John's Gospel." *New Testament Studies* 6 (1960): 117–31.

Rooke, Deborah W. "Kingship as Priesthood: The Relationship between the High Priesthood and the Monarchy." In *King and Messiah in Israel and the Ancient Near East*. Proceedings from the Oxford Old Testament Seminar, ed. John Day. Sheffield: Sheffield Academic Press, 1998.

Rowland, Christopher. "Christ in the New Testament." In *King and Messiah in Israel and the Ancient Near East*. Proceedings from the Oxford Old Testament Seminar, ed. John Day. Sheffield: Sheffield Academic Press, 1998.

Ruddick, C. T. "Feeding and Sacrifice: The Old Testament Background of the Fourth Gospel." *Expository Times* 79 (August 1968): 340–41.

Ruland, Vernon. "Sign and Sacrament: John's Bread of Life Discourse (Chapter 6)." *Interpretation* 18 (1964): 450–62.

Russell, D. S. *The Method and Message of Jewish Apocalyptic: 200 BC–AD 100*. The Old Testament Library, ed. Peter Ackroyd, James Barr, Bernhard W. Anderson, and James L. Mays. Philadelphia: Westminster, 1964.

Ryrie, Charles C. *Biblical Theology of the New Testament*. Chicago: Moody, 1959.

———. *The Miracles of Our Lord*. Neptune, NJ: Loizeaux Brothers, 1984.

Saldarini, Anthony J. "Judaism and the New Testament." In *The New Testament and Its Modern Interpreters*, edited by Eldon Jay Epp and George W. MacRae. Atlanta: Scholars Press, 1989.

Saucy, Mark R. *The Kingdom of God in the Teaching of Jesus: In 20th Century Theology*. Dallas: Word, 1997.

———. "Miracles and Jesus' Proclamation of the Kingdom of God." *Bibliotheca Sacra* 153 (July-September 1996): 281–307.

Scannell, Timothy Joseph. "Fulfillment of Johannine Signs: A Study of John 12:37–50." PhD diss., Fordham University, 1998.

Schein, Bruce E. *Following the Way: The Setting of John's Gospel*. Minneapolis: Augsburg, 1980.

Schnackenburg, Rudolph. "Der Menschensohn im Johannesevangelium." *New Testament Studies* 11 (1965): 123–37.

———. *God's Rule and Kingdom*. New York: Herder & Herder, 1963.

———. *The Gospel According to St. John: Commentary on Chapters 5–12*. Translated by Kevin Smyth. Vol. 2. New York: Crossroad, 1982.

———. *The Gospel According to St. John: Commentary on Chapters 13–21*. Translated by Kevin Smyth. Vol. 3. New York: Crossroad, 1984.

———. *The Gospel According to St. John: Introduction and Commentary on Chapters 1–4*. Translated by Kevin Smyth. Vol. 1. New York: Crossroad, 1982.

Schnelle, Udo. *Antidocetic Christology in the Gospel of John*. Translated by Linda M. Maloney. Minneapolis, MN: Fortress, 1992.

———. Schnelle, Udo. *Das Evangelium nach Johannes*. Theologischer Handkommentar zum Neuen Testament, ed. Erich Fascher, vol. 4. Leipzig: Evangelische Verlagsanstalt, 1998.

Schuchard, Bruce G. *Scripture within Scripture: The Interrelationship of Form and Function in the Explicit Old Testament Citations in the Gospel of John.* Dissertation Series, no. 133. Atlanta: Scholars Press, 1993.

Schürer, Emil. *The History of the Jewish People in the Age of Jesus Christ.* Revised and translated by Geza Vermes and Fergus Millar. Vol. 1. Edinburgh: T. & T. Clark, 1973.

Schweitzer, Albert. *The Kingdom of God and Primitive Christianity.* Translated by L. A. Garrard. New York: Seabury, 1968.

Scott, E. F. *The Fourth Gospel: Its Purpose and Theology.* Edinburth: T. & T. Clark, 1906.

————. *The Historical and Religious Value of the Fourth Gospel.* London: Constable & Company, 1910.

Scott, Martin. *Sophia and the Johannine Jesus.* Journal for the Study of the New Testament Supplement Series, ed. Stanley E. Porter, vol. 71. Sheffield: Sheffield Academic Press, 1992.

Scott, R. B. Y. "Weights and Measures in the Bible." *Biblical Archaeologist* 22 (May 1959): 22–40.

Scroggie, Graham. *A Guide to the Gospels.* London: Pickering & Inglis LTD., 1948.

Shafto, G. R. H. *The Wonders of the Kingdom: A Study of the Miracles of Jesus.* London: Student Christian Movement, 1924.

Simpson, A. B. *The Word Made Flesh: A Christ-Centered Study of the Book of John.* Camp Hill, PA: Christian Publications, 1995.

Sloan, Robert B. "The Absence of Jesus in John." In *Perspectives on John: Method and Interpretation in the Fourth Gospel,* edited by Robert B. Sloan and Mikeal C. Parsons. Lewiston, NY: Edwin Mellen, 1993.

Smalley, Stephen S. "Johannes 1, 51 und die Einleitung zum vierten Evangelium." In *Jesus und der Menschensohn,* edited by Rudolf Pesch and Rudolf Schnackenburg. Freiburg: Herder, 1975. 300–313.

————. *John: Evangelist & Interpreter.* 2nd. ed. Downers Grove, IL: InterVarsity Press, 1998.

————. "Keeping up with Recent Studies: St. John's Gospel." *Expository Times* 97 (January 1986): 102–8.

Smith, D. Moody. *The Composition and Order of the Fourth Gospel: Bultmann's Literary Theory.* Yale Publications in Religion, ed. David Horne, vol. 10. New Haven and London: Yale University Press, 1965.

————. *Johannine Christianity: Essays On Its Setting, Sources, and Theology.* Columbia, SC: University of South Carolina Press, 1984.

————. "Johannine Studies." In *The New Testament and Its Modern Interpreters,* edited by Eldon Jay Epp and George W. MacRae. Atlanta: Scholars Press, 1989.

————. *John.* Proclamation Commentaries, ed. Gerhard Krodel. Philadelphia: Fortress, 1976.

————. *John among the Gospels: The Relationship in Twentieth-Century Research.* Minneapolis, MN: Fortress, 1992.

————. "Judaism and the Gospel of John." In *Jews and Christians: Exploring the Past, Present, and Future,* edited by James H. Charlesworth. New York: Crossroad Publishing, 1990.

————. *The Theology of the Gospel of John.* New Testament Theology, ed. James D. G. Dunn. New York: Cambridge University Press, 1995.

Smith, Robert Houston. "Exodus Typology in the Fourth Gospel." *Journal of Biblical Literature* 81 (December 1962): 329–42.

Smith, T. C. "The Book of Signs: John 2–12." *Review and Expositor* 62 (fall 1965): 441–57.

———. *Jesus in the Gospel of John: Study of the Evangelist's Purpose and Meaning.* Nashville, TN: Broadman, 1959.

———. "The Secondary Purpose of the Fourth Gospel." *Review and Expositor* 50 (January 1953): 67–86.

Smitmans, Adolf. *Das Weinwunder von Kana: Die Auslegung von Jo 2, 1–11 bei den Vatern und heute.* Beitrage zur Geschichte der Biblischen Exegese, ed. Oscar Cullman, Ernst Käsemann, Hans-Joakim Kraus, Harold Riesenfeld, Karl Hermann Schelkle, and Ernst Wolf, vol. 6. Tübingen: J. C. B. Mohr (Paul Siebeck), 1966.

Songer, Harold S. "John 5–12: Opposition to the Giving of True Life." *Review and Expositor* 85 (summer 1988): 459–71.

Staley, Jeff. "The Structure of John's Prologue: Its Implications for the Gospel's Narrative Structure." *Catholic Biblical Quarterly* 48 (April 1986): 241–63.

Stauffer, Ethelbert. *Jesus and His Story.* Translated by Richard Winston and Clark Winston. New York: Alfred A. Knopf, 1960.

Stedman, Ray C. *God's Loving Word: Exploring the Gospel of John.* Grand Rapids, MI: Discovery, 1993.

Stensvad, Allan Maurice. "Christ's Claim to Deity in the Fourth Gospel." ThM thesis, Dallas Theological Seminary, 1960.

Stevens, Calvin T. "The 'I AM' Formula in the Gospel of John." *Studia Biblica et Theologica* 7–8 (October 1977): 19–30.

Stevens, Daniel C. "Light and Life in the Gospel of John." ThM thesis, Dallas Theological Seminary, 1973.

Story, Cullen I. K. *The Fourth Gospel: Its Purpose, Pattern, and Power.* Shippensburg, PA: Ragged Edge, 1997.

Strachan, R. H. *The Fourth Gospel: Its Significance and Environment.* London: Student Christian Movement Press, 1941.

Strickland, Wayne G. "Isaiah, Jonah, and Religious Pluralism." *Bibliotheca Sacra* 153 (January-March 1996): 24–33.

Talbert, Charles H. *Reading John: A Literary and Theological Commentary on the Fourth Gospel and the Johannine Epistles.* Reading the New Testament Series, ed. Charles H. Talbert. New York: Crossroad, 1992.

Tasker, R. V. G. *The Gospel According to St. John: An Introduction and Commentary.* Tyndale New Testament Commentaries, ed. R. V. G. Tasker. Grand Rapids, MI: Eerdmans, 1960. Reprint, 1980.

Taylor, Vincent. *The Names of Jesus.* New York: St Martin's Press, 1953.

Taylor, William M. *The Miracles of Our Saviour.* New York: A. C. Armstrong & Son, 1890.

Tenney, Merrill C. "The Gospel of John." In *The Expositor's Bible Commentary*, edited by Frank E. Gaebelein, vol. 9. Grand Rapids, MI: Zondervan, 1981.

———. *John: The Gospel of Belief.* Grand Rapids, MI: Eerdmans, 1948.

———. *New Testament Survey.* Rev. ed. Grand Rapids, MI: Eerdmans, 1985.

———. *New Testament Times.* Grand Rapids, MI: Eerdmans, 1965.

———. "The Old Testament and the Fourth Gospel." *Bibliotheca Sacra* 120 (October-December 1963): 300–308.

———. "Topics from the Gospel of John—Part II: The Meaning of the Signs." *Bibliotheca Sacra* 132 (April-June 1975): 145–60.

———. "Topics from the Gospel of John—Part III: The Meaning of 'Witness' in John." *Bibliotheca Sacra* 132 (July-September 1975): 229–41.

———. "Topics from the Gospel of John—Part IV: The Growth of Belief." *Bibliotheca Sacra* 132 (October-December 1975): 343–57.

Tew, William Mark. "Judgment as Present and Future in the Gospel of John." PhD diss., New Orleans Baptist Theological Seminary, 1988.

Thomas, Robert L. "The Mission of Israel and of the Messiah in the Plan of God." In *Israel: The Land and the People*, edited by H. Wayne House. Grand Rapids, MI: Kregel, 1998.

Thompson, Marianne Meye. "The Historical Jesus and the Johannine Christ." In *Exploring the Gospel of John: In Honor of D. Moody Smith*, edited by R. Alan Culpepper and C. Clifton Black. Louisville, KY: Westminster John Knox, 1996.

———. "The Humanity of Jesus in the Gospel of John." PhD diss., Duke University, 1985.

———. "John, Gospel of." In *Dictionary of Jesus and the Gospels*, edited by Joel B. Green, Scot McKnight, and I. Howard Marshall. Downers Grove, IL: InterVarsity, 1992.

Toussaint, Stanley D. "The Contingency of the Coming of the Kingdom." In *Integrity of Heart, Skillfulness of Hands: Biblical and Leadership Studies in Honor of Donald K. Campbell*, edited by Charles H. Dyer and Roy B. Zuck. Grand Rapids, MI: Baker, 1994.

———. "The Kingdom and Matthew's Gospel." In *Essays in Honor of J. Dwight Pentecost*, edited by Stanley D. Toussaint and Charles H. Dyer. Chicago: Moody, 1986.

———. "The Significance of the First Sign in John's Gospel." *Bibliotheca Sacra* 134 (January-March 1977): 45–51.

Towner, Philip H. "Christ the Lamb: The Relationship Between the Presentation of Christ as Lamb in the Fourth Gospel and Revelation." MA thesis, Trinity Evangelical Divinity School, 1981.

Towns, Elmer. *The Gospel of John: Believe and Live*. Old Tappan, NJ: Fleming H. Revell, 1990.

Trench, Richard Chenevix. *Notes on the Miracles of Our Lord*. New York: D. Appleton & Company, 1857.

Trudinger, L. Paul. "An Israelite in whom there is no Guile: An Interpretative Note on John 1:45–51." *Evangelical Quarterly* 54 (April-June 1982): 117–20.

———. "The Seven Days of the New Creation in St. John's Gospel: Some Further Reflections." *Evangelical Quarterly* 44 (July-September 1972): 154–58.

Turner, John D. "The History of Religions Background of John 10." In *The Shepherd Discourse in John 10 and its Context: Studies by members of the Johannine Writings Seminary*, edited by Johannes Beutler and Robert T. Fortna. Cambridge: Cambridge University Press, 1991.

Turner, G. A. "The Date and Purpose of St. John's Gospel." *Journal of Evangelical Theological Society* 6 (1963): 82–85.

Uomoto, George Yoshinori. "The Logos Doctrine in John." ThM thesis, Dallas Theological Seminary, 1946.

Van Belle, Gilbert. *Johannine Bibliography 1965–1985: A Cumulative Bibliography on the Fourth Gospel*. Leuven: University Press, 1988.

———. *The Signs Source in the Fourth Gospel: Historical Survey and Critical Evaluation of the Semeia Hypothesis.* Bibliotheca Ephemeridum Theologicarum Lovaniensium, vol. 116. Leuven: University Press, 1994.

Van der Waal, C. "The Gospel According to John and the Old Testament." *Neotestamentica* 6 (1972): 28–47.

Vermes, Geza. *The Dead Sea Scrolls in English.* 3rd ed. New York: Penguin, 1987.

———. *The Dead Sea Scrolls: Qumran in Perspective.* Rev. ed. Philadelphia: Fortress, 1977.

Villescas, John. "John 2.6: The Capacity of the Six Jars." *Bible Translator* 28 (October 1977): 447.

Von Harnack, Adolf. "Über das Verhältnis des Prologs des vierten Evangeliums zum ganzen Werke." *Zeitschrift für Theologie und Kirche* 2 (1892), 189–231.

Wallace, Ronald S. *The Gospel Miracles: Studies in Matthew, Mark, and Luke.* Grand Rapids, MI: Eerdmans, 1960.

Waltke, Bruce K. "The Creation Account in Genesis 1:1–3—Part IV: The Theology of Genesis 1." *Bibliotheca Sacra* 132 (October-December 1975): 327–42.

———. "The Creation Account in Genesis 1:1–3—Part V: The Theology of Genesis 1—Continued." *Bibliotheca Sacra* 133 (January-March 1976): 28–41.

Walvoord, John F. "Biblical Kingdoms Compared and Contrasted." In *Issues in Dispensationalism,* edited by Wesley R. Willis and John R. Master. Chicago: Moody, 1994.

———. *The Millennial Kingdom.* Grand Rapids, MI: Zondervan, 1959.

———. *The Nations, Israel and the Church in Prophecy.* Grand Rapids, MI: Zondervan, 1988.

———. "The New Covenant." In *Integrity of Heart, Skillfulness of Hands: Biblical and Leadership Studies in Honor of Donald K. Campbell,* edited by Charles H. Dyer and Roy B. Zuck. Grand Rapids, MI: Baker, 1994.

———. "The Theological Significance of Revelation 20:1–6." In *Essays in Honor of J. Dwight Pentecost,* edited by Stanley D. Toussaint and Charles H. Dyer. Chicago: Moody, 1986.

Warden, Francis M. "'Monogenes' in the Johannine Literature." PhD diss., Southern Baptist Theological Seminary, 1939.

Watson, D. F. "Wine." In *Dictionary of Jesus and the Gospels,* edited by Joel B. Green and Scot McKnight. Downers Grove, IL: InterVarsity Press, 1992.

Weiss, Johannes. *Jesus' Proclamation of the Kingdom of God.* Translated by Richard Hyde Hiers and David Larrimore Holland. Philadelphia: Fortress, 1971.

Westcott, B. F. *The Gospel According to St. John.* 1894. Reprinted, Grand Rapids, MI: William B. Eerdmans, 1973.

Westermann, Claus. *Das Johannesevangelium aus der Sicht des Alten Testaments.* Stuttgart: Calwer Verl., 1994.

———. *The Gospel of John: In the Light of the Old Testament.* Translated by Siegfried S. Schatzmann. Peabody, MA: Hendrickson, 1998.

Whitacre, Rodney A. *John.* IVP New Testament Commentary Series, ed. Grant R. Osborne. Downers Grove, IL: InterVarsity, 1999.

White, Roland John. "The Kingdom of God in the Fourth Gospel." PhD diss., Southern Baptist Theological Seminary, 1982.

Wigram, George V. *The Englishman's Greek Concordance of the New Testament.* 9th ed. Grand Rapids, MI: Zondervan, 1970.

Wilkens, Wilhelm. *Zeichen und Werke*. Abhandlungen zur Theologie des Alten und Neuen Testaments, ed. O. Cullmann and H. J. Stoebe, vol. 55. Zurich: Zwingli Verlag, 1969.

Williamson, H. G. M. "Messianic Texts in Isaiah 1–39." In *King and Messiah in Israel and the Ancient Near East*. Proceedings from the Oxford Old Testament Seminar, ed. John Day. Sheffield: Sheffield Academic Press, 1998.

Williford, Donald Dee. "A Study of the Religious Feasts as Background for the Organization and Message of the Gospel of John." PhD diss., Southwestern Baptist Theological Seminary, 1981.

Wind, A. "Destination and Purpose of the Gospel of John." *Novum Testamentum* 14 (January 1972): 26–69.

Windisch, Hans. *Johannes und die Synoptiker: Wollte der vierte Evangelist die alteren Evangelien erganzen oder ersetzen?* Untersuchungen zum Neuen Testament 12. Leipzig: J. C. Hinrichs, 1926.

Witherington, Ben III. *John's Wisdom: A Commentary on the Fourth Gospel*. Louisville, KY: Westminster John Knox, 1995.

Witmer, John A. *Immanuel*. Swindoll Leadership Library, ed. Charles R. Swindoll. Nashville, TN: Word, 1998.

Wright, R. B. "Psalms of Solomon." In *The Old Testament Pseudepigrapha: Expansions of the "Old Testament" and Legends, Wisdom and Philosophical Literature, Prayers, Psalms, and Odes, Fragments of Lost Judeo-Hellenistic Works*, edited by James H. Charlesworth, vol. 2. Garden City, NY: Doubleday & Company, 1985.

Woods, M. W. "The Use of the Old Testament in the Fourth Gospel. The Hermeneutical Method Employed in the Semeia and Its Significance for Contemporary Biblical Interpretation." PhD diss., Southwestern Baptist Theological Seminary, 1980.

Yee, Gale A. *Jewish Feasts and The Gospel of John*. Zacchaeus Studies: New Testament, ed. Mary Ann Getty. Wilmington: Michael Glazier, 1989.

Zeretsky, Tuvya. "Israel the People." In *Israel: The Land and the People*, edited by H. Wayne House. Grand Rapids, MI: Kregel, 1998.